L'Académie de droit international de La Haye

honorée du prix Wateler de la Paix (1936, 1950), du prix Félix Houphouët-Boigny pour la recherche de la paix (1992), de l'ordre du Rio Branco, Brésil (1999), et de la médaille de l'Institut royal d'études européennes, Espagne (2000)

The Hague Academy of International Law

awarded the Wateler Peace Prize (1936, 1950), the Félix Houphouët-Boigny Peace Prize (1992), the Order of Rio Branco, Brazil (1999), and the Medal of the Royal Institute of European Studies, Spain (2000)

ISBN 978-90-04-77122-2

International Arbitration

Its Legitimacy, Efficiency and Place within International Law

THE HAGUE ACADEMY OF INTERNATIONAL LAW
ACADEMIE DE DROIT INTERNATIONAL DE LA HAYE

International Arbitration

Its Legitimacy, Efficiency and Place within International Law

Dominique Hascher

Jean-Michel Jacquet

Gabrielle Kaufmann-Kohler

Alexis Mourre

Foreword by Diego P. Fernández Arroyo

BRILL | NIJHOFF

2026

Leiden/Boston

GENERAL TABLE OF CONTENTS

FOREWORD

by

DIEGO P. FERNÁNDEZ ARROYO [1]

No one of the best internationalists doubts the excellence and powerful influence that the courses at The Hague Academy of International Law have had on the evolution of international law and each of its branches. Furthermore, without exaggerating in the slightest, it can be said that everything essential to international law is contained in the famous *Recueil des cours*, to such an extent that one could obtain an excellent education as an internationalist simply by studying the nearly 450 volumes that this famous collection contains today. The most courageous could complete their knowledge with the other publications that the Academy has given us throughout its more than 100 years of fruitful existence.

Among the countless issues of international law addressed over the years, international arbitration has, unsurprisingly, always been a topic of particular interest to the Academy, as reflected in the early volumes of the *Recueil des cours*. Thus, already in 1928, we find two special courses on arbitration, covering its public and private aspects, respectively [2]. This is not surprising. On the one hand, arbitration was frequently used to resolve interstate disputes, as underscored by the developments regarding this theme at the Institut de droit international since its creation in 1873 and by the institutionalization of arbitration in 1899 following the creation of the Permanent Court of Arbitration [3]. On the other hand, the international community had just consolidated a specific legislative task aimed at harmonizing the law governing international arbitration, an agenda materialized in the League of Nations's work on arbitration clauses and arbitral awards in the 1920s

1. Professor, Sciences Po Law School, Paris; President of the Curatorium of The Hague Academy of International Law.
2. See D. Schindler, "Les progrès de l'arbitrage obligatoire depuis la création de la société des nations", *Recueil des cours*, Vol. 25 (1928), 233-364 and S. Rundstein, "L'arbitrage international en matière privée", *Recueil des cours*, Vol. 23 (1928), 327-462.
3. See B. Sousa Rodrigues, *The Transnational Codification of International Arbitration. Uniformisation under the Shadow of War and Commerce*, Brill/Nijhoff, 2025, particularly 67-95.

and crowned three decades later with the adoption of the New York Convention under the auspices of the United Nations in 1958.

Since then, interest in arbitration has never waned. On the contrary, all the issues that have marked the evolution of arbitration in its various forms (interstate, public-private and private) have been addressed from a variety of perspectives. However, it has been since 2011 that activities related to arbitration have multiplied in the Academy. This can be easily corroborated by a perfunctory analysis of the Academy's publications, as many of the published courses have the word arbitration in their title. But the reality is much broader than what is evident. In fact, there are instances where, even though the course refers significantly, if not primarily, to arbitration, such reference is more implicit [4]. Such has been the significance of arbitration in the Academy's curriculum in recent years that even a general course on private international law has had arbitration as its central theme [5]. In fact, had it not been for unforeseen circumstances, there would have been two, as another general course was announced for 2022 with the same main object, although presumably with a different approach [6].

Of course, the *Recueil des cours* is the Academy's flagship publication and can undoubtedly be considered its most visible legacy. However, in addition to being the subject of the occasional unpublished courses, arbitration is also featured in the Academy's other programs. Thus, a recent program of its Centre for Studies and Research was devoted exclusively to the crucial issue of determining the applicable law in international arbitration, covering both investment arbitration and commercial arbitration [7]. The same can be said of the Academy's programs that take place beyond the gates surrounding the Peace Palace – in fact, far beyond – in which arbitration often plays a starring role [8]. Finally, it is important to highlight the close collaboration that

---

4. Among many other examples, see Ch. N. Brower, "The Iran-United States Claim Tribunal", *Recueil des cours*, Vol. 224 (1990), 123-396.

5. G. A. Bermann, "International Arbitration and Private International Law", *Recueil des cours*, Vol. 381 (2015), 41-478.

6. I am talking of a course which had to be delivered by Emmanuel Gaillard, who passed away in 2021. The Academy has paid tribute to his work in a volume containing several works that analyze his invaluable contribution to international law, which highlights his famous course on the "Aspects philosophiques du droit de l'arbitrage international", *Recueil des cours*, Vol. 329 (2007), 49-216. See *The Hague Academy's Lectures on Emmanuel Gaillard's Legacy*, Brill/Nijhoff, 2023.

7. G. Cordero-Moss and D. P. Fernández Arroyo (eds.), *Applicable Law Issues in International Arbitration*, Brill/Nijhoff, 2023.

8. In addition to the External Programme, which has been taking place annually in Africa, Asia and Latin-America for almost sixty years, the Academy has launched the

the Academy maintains with its neighboring institution, the Permanent Court of Arbitration.

If the number of Academy activities devoted to international arbitration has increased so much in recent decades, it is due to the growing importance that this mechanism has gained among peaceful means of resolving international disputes. In many fields, particularly in areas such as international business, investment and sports, arbitration has become the predominant mechanism, creating in some cases a sort of *de facto* quasi-exclusive jurisdiction. Obviously, this preeminence is not without consequences. In fact, because of this growing importance and the rise of certain phenomena fairly or unfairly associated with it, international arbitration is now at the center of a debate that often goes beyond the legal sphere. In this regard, there is a striking paradox: a dispute resolution mechanism of proven effectiveness and undeniable success – which is due, in large part, to the sustained support of States that have developed a highly favorable legal framework – is increasingly subject to sharp criticism and high demands [9].

All of the above serves to confirm that it is no coincidence that several of the Academy's recent programs have opened with inaugural lectures specifically addressing international arbitration. This book brings together four of these lectures, originally delivered and published in French and now available in English in a single volume. As with all those invited to open the Academy's programs, the level and prestige of the authors featured in this work are superlative. Although all of them are very familiar with the practice of international arbitration, their profiles are different: Gabrielle Kaufmann-Kohler and Jean-Michel Jacquet are renowned professors and have played an outstanding role in the last generation of international arbitration rules by UNCITRAL; Alexis Mourre is one of the most reputable practitioners and has served two terms as president of the most cosmopolitan and influential of arbitration institutions, the International Court of Arbitration of the International Chamber of Commerce; and Dominique Hascher has contributed significantly to the development of arbitration case law as a senior judge, both in France (as an appeals and cassation judge) and in Singapore (as a judge of the International Commercial Court).

Programmes on Demand one decade ago. Most of the latter have been organized in Asia.

9. See D. P. Fernández Arroyo, "Nothing Is for Free: The Prices for Arbitralizing Legal Disputes", in L. Cadiet, B. Hess and M. Requejo Isidro (eds.), *Privatizing Dispute Resolution*, Nomos, 2019, 617-646.

The works offered by these distinguished lecturers reflect a diversity of perspectives, among the many that international arbitration allows today. Interestingly, the topics addressed complement each other, as if the contributions gathered in this book had been deliberately requested, following the design of a homogeneous thematic index. Thus, while Mourre addresses the issue of the legitimacy of arbitration from a broad perspective with a marked political and sociological content, Kauffman-Kohler focuses on a specific aspect of legitimacy, that of the adjudicator's accountability, comparing the independence and impartiality of judges and arbitrators in the context of investor-State disputes. Similarly, while Hascher analyzes the imbrication of arbitration into general international law from the perspective of the control of arbitral awards, Jacquet offers a more academic view within the framework of private international law, based on an irrefutable practical observation: the routine and systematic submission of international commercial disputes to arbitration.

All in all, these four high-level contributions accurately summarize the Academy's permanent interest in the evolution of international arbitration and how it relates to international law. These are reflections intended to endure, in line with the spirit that has always characterized this more than century-old institution.

THE ROLE OF INTERNATIONAL LAW IN THE SUPERVISION OF ARBITRAL AWARDS

by

DOMINIQUE HASCHER

TABLE OF CONTENTS

INTRODUCTION

1. The role of national or international supervisory bodies [1] is to stabilize arbitral justice by ensuring the integrity of the awards submitted to them and, beyond that, to preserve the integrity of the arbitration system in which the award was made. The importance of the issues entrusted to arbitral tribunals, whose decisions have repercussions that go beyond the disputes entrusted to them [2], makes it easier to assess the gravity of this mission.

2. The grounds for challenging awards which are mainly set out in the New York Convention of 10 June 1958 on the Recognition and Enforcement of Foreign Arbitral Awards, the Washington Convention of 18 March 1965 on the Settlement of Investment Disputes between States and Nationals of Other States (ICSID) and the Model Law on International Commercial Arbitration of the United Nations Commission on International Trade Law (UNCITRAL) are well known. None in particular favors the intervention of international law.

3. The text of this inaugural lecture invites you to reflect on the regulation of a universal system of arbitral justice. How do the supervisory bodies establish connections between national and international legal orders to control awards by transferring them from one legal order to another? Their ability to mobilize principles from a plurality of legal orders reveals their strengths and weaknesses in carrying out their task. In the international order, there are many interconnected suborders: the international interstate legal order, the transnational legal order which transcends the legal orders of States (*lex mercatoria* or the legal order specific to international trade [3], international contract

---

1. This lecture does not deal with the International Court of Justice. See W. M. Reisman,"The Supervisory Jurisdiction of the International Court of Justice: International Arbitration and International Adjudication", *Collected Courses*, Vol. 258 (1996), p. 9. The theme of the lecture emerged from discussions held with the late Professor Fadlallah during the writing of the book *Les grandes décisions du droit de l'arbitrage commercial international*, Dalloz, 2019.

2. A. Plantey, "L'arbitrage dans les échanges internationaux", *Rev. Sciences morales et pol.*, 1995, p. 323. B. Oppetit, "Théorie de l'arbitrage", PUF, 1998; G. Aguilar-Alvarez and W. M. Reisman, "The Reasons Requirement in International Investment Arbitration", Martinus Nijhoff, 2008, p. 2.

3. A. Pellet, "La *lex mercatoria*, tiers ordre juridique ?", Mélanges Kahn, Litec, 2000, p. 53. M. Virally, "Un tiers droit ?", Réflexions théoriques, Etudes Goldman, Litec, 1982, p. 373.

law[4], *lex sportiva*[5]) or the arbitral legal order, which brings together the rules of arbitration to which an international normative value is attributed, derived from the consensus of national legal orders or drawn from international law[6]. Whatever the composition of these legal orders, which varies according to doctrinal constructs[7], we are dealing with pluriverses that coexist and cut across each other, rather than isolated and hierarchically arranged universes[8].To confine oneself to a category or to give a definition of international law would prevent reasoning on the composite nature of this law as it is produced by the supervisory bodies which try to elaborate the rules and whose dynamics would otherwise be broken.

4. The submission of awards to international law is a factor of attraction for international law (Chap. 1), which plays a moderating role (Chap. 2) in a system of supervision based on universally recognized principles, elevated to the rank of principles of international law, as a common language (Chap. 3).

4. *Texaco* v. *Libya*, Award of 19 January 1977, *JDI*, 1977, 350, ILM, Vol. 17 (1978), p. 1, *International Law Reports*, Vol. 53, p. 389, paras. 32, 44.

5. M. Maisonneuve, "L'arbitrage des litiges sportifs", LGDJ, 2011; A. Rigozzi, "L'arbitrage international en matière de sport", Bruylant, LGDJ, Helbing & Lichtenhahn, 2005, No. 1222.

6. The representation of the arbitral legal order in no way excludes State norms, but the legal positivism of this vision takes into consideration the normative activity of States in their entirety, E. Gaillard, "Legal Theory of International Arbitration", Martinus Nijhoff, 2010 ("Aspects philosophiques du droit de l'arbitrage international", Adi-poche, Martinus Nijhoff, 2008), para. 50; E. Gaillard, "Transcending National Legal Orders", in *International Arbitration: The Coming of a New Age*, ICCA Congress Series, No. 17, Wolters Kluwer, 2013, p. 371. The Hague Academy's Lectures on the Scientific Legacy of Emmanuel Gaillard, Brill Nijhoff, 2023.

7. E. Loquin, "L'ordre juridique arbitral", *JDI*, 2022, p. 1157; J.-B. Racine, "Réflexions sur l'autonomie de l'arbitrage commercial international", *Rev. arb.*, 2005, p. 305.

8. F. Ost and M. de Kerchove, "De la pyramide au réseau ?", *Publications des Facultés universitaires Saint Louis*, No. 94, 2002.

CHAPTER 1

THE ATTRACTION OF INTERNATIONAL LAW

International law governs the award

5. The fact that awards are subject to international law is a factor that attracts international law to the review process. Although governed by international law, arbitration proceedings are not the place where international law manifests itself most specifically. Many procedural rules are international in origin, but this does not mean that international law has any influence on the award. A typology based on the rules applicable to the dispute better reflects the international basis of awards. The permissive choice of substantive rules gives way to the application of rules of international law, in international commercial contracts with the *lex mercatoria*, in sports disputes with the *lex sportiva* [9] or in investment matters [10]. Their application is characterized by decompartmentalization and extension. The *El Paso* v. *Argentina* award relies on the UNIDROIT Principles to support the identification of a general principle of international law on the exemption from liability [11]. More broadly, there is nothing to prevent the choice of international law as the law of the contract or in conjunction with national law. Grossen observes that "[t]he election of a particular legal system entails the concurrent designation of international law in so far as international law is deemed to form part of that system or is

9. F. Latty, "La *lex sportiva*", Martinus Nijhoff, 2007; CAS Award No. 98/200 of 20 August 1999, para. 156: "Sports law has developed and consolidated along the years, particularly through the arbitral settlement of disputes, a set of unwritten legal principles – a sort of *lex mercatoria* for sports or, so to speak, a *lex ludica*" (*Digest of CAS Awards*, II, 1998-2000, M. Reeb (ed.), Kluwer Law International, 2002, p. 38); CAS Award No. 2014/A/3505 of 3 December 2014, paras. 85-87.

10. A. Carlevaris, "General Principles of Commercial Law and International Investment Law", in General Principles and the Coherence of International Law, Queen Mary Studies in International Law, M. Andenas, M. Fitzmaurice, A. Tanzi and J. Wouters (eds.), Vol. 37, Brill Nijhoff, 2019, p. 205. Resolution of the Institute of International Law on The Proper Law of the Contract in Agreements between a State and a Foreign Private Person, Athens Session, 1979, S. Karger, Vol. 58, tome II, p. 193. P. Juillard, "L'évolution des sources du droit des investissements", *Collected Courses*, Vol. 250 (1994), p. 9.

11. *El Paso* v. *Argentina*, ICSID Award of 31 October 2011, ARB/03/15, paras. 621-624.

incorporated into it by provisions of domestic law" [12]. Plantey explains that "[i]t is often appropriate to raise the dispute above the legal system of one of the States concerned in order to subject it to major principles of an international nature" [13].

6. The application of national law is not exclusive of the general principles of international law, as stated in *Texaco* v. *Libya* [14]. Research into the fundamental legal system corresponds to theories constructed for specific purposes to internationalize contracts and justify that the investor be considered a subject of public international law [15]. Today, this is accepted and many international conventions protect investment under international law.

7. Some investment protection treaties contain choice of law clauses which, in addition to the provisions of the treaty and the law of the host State, mention the principles of international law [16]. But in all cases, as the arbitral tribunal in *AAPL* v. *Sri Lanka* explained that

> "the Bilateral Investment Treaty is not a self-contained closed legal system limited to provide for substantive material rules of direct applicability, but it has to be envisaged within a wider juridical context in which rules from other sources are integrated through implied incorporation methods, or by direct reference to certain supplementary rules, whether of international law character or of domestic law nature" [17].

---

12. J.-M. Grossen, "La prise en compte du droit international public dans l'arbitrage commercial international", Festschrift für Franz Kellerhals, Stämpfli Verlag Bern, 2005, p. 35.

13. A. Plantey, "Le rôle de l'arbitrage dans le développement de l'économie", IDEF, 29 March 1996.

14. *Texaco* v. *Libya*, Award, JDI, 1977, 350, ILM, Vol. 17 (1978), p. 1, *International Law Reports*, Vol. 53, p. 389:

> "[a]ny national law embodies general principles of law as provided for in Article 38 of the Statute of the International Court of Justice. The generic term 'general principles of law' refers to certain principles common to the legal systems of the various States of the world. They constitute a source of international law which has its origin in the various national laws: therefore, the application of national law does not exclude that of the general principles of law, which are themselves part of the principles of international law" (para. 50).

15. Ch. Leben, "Quelques réflexions théoriques à propos des contrats d'Etat" Mélanges Kahn, Litec, 2000, p. 119; "La théorie du contrat d'Etat et l'évolution du droit international des investissements", *Collected Courses*, Vol. 302 (2003), p. 197; P. Weil, "Ecrits de droit international", PUF, 2000, pp. 351, 379, 409.

16. Y. Banifatemi and E. Gaillard, "The Meaning of 'and' in Article 42 (1), Second Sentence, of the Washington Convention: The Role of International Law in the ICSID Choice of Law Process", 18 (2) ICSID Review (2004), p. 375.

17. ICSID Award of 27 June 1990, *Asian Agricultural Products Ltd* v. *Sri Lanka*, ARB/87/3, para. 21.

Moreover, it is settled case law since the *Georges Pinson* award that a treaty is regulated by international law [18].

8. The ICSID Convention lays the foundations for an organized arbitration system leading to the application of international law, whether with regard to jurisdiction [19] or the merits. By directing the arbitrators to "the rules of international law as may be applicable" to decide the dispute, the Convention refers to the sources of international law identified in Article 38 (1) of the Statute of the International Court of Justice (ICJ) [20].

9. Not all international law can be used to review awards. Not all violations of international law are violations of substantive public policy; the Swiss Federal Tribunal reminds us in relation to an arbitration under the European Energy Charter:

> "The primacy of international law over domestic law is undoubtedly a generally accepted principle, including in Switzerland . . . It does not follow, however, that an award imposing an obligation on a party to compensate the opposing party in an equitable manner should necessarily be regarded as incompatible with the restrictive definition of substantive public policy. . ., even if that injunction contradicted a rule derived from supranational law." [21]

10. The imperative nature of certain rules is not excluded. Encouraged by legal doctrine, such as the resolution of the Institute of International Law on Arbitration between States and Foreign Enterprises [22], arbitral case law clearly establishes the need to respect

---

18. Franco-Mexican Claims Commission, Decision No. 1 of 19 October 1928 *(Georges Pinson)*, RSA, p. 422, No. 50 (4), "[a]n international convention must be deemed to refer tacitly to common international law in respect of all matters which it does not itself resolve in express terms and in a different manner".

19. ICSID Award of 15 April 2009, No. ARB/06/5 *Phoenix Action* v. *Czech Republic*, paras. 74-75; Decision of the Tribunal on Objections to Jurisdiction of 24 May 1999, *CSOB* v. *Slovakia*, ICSID No. ARB/97/4, para. 35.

20. *Ad hoc* Committee, *Wena* v. *Egypt*, Decision of 28 January 2002, ICSID No. ARB/98/4, paras. 37-46. Y. Banifatemi and E. Gaillard, "The Meaning of 'and' in Article 42 (1)", Second Sentence, of the Washington Convention: The Role of International Law in the ICSID Choice of Law Process, 18 (2) *ICSID Review* (2004), p. 375. W. M. Reisman, "The Regime for *Lacunae* in the ICSID Choice of Law Provision and the Question of Its Threshold", 15 *ICSID Review* (2000), p. 362. H. Slim, "Host State's Liability in Investment Dispute Arbitration: The Role of Domestic Law", Mélanges El Kosheri, Wolters Kluwer, 2015, p. 345.

21. TF Judgment of 6 October 2015, 4A_34/2015, para. 5.31.

22. "In no case shall an arbitrator violate principles of international public policy as to which a broad consensus has emerged in the international community" (Art. 2), *Institute of International Law Yearbook*, Santiago de Compostella Session, 1989, Pedone, 1990, Vol. 63-II, p. 216.

the principles of international law that are peremptory, whether in the field of international commercial law [23], sports law [24] or investment law [25]. The security of transactions is identified as a principle of public policy of the *lex mercatoria* [26], good faith as a principle of transnational public policy reflected in the *jus cogens* of international arbitration [27]. In his lecture to the Academy, Gaillard emphasized the extent to which the method of transnational rules makes it possible to identify "truly international public policy rules, which correspond to the public international law concept of *jus cogens*" [28]. French and Swiss case law include in international public policy the principles of good faith performance of contracts [29] and *pacta sunt servanda* [30]. There is, therefore, a need for rules of international law that are binding on arbitrators.

The attractive force of international law

11. The application of international law is not always singled out and is not systematically explicit. Other sources are also involved, such as transnational substantive rules [31], which need not be dwelt on since

---

23. ICC Award 2730 of 1982 (Merits), S. Jarvin and Y. Derains, *Collection of ICC Arbitral Awards*, 1974-1985, Kluwer, 1990, p. 490; ICC Awards 7047 of 1994 (Merits) and 6474 of 1992 (Jurisdiction), J.-J. Arnaldez, Y. Derains and D. Hascher, *Recueil des sentences arbitrales de la CCI*, 1996-2000, Kluwer Law International, 2003, pp. 32, 341.

24. CAS Award 2002/A/431 of 23 May 2003, *Digest of CAS Awards*, M. Reeb (ed.), III, 2001-2003, Kluwer Law International, Staempfli, 2004, p. 410.

25. Award NAFTA *Methanex* v. *United States*, 3 August 2005, ". . . as a matter of international constitutional law a tribunal has an independent duty to apply imperative principles of law or *jus cogens* and not to give effect to parties' choice of law that are inconsistent with such principles" (Part IV, Chap. C, p. 11, para. 24); ICSID Award of 11 June 2012, No. ARB/03/23, *EDF, Saur* et al v. *Argentina*, "It is common ground that the Tribunal should be sensitive to international *jus cogens* norms, including basic principles of human rights" (para. 909).

26. ICC Award No. 3267 of 1979 and commentary, S. Jarvin and Y. Derains, *Collection of ICC Arbitral Awards*, 1974-1985, Kluwer, 1990, p. 376.

27. ICC Award No. 6474 of 1992, paras. 36-38, J.-J. Arnaldez, Y. Derains and D. Hascher, *Collection of ICC Arbitral Awards*, 1996-2000, Kluwer Law International, 2003, p. 341. A. Gomez Robledo, "Le *ius cogens* international : sa genèse, sa nature, ses fonctions", *Collected Courses*, Vol. 172 (1981), p. 9.

28. E. Gaillard, "Legal Theory of International Arbitration", Martinus Nijfhoff, 2010 (Aspects philosophiques du droit de l'arbitrage international, Adi-poche, Martinus Nijhoff, 2008), para. 61.

29. CA Paris, Judgment of 29 March 1991, *Rev. arb.*, 1991, p. 478, note L. Idot; 12 January 1993, *Rev. arb.*, 1994, p. 685; 20 June 1996, *Rev. arb.*, 1996, p. 657, obs. DB.

30. TF Judgment of 8 April 2021, 4A_516/2020, para. 4.2.2.

31. E. Gaillard, "Les vertus de la méthode des règles matérielles appliquées à la convention d'arbitrage", *Rev. arb.*, 2020, p. 701.

it suffices to point out that the validity of the award is examined in the light of the rules of the country where recognition and enforcement are sought.

12. The contractual basis of arbitration in no way detracts from the force of international law. The *ad hoc* committee in *Duke* v. *Peru* invoked the will of the parties and the principle of good faith to interpret the arbitration clause in a contract governed by Peruvian law:

> "In addressing this question of consent under Article 25 [of the ICSID Convention], a tribunal is not bound to apply host state law, even in a case where the parties' consent derives from or relates to an agreement under host state law. Thus, in *SPP* v. *Egypt*, the source of the state's consent was a provision in its investment law. Egypt submitted that the jurisdictional issues were governed by Egyptian law, and that, pursuant to the Egyptian Civil Code, no effective arbitration agreement had been concluded. This submission was rejected by a Tribunal presided by Jiménez de Aréchaga. It applied instead general principles of interpretation and international law to the question of consent. In *CSOB* v. *Slovakia*, the Tribunal's jurisdiction was derived from a contract. The Tribunal held nevertheless, citing Amco with approval, that: The question of whether the parties have effectively expressed their consent to ICSID jurisdiction is not to be answered by reference to national law. It is governed by international law as set out in Article 25 (1) of the ICSID Convention.
>
> Thus, an ICSID tribunal determining its jurisdiction is not required to interpret the instrument of consent according solely to national law, but rather it is to consider directly whether there is the requisite evidence of consent required by Article 25 (1) of the ICSID Convention, having regard to the common will of the parties on which arbitration is grounded and the general principle (widely applied in municipal law as well as in international law) of good faith." [32]

13. While subjecting jurisdiction to rules rooted in international law is consistent for an *ad hoc* committee because of its role as guarantor of the integrity of the ICSID Convention [33], the application of international

32. Decision of 1 March 2011, ICSID No. ARB/03/28, paras. 141-142.
33. Decision of the *ad hoc* Committee of 5 June 2007, *Soufraki* v. *UAE*, ARB/02/7:

> "[T]he object and purpose of an ICSID annulment proceeding may be described as the control of the fundamental integrity of the ICSID arbitral process in all its

law is more remarkable when the conflict rules of the forum are called upon.

14. The agreement to arbitrate between the investor and the host State based on the provisions of an investment protection treaty is not a treaty, the English judge reminds us [34]. For all that, and independently of any ratification of such a treaty by the United Kingdom, this agreement is governed by international law:

> "The question may then arise: under what law is that agreement to arbitrate to be regarded as subject, applying the principles of private international law of the English forum? . . . It is common ground that English private international law recognises an agreement to arbitrate substantive issues such as the present according to international law (cf. *Orion* v. *Belfort* [1962] 2 Ll.R. 257, 264, per Megaw J, Dicey & Morris, The Conflict of Laws, Vol. 1, para. 16-031 and Mustill & Boyd's Commercial Arbitration (2nd ed.), pp. 80-81), and it is also clear that the present is such. (The words 'in accordance with the law' in s. 46 (1) *(a)* and 'the law determined by the conflict of laws rules which it considers applicable' in s. 46 (3) of the Arbitration Act 1996 are capable of having this broad meaning, and s. 46 (1) *(b)* now adds further to the flexibility of arbitration, by permitting an agreement to arbitrate issues in accordance with other, non-legal considerations.) All this being so, we would be minded to accept that, under English private international law principles, the agreement to arbitrate may itself be subject to international law, as it may be subject to foreign law. That possibility also appears to us to have been embraced as long ago as 1962 by J. Megaw, in *Orion* v. *Belfort* (above). And, if one assumes that this is possible, then that is the view that we would, like the judge, take of this particular arbitration agreement. Although it is a consensual agreement, it is closely connected with the international Treaty which contemplated its making, and which contains the provisions defining the scope of

facets . . . Integrity of the dispute settlement mechanism, integrity of the process of dispute settlement and integrity of solution of the dispute are the basic interrelated goals projected in the ICSID annulment mechanism" (para. 23).

34. CA England and Wales, Judgment of 9 September 2005, *Occidental* v. *Republic of Ecuador* [2005] EWCA Civ. 1116: "the agreement to arbitrate which results by following the Treaty route is not itself a treaty. It is an agreement between a private investor on the one side and the relevant State on the other" (No. 33). See also ICJ, Judgment of 22 July 1952, *Anglo-Iranian Oil Co.* [1952] ECR 93.

the arbitrators' jurisdiction. Further, the protection of investors at which the whole scheme is aimed is likely to be better served if the agreement to arbitrate is subject to international law, rather than to the law of the State against which an investor is arbitrating." [35]

15. The same orientation in favor of international law can be found in the case law of the Swiss Federal Tribunal:

> "The Arbitral Tribunal, whose seat was fixed in Zurich, ruled on its own jurisdiction and judged the case in the light of the ECT *[European Energy Charter]*, a Convention which is an integral part of Swiss law, and which does not refer to the law of another State for the interpretation and application of its jurisdictional clause. In the absence of a choice of law relating to that clause, Swiss law is therefore both the *lex causae* and the *lex fori* in this case. The Federal Tribunal's review will therefore be limited to the question of whether the Arbitral Tribunal disregarded Swiss law – specifically, the ECT – by accepting jurisdiction." [36]

16. The monist/dualist distinction is no longer a clear line, as there are so many ways of integrating international law into domestic law [37]. The Swiss Federal Tribunal does not accept the direct application of international law, even though it is a treaty ratified by Switzerland. Instead, it applied Article 178 of the LDIP [38] as if it were a conflict of laws to apply the Energy Charter as part of Swiss law. Although complicated, the demonstration is nonetheless satisfactory. The expression "closely connected with the international Treaty" in the

---

35. CA England and Wales, Judgment of 9 September 2005, *Occidental* v. *Republic of Ecuador* [2005] EWCA Civ 1116, No. 33. Resolution of the Institute of International Law on The Proper Law of the Contract in Agreements between a State and a Foreign Private Person, Athens Session 1979, S. Karger, Vol. 58, Part II, p. 193.

36. *Supra* note 22, TF, Judgment of 6 October 2015, No. 4A-34/2015, para. 3.4.2.

37. H. Triepel, "Les rapports entre le droit interne et le droit international", *Collected Courses*, Vol. 1 (1923) p. 73; G. A. Walz, "Les rapports du droit international et du droit interne", *Collected Courses*, Vol. 61 (1937), p. 375; Y. Iwasawa, "Domestic Application of International Law", *Collected Courses*, Vol. 378 (2015), p. 9. On the integration of international custom into the common law, see the 25 November 2015 Judgment of the UK Supreme Court, *Keyu* et al. v. *Secretary of State for Foreign and Commonwealth Affairs* [2015] UKSC 69, Nos. 142-151.

38. Article 178 LDIP with its alternative connections to the law chosen by the parties, to the law governing the subject matter of the dispute or to Swiss law validates the arbitration clause as well as a substantive rule would (E. Gaillard and P. Lalive, "Le nouveau droit de l'arbitrage international en Suisse", *JDI*, 1989, p. 905; see also B. Oppetit, "Le développement des règles matérielles", *Trav. Com. fr. DIP*, Journée du cinquantenaire, CNRS, 1988, p. 121).

judgment of the English Court of Appeal refers to the conflict of laws technique, but the English judge rejects any mechanistic approach and prefers a subtle flexibility. It is everyone's responsibility to maintain the equilibrium of the international justice system [39] and not to get bogged down in formalism, even if it is a matter of private international law. A rule derived from various sources, with the possibility of nuances and different contents, provides flexibility to those applying the rule by distancing themselves from a mechanical application that would limit them to a single source. This is similar to the reasoning of arbitrators in determining the applicable law when they endeavor to select rules that correspond to the legitimate expectations of the parties. The attraction of international law as a source of inspiration encourages reasoning that goes beyond the search for formal sources and their hierarchies, which do not allow the international situation of the award to be considered in all its dimensions.

17. The attraction of international law must be equally manifest when reviewing awards made in arbitrations based on a national investment law. Reasoning in terms of the application of foreign law, as in an English decision on an award based on Kyrgyz investment law [40], leaves less room for unity of interpretation of investment law concepts than in the case of treaty-based arbitration. How can a harmonizing interpretation be encouraged when the generally accepted rule is that the application and interpretation of foreign law by the trial judge as factual findings is not subject to review [41]? National investment laws have a broadly uniform content, with concepts that overlap with those used in treaties. It is, therefore, not true that the application of international standards depends solely on the national or international source of investment protection. Notwithstanding a referral to arbitration based on Egyptian investment law, the *SPP* v. *Egypt* award is persuasive in its use of international law rather than Egyptian law [42].

---

39. The English Court of Appeal emphasized this in its Judgment of 9 September 2005 in *Occidental* v. *Republic of Ecuador*: "the protection of investors at which the whole scheme is aimed is likely to be better served if the agreement to arbitrate is subject to international law, rather than to the law of the State against which an investor is arbitrating" ([2005] EWCA Civ 1116, No. 33).

40. Judgment of 13 October 2017, *The Kyrgyz Republic* v. *Stans Energy and Kutisay Mining* [2017] EWHC 2539 (Comm).

41. The Application of Foreign Law in Civil Matters in the EU Member States and Its Perspectives for the Future, Swiss Institute of Comparative Law, Opinion 09-184, 11 July 2011.

42. Decision on Jurisdiction, 14 April 1988, *SPP* v. *Egypt*, ARB/84/3, para. 61, E. Gaillard, *La jurisprudence du CIRDI*, Pedone, 2004, Vol. 1, p. 347.

When a national law provides protection for investors, it takes its place in international relations. If that law violates the minimum requirements of protection, it must be sanctioned by the arbitral tribunal. Supervisory bodies are also encouraged to place their solutions under the banner of international law.

18. The attractive force of international law is best explained if we accept that the function of international law in the control of awards is not the same as its function in relations between States. While its role is no different from that of foreign law, the application of international law shows that the international legal order which gave rise to the award cannot be disregarded, the objectives and coherence of which are better preserved than with the application of national law. The fact that international law does not always have the same character is not a problem.

CHAPTER 2

INTERNATIONAL LAW AS A MODERATING FACTOR IN REVIEW

19. Review in the light of international law does not require that the award be governed by international law. International law may be involved in the review of an award that was not submitted to it or for a question that was not submitted to it. A more assertive application of international law must not be the cause of excesses. Control of an award must be necessary to avoid anything that could cause disruption to a peaceful international legal order. To restore harmony, the supervisory bodies have at their disposal global legal instruments, the New York Convention or the Washington Convention, neither of which authorizes them to review the arbitrators' decisions on the merits [43]. The weight of international law must not be allowed to restrict the freedom of arbitrators, especially since once the existence of an arbitral legal order has been recognized, it must be given free rein in all areas where there is no need for control.

Getting involved in the merits?

20. Of interest here is the Vienna Convention on the Law of Treaties of 23 May 1969 as an interpretative tool to balance control, and proportionality as a methodological tool, particularly for confronting pecuniary obligations and corruption issues with public policy.

21. The Vienna Convention represents a codification of international custom [44] whose rules of interpretation can be applied independently of its ratification by the host State signatory to the investment protection treaty [45]. As the Vienna Convention applies to the interpretation of any

43. W. M. Reisman, *Systems of Control in International Adjudication & Arbitration*, Duke University Press, 1992.

44. M. Villiger, *Commentary on the 1969 Vienna Convention on the Law of Treaties*, Martinus Nijhoff, 2009, Article 31, para. 25, p. 433. See also G. Berlia, "Contribution à l'interprétation des traités", *Collected Courses*, Vol. 114 (1965), pp. 287-334; L. Ehrlich, "L'interprétation des traités", *Collected Courses*, Vol. 24 (1928), pp. 1-146; H. Lauterpacht, "De l'interprétation des traités", session de Bath, 1950, *Annuaire de l'Institut de droit international*, Bâle, 1950, tome 1, p. 366.

45. TF, Judgment of 25 March 2020, 4A_306/2019, para. 3.4.1.

treaty, the ratification by the supervising court forum country of the investment protection treaty in respect of which the arbitrators are ruling is irrelevant to its application.

22. It should not be possible to go into the merits on the pretext of reviewing jurisdiction [46]. The case law of the main European countries in which investment arbitrations are held shows that recourse to the Vienna Convention to interpret the clauses of the treaty maintains control within the permissible limits of jurisdiction, without invading the merits [47]. The lines of control are, therefore, not altered by the intervention of the Vienna Convention. But in the absence of a preliminary ruling mechanism, how can different national interpretations of international conventions be avoided? Without the support of such a mechanism, the search for a coherent interpretation increases the importance of comparative reasoning. Consensus is not always reached [48]. National judges should strive to interpret treaties as if they were international judges [49], especially higher courts, which, through their regulatory action, deepen the control of awards by unifying it.

23. This proposition remains valid in the event of non-ratification of the investment protection treaty by the forum supervisory court country. Equating a treaty to which the forum is not a party with foreign law, the determination of which is exclusively within the powers of the trial judges, does not reflect the fact that a treaty cannot be given a meaning that is contrary to international law [50]. What matters is the application of international law, of which treaties are a source and to which they are subject. There is an obligation to respect international law and therefore to verify whether the provisions of the treaty have been observed. The

46. A limitation period is an issue of admissibility, the court hearing the annulment is not allowed, under the guise of jurisdiction *ratione temporis*, to trim through the merits of the arbitral tribunal's decisions on harmful acts for finding them time-barred, Civ. 1re, Judgment of 31 March 2021, *Rusoro Mining* v. *Venezuela*, No. 19-11.551.

47. "International Investment Law in European Courts", in *International Investment Law: An Analysis of the Major Decisions*, H. Ruiz Fabri and E. Stoppioni (eds.), Oxford, Hart Publishing, 2022, p. 617.

48. For example, in *PAO Taneft* v. *Ukraine*, the abuse of the right to bring proceedings before the investment tribunal is considered a question of admissibility by the English judge (Judgment of 13 July 2018 [2018] EWHC 1797 (Comm), paras. 99-100) and therefore not subject to review but treated by the French judge as a question of jurisdiction subject to review (CA Paris, Judgment of 29 November 2016, No. 14/17964).

49. B. Conforti, "L'activité du juge interne et les relations internationales de l'Etat", *Institute of International Law*, Milan Session, 1993, Vol. 65-I, Pedone, 1993, p. 328; H. Mosler, "L'application du droit international public par le juge interne", *Collected Courses*, Vol. 91 (1957), p. 619.

50. There is no question of applying rules of foreign law which have their origin in an unratified treaty by the forum, Civ. 1re, Judgment of 1 February 1972, *Rev. crit. DIP* 1973, p. 313, note G. Droz; D. 1973.59, note P. Lagarde; JCP 1973 II 17406, note M. G.

opposite solution would reflect a lack of responsibility by refusing to be part of a universal application of the principles of good governance that rule investments and shape international economic relations [51].

24. Proportionality is a principle of reasoning in the international legal order, but it does not systematically apply to the interpretation of every treaty. Admittedly, the admission of proportionality as a rule of law in major domestic legal systems [52] is not sufficient to make it a general principle of international law within the meaning of Article 38 (1) *(c)* of the ICJ Statute [53]. But proportionality is not only a principle common to national legal systems; it can also be identified as a principle formed in several international legal suborders: the World Trade Organisation [54], the European Union [55] and the European Convention on Human Rights [56] or even the sports legal order [57]. Arbitral case law on investment also uses it as a method of interpreting the rules of protection [58].

---

51. G. Canivet, "Rôle et responsabilité des juridictions dans la mise en œuvre des principes de la gouvernance mondiale", Mélanges E. Zoller, p. 543.

52. A. Barak, *Proportionality*, Cambridge University Press, 2012 ("Democracy, the rule of law, principle theory, and constitutional interpretation are all legal sources from which proportionality may be derived as a constitutional concept", p. 240). S. Breyer, *La Cour suprême, le droit américain et le monde*, pref. G. Canivet and O. Jacob, 2015, p. 268 (The Court and the World, 2015).

53. M. Vazquez-Bermudez, *Second Report on General Principles of Law*, International Law Commission, 9 April 2020, A/CN.4/741 (Second Part, pp. 5- 37).

54. M. Andenas and S. Zleptnig, "Proportionality and Balancing in WTO Law: A Comparative Law Perspective", 2007, *Texas Intl. Law Journal*, Vol. 42.371.

55. ECJ, Judgment of 13 November 1990, Fedesa, aff. C-331-88, para. 13. G. Canivet, "La fonction du principe en droit constitutionnel français et en droit européen" Regards croisés sur l'internationalisation du droit : France-Etats-Unis, M. Delmas-Marty and S. Breyer (eds.), SLC, UMR de droit comparé de Paris, Vol. 18, 2009, p. 140.

56. S. van Drooghenbroek, "La proportionnalité dans le droit de la Convention européenne des droits de l'homme : prendre l'idée simple au sérieux", *Publications des Facultés universitaires Saint Louis*, No. 90, 2001.

57. CAS Award 2018/0/5794 & 5798 of 30 April 2019, paras. 582-586; CAS Award 2016/A/4745 of 30 August 2016, paras. 73-85; CAS Award 2016/O/4684 of 10 October 2016, paras. 129-132; CAS Award No. 2014/A/3665, 3666 & 3667 of 2 December 2014, paras. 91-108; CAS Award JO 00/04 of 18 September 2000, paras. 11-12.

58. Expropriation: *Tecmed* v. *Mexico* Award of 29 May 2003, ICSID No. ARB(AF)/00/2, para. 122; *LG&E* v. *Argentina*, Award of 25 July 2007, ARB/02/1, para. 195; *El Paso* v. *Argentina*, Award of 31 October 2011, ARB/03/15, paras. 241, 243 (ICSID); *Azurix* v. *Argentina*, Award of 14 July 2006, ARB/01/12, paras. 311-312; *Siemens* v. *Argentina*, Award of 17 January 2007, ICSID No. ARB/02/8, para. 354; *PL Holdings* v. *Poland*, SCC aff. No. 2014/13, Award of 28 June 2017, paras. 354-391.

The obligation of full protection and security (FPS) and fair and equitable treatment (FET): *Occidental* v. *Ecuador*, Award of 5 October 2012, ARB/06/11, paras. 402-452; *MTD* v. *Chile*, ARB/01/7, Award of 25 May 2004, para. 109; *Marfin* v. *Cyprus*, Award of 26 July 2018, ARB/13/27, paras. 1211-1213; *Joseph Lemire* v. *Ukraine*, Decision on Jurisdiction and Liability of 14 January 2010, ARB/06/18, para. 285; *Saluka*

25. It is difficult to characterize a violation of public policy [59] or an excess of power [60] over an interpretation. The application of proportionality by the arbitral tribunal is difficult to control because it quickly comes up against the substance, which is not controlled. Can one slip into the merits of the case by using proportionality when reviewing an award? There are examples [61]. Proportionality is not about reversing even the best-established solutions. However, the methodological usefulness of proportionality in handling the public policy exception must not be disregarded. An example of this is the case law of the Swiss Federal Tribunal concerning a disciplinary sanction imposed in a sports arbitration, the proportionality of which could not be considered "from the limited perspective of incompatibility with public policy, unless the award constituted a violation of personality that was extremely serious and out of all proportion to the conduct it sanctioned" [62]. Refusal to accept the award is an interference with the right to effective enforcement of decisions [63]. As an aspect of the right to a fair

Investments v. *Czech Republic*, UNCITRAL Partial Award of 17 March 2006, para. 306; *Total* v. *Argentina*, Decision on Liability of 27 December 2010, No. ARB/04/01, paras. 123, 162, 164; *Belenergia* v. *Italy*, aff. ARB/15/40, Award of 6 August 2019, paras. 605, 606; *Electrabel* v. *Hungary*, Award of 25 November 2015, ARB/07/19, paras. 179, 219; *Stadtwerke München* v. *Spain*, Award of 2 December 2019, ARB/15/1, paras. 323-355; *RWE Innogy* v. *Spain*, Decision, 30 December 2019, ARB/14/34, paras. 550-600; *Antaris & Göde* v. *Czech Rep.*, PCA aff. 2014-01, Award of 2 May 2018, paras. 444-445; *EDF* v. *Romania*, Award of 8 October 2009, ARB/05/13, para. 293. G. Bücheler, Proportionality in Investor-State Arbitration, Oxford University Press, 2015.

Non-precluded measures clause (NPM): *Continental Casualty* v. *Argentina*, Award of 5 September 2008, ICSID No. ARB/03/9, para. 227.

59. TF Judgment of 25 August 2020, 4A_248/2019 and 4A_298/2019, paras. 9.8.2-9.8.3.

60. Decision of the *ad hoc* Committee 2 November 2015, *Occidental Petroleum Corp. & Occidental Petroleum Cie* v. *Republic of Ecuador*, ARB/06/11, paras. 343-351.

61. CA Cairo, Judgment of 3 June 2020, No. 39/130, para. 22:

> "the compensation awarded by the Award as compensation for lost profit, exceeded reasonable limits and contradicted its objectives, becoming an unjust, inequitable, ill-founded compensation, not taking into account the legal aims of the parties to the arbitration. This is because the award violates the guarantees of legal certainty aimed at by any legislator. This unfair exceedance of any limit has had a negative impact on the arbitration award and the structure of its making".

62. TF Judgment of 31 March 1999, 5P.83/1999, para. 3 *(c)*, Digest of CAS Awards, M. Reeb (ed.), II, 1998-2000, Kluwer Law International, 2002, p. 767. See also TF Judgment of 25 August 2020, 4A_248_2019 & 4A_398_2019 for the proportionality of a hormone treatment measure imposed by a sports regulation with the principle of prohibition of discrimination.

63. ECHR, Judgments of 29 April 2008, *McDonald* v. *France*, Appl. No. 18648/04; 3 May 2011, *Negropontis* v. *Greece*, Appl. No. 56759/08, paras. 89-92; 18 December 2008, *Sacoccia* v. *Austria*, Appl. No. 69917/01, paras. 60-62.

trial[64], the right to enforcement is not absolute[65], but the interference must remain proportionate and legitimate.

26. In the case of pecuniary awards, which are the most frequent in arbitration, it should be remembered that *restitutio in integrum*[66] is a principle of reasoning[67]. While it is also a general principle aimed at avoiding double compensation[68], the obligation to make full reparation is not a fundamental principle[69]. An award of punitive damages is not in itself contrary to international public policy, except "where the amount awarded is disproportionate to the loss suffered and to the debtor's breach of contractual obligations", as the French Court of Cassation has ruled[70]. This is not an invitation to revisit the amount of the award in the light of the debtor's ability to pay but to check whether the award is commensurate with the contractual nonperformance in the circumstances of the case[71]. Does the nonrecognition of the award

---

64. ECHR, Judgments of 19 March 1997, *Hornsby*, Appl. No. 18357/91, para. 40; 31 October 2006, *Jelicic* v. *Bosnia and Herzegovina*, Appl. No. 41183/02, para. 38; 15 January 2009, *Bourdov* v. *Russia*, Appl. No. 33509/04, para. 65; 7 January 2014, *Fondation foyer de l'église réformée* v. *Romania*, Appl. No. 2699/03, para. 55.

65. ECHR, 18 February 1999, *Waite and Kennedy* v. *Germany*, Appl. No. 26083/94, para. 59.

66. ICJ, Judgment of 13 September 1928, *The Factory at Chorzow* Series A, No. 17, 1928, Leiden, Sijthoff.

67. *Texaco* v. *Libya, ad hoc* Award of 19 January 1977, para. 98.

68. J. Crawford, The International Law Commission's Articles on State Responsibility, Introduction, Text and Commentaries, Cambridge University Press, 2005, Article 36, p. 218.

69. TF Judgment of 8 April 2021, 4A_516/2020

> "The principles of international law do not, moreover, confer an absolute right to full compensation (above-mentioned Judgment 4P.200/2001 let. B and Recital 2 *c)*. For the rest, the Federal Tribunal does not have to sanction, on grounds of public policy, an erroneous or even arbitrary interpretation of a clause in a BIT; it cannot be required to examine whether or not the compensation provided for in the BIT includes loss of profit (Judgment cited above in 4P.200/2001, para. 2*c* in fine; Judgment 4A_157/2017 of 14 December 2017, para. 3.3.4)" (para. 4.2.3)
>
> ". . . In the present case, public policy is not necessarily breached because the Turkish investor does not obtain full compensation for its loss, because it is awarded compensation that does not fully cover the loss suffered – or that is not in reasonable proportion to the value of the lost investments. However, taking into account all the specific circumstances, the compensation must appear to be out of all proportion to the value of the lost investment, and there must be such extreme disproportion between the two that the most essential principles of the legal system are shockingly violated. As will be shown below, such a situation has not arisen" (para. 4.4).

70. Civ. 1re, Judgment of 1 December 2010, No. 09-13.303; Civ. 1re, Judgment of 7 November 2012, No. 1123871.

71. Civ. 1re, Judgment of 17 October 2018, No. 17-18.995, *Rev. crit. DIP*, 2019, p. 982, note by P. de Vareilles-Sommières; Civ. 1re, Judgment of 12 January 2022, No. 2016189; Civ. 1re, Judgment of 28 January 2009, No. 07-11.729.

violate the creditor's right to property [72]? Protection of property is an essential value protected by international public policy and fundamental rights. The claim for compensation which forms part of the award beneficiary's proprietary rights is thus a protected asset, and any interference caused by nonrecognition must remain proportionate [73].

27. Is a more discreet application of international law still appropriate today, even when a criticism of a breach of public policy is raised? Public policy has always emphasized the fight against corruption, influence peddling and money laundering, as can be seen from the arbitral case law [74]. The condemnation of such conduct is based on the general principle of the illegality of corruption in the *lex mercatoria* and in international law, where it is expressed in several international conventions [75]. Even if these conventions are not directly applicable, the values they protect are undoubtedly essential to the legal order of any forum. The review of corruption issues in the award, as it appears before certain courts under their national law, is destructive of the distinction between review of public policy and review of the merits [76]. International law does not require that the correctness of the award is ensured as in an appeal. It is through the prism of the challenge to the award that the judge must carry out any assessment of corruption, and not directly, as the arbitrator would do.

28. Here are the relevant questions to be answered. Does an award which gives rise to a right to compensation in favor of the party accused of unlawful conduct infringe the right to respect for the property of the party ordered to pay compensation? Or is the latter entitled, without exceeding the right to respect for its property, to a confiscatory

72. This issue has been remarkably developed by Professor P. de Vareilles-Sommières, *Rev. crit. DIP*, 2019, p. 982, No. 19.

73. ECHR, Judgments of 30 June 2022, *BTS Holding* v. *Slovak Republic*, Appl. No. 55617/17, para. 53; *Greek Refineries Stran and Stratis Andreadis* v. *Greece*, 9 December 1994, paras. 58-62, Series A, No. 301-B; also ECHR, Judgment of 24 September 2013, *Pennino* v. *Italy*, Appl. No. 42892/04, paras. 54-60 (concerning a court judgment).

74. ICSID Award ARB/00/7 of 4 October 2006, *Work Duty Free Ltd.* v. *Republic of Kenya*; ICC Award 12290 of 2005, J.-J. Arnaldez, Y. Derains and D. Hascher, *Collection of ICC Arbitral Awards*, 2008-2011, Kluwer, p. 831. E. Gaillard, "La corruption saisie par les arbitres du commerce international", *Rev. arb.*, 2017, p. 805; A. Llamzon, "Corruption in International Investment Arbitration", OUP, 2014.

75. United Nations Conventions against Corruption of 9 December 2003 (Merida) and against Transnational Organized Crime of 15 November 2000 (Palermo), the OECD Convention on Combating Bribery of Foreign Public Officials in International Business Transactions of 17 December 1997.

76. I. Fadlallah, "L'ordre public dans les sentences arbitrales", *Collected Courses*, Vol. 249 (1994), p. 369, La corruption corrompt l'arbitrage, *Rev. arb.*, 2022, 620.

solution consisting of keeping the investment without compensation? This question is all the more pressing given that the public authorities of the host country are often complicit in the illegality of which the investor who won the arbitration is accused. By surrendering to the State the investment and the acquisition price paid by the investor attracted by the climate of corruption fostered by the host State, which still confiscates the profits of the investor's money laundering activities in which it actively participated, the Belokon [77] case law represents a strong incentive to institutionalized corruption. In answering these questions, it will be necessary to examine the respective conduct of the parties in order to assess whether the infringement of a party's right to respect for its possessions is legitimate and proportionate.

29. Proportionality reduces the imperative nature of norms in order to better channel the confrontation with public policy and avoid a revision of the merits of the award [78]. As a technique of reconciling legal systems to resolve conflicts between norms, proportionality encourages dialogue between courts [79]. However, the courts must be accessible to dialogue, which is not possible if a political position is defended.

The limits

30. The Court of Justice of the European Union ("CJEU") challenges the arbitrability of disputes based on investment protection treaties considered to be contrary to the European Treaties. It does not matter whether European law plays a role in the resolution of the dispute. Various reasons are put forward. They range from the absence of a preliminary ruling mechanism for an arbitration tribunal, whereas the interpretation of a Member State's law is always likely to give rise to an interpretation of European law, to the binding nature of European law for the courts and institutions of the Member States, whose full application must be guaranteed, to the exclusion in an international agreement, whether signed by the European Union or not, of the European Union's

77. Cass. Civ. 1re, Judgment of 23 March 2022, *Belokon* v. *Kirghizistan*, No. 17-17.981. For a balanced solution, see *Spentex* v. *Uzbekistan* (ICSID Award of 27 December 2016, No. ARB/13/26); Ch. Jarrosson, La jurisprudence Belokon-Sorelec, ou l'avènement d'un contrôle illimité des sentences, *Rev. arb.*, 2022, 1251.

78. K. Lund-Turner, "The Corruption Defense in Investment-Treaty Arbitration: Tempering the Zero-Tolerance Approach", *Pacific McGeorge School of Law*, Spring 2015.

79. S. W. Schill, "Cross-Regime Harmonization Through Proportionality Analysis: The Case of International Investment Law, the Law of State Immunity and Human Rights", *ICSID Review*, Vol. 27, No. 1 (2012), p. 87.

judicial system [80]. It is as if a treaty to which a Member State is a party were, as far as that State is concerned, like a national law submitted to the European legal order.

31. The case law of the CJEU alters previous balances, returning to the days when arbitrators were prohibited from applying rules of public policy. It takes us back to a conception of international law that is contrary to the very origins of that law [81]. No legal system prohibits others from applying its rules, because there are no rules more dignified than others, especially since European law primarily raises issues of economic regulation that do not lend themselves well to universal recognition [82]. International law would rather dictate dissidence from than obedience to European law.

32. The impact of European case law policy on the international system for the enforcement of awards is measured in the *Micula* case. The enforcement of the ICSID award, made on the basis of the BIT between Sweden and Romania, amounted, for the European Commission, to granting State aid in breach of the Treaty on the Functioning of the European Union, and Romania was therefore prohibited from satisfying the investor [83]. However, in addition to compensating the investor, Romania incurred another international obligation, namely to give effect to the award under Article 53 of the Washington Convention. When asked to enforce the award, the English judge was obliged to

80. CJEU, *Achmea*, Judgment of 6 March 2018, Case C-284/16, *Rev. crit. DIP*, 2018, p. 616, note E. Gaillard; CJEU Judgment of 26 October 2021, *PL Holdings* v. *Poland*, Case C-109/20; CJEU, Judgment of 2 September 2021, *Moldova* v. *Komstroy*, case C-741/19. EU Law and International Investment Arbitration, H. Ruiz-Fabri and E. Gaillard (eds.), IAI 2018; G. Cordero-Moss, "Towards the End of Arbitrability? About Achmea, Komstroy", PL Holdings *et al.*, Brierley Lecture, 19 January 2022.

81. B. Ancel, "Eléments d'histoire du droit international privé", Panthéon-Assas, 2017.

82. TF Judgment of 1 February 2002, 128 III 234:

> "In any event, as the Federal Court has already had occasion to point out, it seems doubtful whether the provisions of national or European competition law form part of the fundamental legal or moral principles recognized in all civilized states to the extent that their violation should be considered contrary to public policy (Judgment 4P.119/1998 of 13 November 1998, Recital 1b/bb, . . .). Moreover, the author cited by the appellant notes, even if he deplores it, that in view of the latter judgment, an arbitrator sitting in Switzerland is certainly obliged to apply Community competition law, but that this obligation cannot be the subject of any sanction at the annulment stage. . ."

W. Ganshof van der Meersch, L'ordre juridique des Communautés européennes et le droit international, *Collected Courses*, Vol. 148 (1975), p. 1; 50th anniversary of the Judgment in van Geend en Loos, 1963-2013, Conference Proceedings, Luxembourg, 13 May 2013, EU Pubs. Office, 2013.

83. Commission Decision (EU) 2015/470 of 30 March 2015, OJ (L 232) 2015, p. 43.

apply Article 54 (1) of the Convention, which requires Contracting States to enforce the pecuniary obligations imposed by the award. In response to Romania's suggestion that the ICSID Convention should be interpreted in accordance with European views, the UK Supreme Court retorted with the principles of interpretation of international law, thereby placing an international commitment of the United Kingdom above European law:

> "The first step in the analysis should be to ask whether the United Kingdom has relevant obligations arising from the ICSID Convention which, by operation of Article 351 TFEU, preclude the application of the Treaties . . . on a proper interpretation of the ICSID Convention, the United Kingdom clearly does have such obligations. Therefore, the Treaties do not have any relevant effect and this court is not bound by EU law to interpret the Convention in the manner for which Romania contends. In any event, the proper interpretation of the Convention is given by principles of international law applicable to all Contracting States and it cannot be affected by EU law." [84]

33. This is a line of reasoning that the European Commission cannot accept and it has opened infringement proceedings against the United Kingdom [85]. We are, therefore, departing from international law to prohibit arbitration under European law.

84. [2020] UKSC 5, Judgment of 19 February 2020, para. 87.
85. European Commission press release of 9 February 2022.

CHAPTER 3

A REVIEW BASED ON UNIVERSALLY RECOGNISED PRINCIPLES, ELEVATED TO THE RANK OF PRINCIPLES OF INTERNATIONAL LAW, AS A COMMON LANGUAGE

34. Principles are a source of law in all legal systems. Because of its universalist premise, it has been noted that "[i]nternational human rights law provides a particularly fertile environment for dialogue between judges" [86]. The most demonstrative is, therefore, to take fundamental rights as a guide to illustrate adherence to unifying values as an example of a common language. The universal values embodied in these rights explain their intervention in relations between sports associations and athletes by means of general principles of law [87].

35. The review of awards unquestionably draws on the human rights treaties in force in the review court forum State [88]. Is it more difficult for an *ad hoc* committee, acting under the aegis of the Washington Convention, to apply international human rights law? With the exception of one *ad hoc* committee which did not know what to do with it, on the pretext that treaties which do not have the protection of investments as their object are of limited use [89], it should be noted that a first *ad hoc* committee in the *Fraport* v. *Philippines* case referred to the main international human rights instruments [90] and that, relying on this decision, another *ad hoc* committee in the *Churchill Mining* v. *Indonesia* case referred to human rights treaties as the source of the content of the right to be heard:

---

86. L. Hennebel and A. van Waeyenberge, "Réflexions sur le commerce transnational entre juges", *Les sources du droit revisitées, Vol. 2, normes internes et infraconstitutionnelles* (I. Hachez, Y. Cartuyvels, H. Dumont, Ph. Gérard, F. Ost and M. van de Kerchove (eds.)), Université Saint-Louis, 2012, p. 713.

87. M. Maisonneuve, "Le TAS et les droits fondamentaux", RDLF 2017, chron. 09.

88. ECHR, 2 October 2018, *Mutu and Pechstein* v. *Switzerland*, Appl. No. 40575/10 and 67474/10; 20 May 2021, *BEG* v. *Italy*, Appl. No. 5312/11.

89. Decision of the *ad hoc* Committee of 1 September 2009, *Azurix* v. *Argentina*, ICSID No. ARB/01/12 (para. 128).

90. *Fraport* v. *Philippines*, Decision of 23 December 2010, ICSID No. ARB/03/25 (Universal Declaration of Human Rights, International Covenant on Civil and Political Rights and European Convention on Human Rights) "The right to present one's case is also accepted as an essential element of the requirement to afford a fair hearing accorded in the principal human rights instruments" (para. 202).

> "Even if *ad hoc* committees operate within the ICSID Convention, the reference to the jurisprudence of specialized courts which are an integral part of human rights treaties fosters the consistency of the content of the right to be heard and strengthens the effectiveness of this concept. It also enhances the legitimacy of the interpretation by linking it to the broader body of international law." [91]

36. It is the *ad hoc* committee in *Tulip Real Estate and Development Netherlands* v. *Republic of Turkey* that, however, systematized the introduction of human rights by resorting to Article 31 (3) *(c)* of the Vienna Convention on the Law of Treaties:

> "Provisions in human rights instruments dealing with the right to a fair trial and any judicial practice thereto are relevant to the interpretation of the concept of a fundamental rule of procedure as used in Article 52 (1) *(d)* of the ICSID Convention. This is not to add obligations extraneous to the ICSID Convention. Rather, resort to authorities stemming from the field of human rights for this purpose is a legitimate method of treaty interpretation." [92]

37. There is also an *ad hoc* committee that has based itself on the international law principle on an independent and impartial judge to extend, beyond the mere constitution of the tribunal mentioned in Article 52 (1) *(a)* of the Washington Convention, the review of the award to the independence and impartiality of the arbitrators [93].

38. While it is true that human rights are not intended to protect investments [94], investors are, however, not excluded from their concerns [95], to the point that one author has referred to a *"bizarre human*

---

91. *Churchill Mining* v. *Indonesia*, Decision of 18 March 2019, ICSID No. ARB/12/14 and 12/40, para. 179.

92. Decision of the *ad hoc* Committee of 30 December 2015, ICSID No. ARB/11/28, paras. 87, 92.

93. *Ad hoc* Committee Decision of 11 June 2020, *Eiser* v. *Spain*, ICSID No. ARB/13/36, paras. 176-178.

94. *Mondev* v. *USA*, Award of 11 October 2002, ARB(AF)/99/2, para. 144; *Veteran Petroleum* v. *Russia*, PCA Award of 18 July 2014, No. AA228, para. 765.

95. *Human Rights in International Investment Law and Arbitration*, P.-M Dupuy, F. Francioni and E.-U. Petersmann (eds.), OUP, 2010; A. Pellet, "Notes sur la fragmentation du droit international : droit des investissements et droits de l'Homme", Ecrits en l'honneur de Pierre-Marie Dupuy, Martinus Nijhoff, 2014, p. 757; V. Kube and E-U Petersmann, "Human Rights Law in International Investment Arbitration", *EUI Working Paper Law* 2016 (2) AJWH, p. 65. G. Puma, "Human Rights Law and Investment Law: Attempts at Harmonization Through a Difficult Dialogue between Arbitrators and Human Rights Tribunals", in *Le dialogue des juridictions dans l'ordre juridique international*, M. Arcari and L. Balmond (eds.), Editoriale Scientifica, 2014, p. 193.

rights treaty" focused solely on the investor's rights [96]. Admittedly, arbitral tribunals can only rule on the basis of the investment protection treaty that gives them jurisdiction [97], but a distinction must be made between jurisdiction and applicable law [98]. A treaty cannot be considered in isolation from international law [99]. Violations of property rights, breach of legal certainty or predictability of the law, damages to reputation and privacy, discrimination and denial of justice [100] infringe values common to a plurality of legal orders as well as to investment law [101]. Awards highlight the importance of human rights, as part of international law, for environmental concerns [102]. What matters is not

---

96. J. E. Alvarez, "Critical Theory and the North American Free Trade Agreement's Chapter Eleven", 28 *U. Miami Inter-Am Law Rev.* 303 No. 2 (1996).

97. *Pezold* v. *Zimbabwe*, Order No. 2 of 26 June 2012, ICSID No. ARB/10/15, para. 57; *Rompetrol* v. *Romania*, Award of 6 May 2013, ICSID No. ARB/06/3, para. 172.

98. C. McLachlan, "The Principle of Systemic Integration and Article 31 (1) *(c)* of the Vienna Convention", ICLQ, Vol. 54, April 2005, pp. 279-320.

99. *Phoenix* v. *Czech Republic*, ICSID Award ARB/06/5 of 15 April 2009:

> "It is evident to the Tribunal that the same holds true in international investment law and that the ICSID Convention's jurisdictional requirements - as well as those of the BIT cannot be read and interpreted in isolation from public international law, and its general principles" (para. 78).

100. C. de Visscher, "Le déni de justice en droit international", *Collected Courses*, Vol. 52 (1935), p. 365; J. Paulsson, "Issues arising from Findings of Denial of Justice", *Collected Courses*, Vol. 405 (2019), p. 9.

101. P. Juillard, "Existe-t-il des principes généraux du droit international économique?", Etudes Alain Plantey, Pedone, 1995, p. 243; M. Paparinskis, "The International Minimum Standard and Fair and Equitable Treatment", OUP, 2013, p. 171; "Convergences et contradictions du droit des investissements et des droits de l'Homme: une approche contentieuse", W. Ben Hamida and F. Coulée (eds.), Pedone, 2017; B. Simma, "Foreign Investment Arbitration: A Place for Human Rights?", ICQL Vol. 60, July 2011, pp. 573-596; C. McLachlan, L. Shore and M. Weiniger, "International Investment Arbitration", OUP, 2010, No. 7.15. In arbitral jurisprudence, see *Saluka* v. *Czech Republic*, PCA Partial Award of 17 March 2006 (UNCITRAL), paras. 308, 309; *Waste Management* v. *Mexico*, Award of 30 April 2004, ARB(AF)/00/3 (NAFTA), para. 98; *Jan de Nul* v. *Egypt*, Award of 6 November 2008, ICSID, ARB/04/13, para. 188; *Victor Pey Casado* v. *Chile*, Award of 8 May 2008, ICSID, ARB/98/2, para. 657; *Alex Genin* v. *Estonia*, Award of 25 June 2001, ICSID, No. ARB/99/2, paras. 348-373. *Robert Azinian* v. *Mexico*, Award of 1 November 1999, No. ARB(AF)/97/2, paras. 97-103; *EDF & Saur* v. *Argentina*, Award of 11 June 2012, ICSID No. ARB/03/23, paras. 909-914; *Rumeli Telekom* v. *Kazakhstan*, Award of 29 July 2008, ICSID No. ARB/05/16, paras. 651-654; *Loewen* v. *USA*, Award of 26 June 2003, ARB(AF)/98/3, para. 129; *Chevron & Texaco* v. *Ecuador*, PCA Partial Award No. 2007-02/AA277 of 30 March 2010, paras. 242-244; *Chevron & Texaco* v. *Ecuador*, PCA Award No. 2009-23 of 30 August 2018, paras. 7.12, 7.13; *Lauder* v. *Czech Republic*, UNCITRAL Award of 3 September 2001, para. 200.

102. *Urbaser* v. *Argentina*, ICSID Award of 8 December 2016, ARB/07/26, paras. 1193-1221; *Saur International* v. *Argentina*, Decision on Jurisdiction and Liability of 6 June 2012, ICSID No. ARB/04/4, paras. 328-332. O. Danic, "Droit international des investissements, droits de l'Homme, droit de l'environnement", in *Droit international des investissements et de l'arbitrage transnational*, Ch. Leben (ed.),

the difference in method or content from one legal system to another but the cross-use of sources [103].

39. Arbitral jurisprudence reveals an analogical work, of inspiration, of transposition, as can also be seen with the methodological use of proportionality [104]. There are arbitral tribunals that have refused to take into account any human rights treaty other than the one ratified by the States concerned by the arbitration [105]. The universality of the values defended should preferably lead to a broader vision which, notwithstanding the status of ratifications or the geographical scope of the treaty, leads to the combined consideration of several instruments, at least by way of reasoning by analogy with the protections of investment treaties [106], otherwise as an expression of general principles of law within the meaning of Article 38 (1) of the ICJ Statute [107]. The case law of the European Court of Human Rights plays an important role in this quest for consistency [108] because unlike other instruments for

Pedone, 2015, p. 531; T. Voon and A. Mitchell, "Community Interests and the Rights to Health in Trade and Investment Law", OUP 2018, p. 249.

103. *Rompetrol* v. *Romania*, Award of 6 May 2013, ICSID No. ARB/06/3, para. 172.

104. Cl. Reiner and Ch. Schreuer, "Human Rights and International Investment Arbitration", in *Human Rights in International Investment Law and Arbitration*, P.-M. Dupuy, F. Francioni and E.-U. Petersmann (eds.), OUP, 2010, p. 82; B. Simma, "Foreign Investment Arbitration: A Place for Human Rights?", ICQL, Vol. 60, July 2011, pp. 573-596; G. Bücheler, *Proportionality in Investor-State Arbitration*, OUP, 2015.

105. Decision on Jurisdiction of 11 September 2009, ICSID No. ARB/07/12, *Toto Costruzioni* v. *Lebanon*, paras. 150, 157-158.

106. Denial of Justice: *Chevron* v. *Ecuador*, PCA Award No. 2009-23 of 30 August 2018, paras. 8.57-8.58 (Universal Declaration of Human Rights of 10 December 1948, International Covenant on Civil and Political Rights of 16 December 1966, American Convention on Human Rights of 22 November 1969).

Presumption of innocence: UNCITRAL Award of 15 December 2014, *Hesham Al Warraq* v. *Indonesia*, paras. 556- 569 (International Covenant on Civil and Political Rights of 16 December1966), paras. 572, 577 (UN Human Rights Committee), para. 574 (Inter-American Court of Human Rights), para. 575 (ECHR, African Charter on Human and Peoples' Rights of 1 June 1981 and African Commission on Human and Peoples' Rights), para. 576 (UN Declaration 1948); *Non bis in idem:* CAS2007/A/1396&1402, Award of 31 May 2010, paras. 116, 117 (1966 Covenant on Civil and Political Rights, Protocol No. 7 ECHR).

Protection of the essential interests of the State and circumstances precluding illegality: *El Paso* v. *Argentina*, Award of 31 October 2011, ICSID No. ARB/03/15, paras. 561, 598 (ECHR (Art. 15), Inter-American Convention (Art. 27)).

107. M. Virally, "Le rôle des 'principes' dans le développement du droit international", Etudes Guggenheim, Faculté de droit de Genève, 1968, p. 531.

108. *Tecmed* v. *Mexico*, Award of 29 May 2003, ICSID No. ARB(AF)/00/2, para. 122; *Philip Morris* v. *Uruguay*, ICSID Award of 8 July 2016, ARB/10/7, para. 531; *El Paso* v. *Argentina*, Award of 31 October 2011, ICSID No. ARB/03/15, para. 598; *Total* v. *Argentina*, Decision on Liability of 27 December 2010, No. ARB/04/01, para. 129; *Perenco* v. *Ecuador*, Decision on Provisional Measures of 8 May 2009, ARB/08/6, para. 70; *Victor Pey Casado*, Award of 8 May 2008, No. ARB/98/2, para. 662; *Saipem* v. *Bangladesh*, Decision on Jurisdiction and Provisional Measures of 21 March 2007,

the protection of fundamental rights, the European Convention protects property and applies to legal persons [109].

40. Arbitral case law reminds us that awards rendered under an investment treaty only protect investments and cannot, as such, remedy a violation of human rights [110]. The mission of arbitrators is not judicial reform [111] and it has been noted that there is no objective of social transformation in investment law, which "is not an instrument of the public policy of the host State's market" [112]. The European Court of Human Rights fulfills a constitutional mission in the service of the objectives of a democratic society. An arbitral tribunal does not perform a constitutional function in the same way as a national court or a regional court of human rights. In the absence of a preliminary ruling mechanism, arbitral tribunals have, moreover, recognized the obstacles to constitutional review [113]. This should not prevent arbitrators from verifying whether a law of the host State is, for the reasons that would

---

ARB/05/07, paras. 130-132; *ADC* v. *Hungary*, Award of 2 October 2006, ARB/03/16, para. 497; *Mondev* v. *USA*, Award of 11 October 2002, ARB(AF)/99/2, paras. 138, 141-144.

109. L. Hennebel and H. Tigroudja, "Traité de droit international des droits de l'homme", Pedone, 2nd ed., 2018; U. Kriebaum, "The European Court of Human Rights' Case Law on International Investment Issues", in *International Investment Law*, H. Ruiz-Fabri and E. Stoppioni (eds.), Hart, 2022, p. 481.

110. *Biloune* v. *Ghana*, Award (UNCITRAL) on Jurisdiction and Liability of 27 October 1989, para. 61; *Loewen* v. *United States*, Award of 26 June 2003, ARB(AF)/98/3, para. 242.

111. *Philip Morris* v. *Uruguay*, ICSID Award of 8 July 2016, ARB/10/7: "arbitral tribunals should not act as courts of appeal to find a denial of justice, still less as bodies charged with improving the judicial architecture of the State", para. 528.

112. E. Castellarin, "Le principe de non-discrimination", in *Convergences et contradictions du droit des investissements et des droits de l'Homme : une approche contentieuse*, W. Ben Hamida and F. Coulée (eds.), Pedone, 2017, pp. 171, 196.

113. ICC Award No. 6320 of 1992:

> "As to the unconstitutionality of a national statute, an international arbitral tribunal might first doubt whether it is empowered to decide upon it, notwithstanding the jurisdiction it has to decide upon the application of the statute. Indeed, to decide that a statute enacted in a sovereign State is unconstitutional, and to refuse to apply it for that reason, would mean that a tribunal rejects the validity and the effects of an element of the law of that State, which is still in force inside the territory of such State, and has not been declared unconstitutional by its competent courts. In the view of this Tribunal, it is highly probable that it does not possess and cannot exercise such an extraordinary power, in any case where the statute in question does not infringe upon transnational public policy. . ."

J.-J. Arnaldez, Y. Derains and D. Hascher, "Collection of ICC Arbitral Awards, 1991-1995", *Kluwer Law International*, ICC Publishing, 1997, p. 336. CA Paris, Judgment of 24 November 2011, *EGPC* v. *NATGAS*, No. 10/16525 (exception of unconstitutionality and mission of the arbitrator). See *Contrôle de constitutionnalité et de conventionalité du droit étranger*, G. Cerqueira and N. Nord (eds.), *Société de Législation Comparée*, Collection Colloques, Vol. 34, 2017.

lead to its unconstitutionality, also contrary to the values protected by the investment protection treaty. The aim is not to end the violation of constitutional or fundamental rights but to draw conclusions as to whether the treaty standards have not been respected. The propensity to respect States cannot prevail over violations of human rights which may, at the same time, constitute a violation of the investor's rights.

41. More generally, there is no obstacle to the defense of objectives and values in assessing the validity of awards. The international nature of supervising bodies does not necessarily predispose them to internationalism in their decisions, but it may encourage them to do so, provided there is a desire to contribute to a universal system of justice. They must, therefore, adopt universally recognized principles. Review of awards must not ignore these rules, which lie at the intersection of several legal orders.

42. The refusal to apply the requirements of the investment protection treaty to situations that call into question the good governance of the State [114], such as expropriation in defiance of the principle of legality [115], the abusive application of a law or procedure to serve particular ends or the denial of justice, constitutes a violation by the arbitral tribunal of its duties due to the neglect of the norms on which its authority is based. It would also be possible to see in the violation of *jus cogens* norms a failure to apply international law [116]. There would then not be a simple misjudgment by an error of law but a disregard of the power to adjudicate [117]. Moreover, the award would be vitiated by the use of reasons that were elliptical on these issues or inadequate to justify the application of the treaty provisions because of the absence or inadequacy of the research carried out by the arbitral tribunal into the facts of the case.

43. The universality of the values protected by nondiscrimination, access to justice, fair trial and legality or legal certainty cannot be disregarded. The inclusion of these values in public policy can be explained in many ways, whatever their source: constitutional law,

---

114. *Cargill* v. *Mexico*, Award of 18 September 2009, ARB(AF)/05/2, para. 276; ECHR 15 September 2009, *Moskal* v. *Poland*, req. No. 10373/05, para. 51.

115. See ECHR 4 November 2014, *Sociedad Anonima Del Ucieza* v. *Spain*, Appl. No. 38963/08, para. 74.

116. Ch. Schreuer (with L. Malintoppi, A. Reinisch and A. Sinclair), "The ICSID Convention", CUP, 2nd ed., 2010, pp. 975-976 (No. 263-264).

117. F. Catsberg, "L'excès de pouvoir dans la justice internationale", *Collected Courses*, Vol. 35 (1931), p. 353.

general principles of law, human rights law or *jus cogens* norms [118]. It matters little what distortions a rule undergoes through its use outside the legal order that gave rise to it or the particular meaning given to it in one legal order or another. The strength of the content of the rule derived from its universality counts, not the source from which the rule derives.

44. As pointed out by Batiffol and Professor Lagarde, if there is any doubt as to whether rules form part of public policy, "[a] comparative approach seems more fruitful. The idea would be to subject to a comparative law test the provisions of foreign law that depart from the provisions of the forum and to invoke public policy against them where they depart substantially from the comparative law standard" [119]. The distinction between international and transnational public policy, which has happened to been used in case law [120], is of no great interest here, except that with a universal concept, the reference point is no longer national. The content is the same, unless there is a difference with the national system, the influence of which would remain marginal, given that we are dealing with peremptory norms at the intersection of a majority of legal orders. The decisions of national and international courts serve as evidence of the recognition of an international norm as a *jus cogens* norm [121]. Formal sources of law are not a limit. Codes

118. Inter-American Court of Human Rights, Judgment of 23 June 2005, *Yatama* v. *Nicaragua*, Series C, No. 127, paras. 184-186; Second Report on *Jus Cogens*, International Law Commission, 16 March 2017 (No. 84, 85) A/CN.4/706 (however: ECHR, Judgment of 21 June 2016, *Al-Dulimi and Montana Management* v. *Switzerland* Appl. No. 5809/08, para. 136). Bruxelles, Trib. 1re instance, 18 February 2022, No. 19/3390/A, *Rép. de Pologne* v. *Manchester Securities*; CA Québec, No. 500-09-009391-004, *Air France* v. *Libyan Arab Airlines*, Judgment of 31 March 2003; H. Lords, Judgment of 16 May 2002, *Kuwait Airways Corporation* v. *Iraqi Airways Company*, [2002] UKHL 19; CA Alger, Judgment of 20 February 1925, JDI, 1926.701. J.-M. Grossen, "La prise en compte du droit international public dans l'arbitrage commercial international", *Festschrift für Franz Kellerhals*, Stämpfli Verlag Bern, 2005, p. 35; M. Forteau, "L'ordre public international face à l'enchevêtrement croissant du droit international public", JDI, 2011.3; E. Gaillard, "Dialogue des ordres juridiques : ordre juridique arbitral et ordres juridiques étatiques", *Rev. arb.*, 2018, p. 493.

119. H. Batiffol and P. Lagarde, "Traité de droit international privé", tome 1, LGDJ, 8th ed. 1993, No. 363.

120. CA Paris, Judgment of 25 May 1990, *Rev crit DIP*, 1990, p. 753, note B. Oppetit; TF Judgment of 19 April 1994, Westland, ATF 120 II 155, para. 6; P. Lalive, "Ordre public transnational (ou réellement international) et arbitrage international", *Rev. arb.*, 1986, p. 329; J.-F. Poudret and S. Besson, "Droit comparé de l'arbitrage international", Bruylant, LGDJ, Schulthess, 2002, No. 824-826.

121. Second Report on *Jus Cogens*, International Law Commission, 16 March 2017, A/CN.4/706 (No. 91, draft Conclusion 9); M. Andenas and J. R. Leiss, "The Systemic Relevance of 'Judicial Decisions' in Article 38 of the ICJ Statute", HJIL, 4/2017, p. 907.

of conduct can signal the emergence of legal standards with a strong common identity. Generally speaking, *soft law* accompanies the universality of fundamental rights and specifies the content of new rights, such as those on the environment [122].

45. The mobilization of principles on which there is the broadest consensus strengthens the control of awards and, in turn, contributes to the development of the legal orders whose standards are concerned. Not only do principles strengthen the cohesion of solutions, but they are also channels of communication. The search for greater coherence or the promotion of the objectives of principles common to a plurality of legal orders only takes full effect if the supervisory bodies have the will and the understanding to participate in making arbitral justice more secure [123]. But a common language only makes sense if one talks to another.

---

122. B. Frydman and G. Lewkowicz, "Les codes de conduite, source du droit global ?", in *Les sources du droit revisitées* (I. Hachez, Y. Cartuyvels, H. Dumont, Ph. Gérard, F. Ost and M. van de Kerchove (eds.)), Vol. 3, normativités concurrentes, Anthémis, Université St-Louis, 2012, p. 179; *Soft Law* et droits fondamentaux, M. A. Ailincai (ed.), Pedone, 2017.

123. A. M. Slaughter, "A Global Community of Courts" (2003) 44 *Harvard International Law Journal*, No. 1, p. 191: "Common Principles and an awareness of a common enterprise will help make simple participation in transnational litigation into an engine of common identity and community".

CONCLUSION

46. Involving international law in the review of awards helps to increase their legitimacy and effectiveness. The connections made between different legal orders as a consequence of the plurality of the sources of international law require, in order to be successful, a supervisory body which is sufficiently skilful or determined to draw on principles borrowed from several legal orders. In all cases, the approach presupposes a spirit of openness in the exercise of adjudcative functions.

47. The review of awards was conceived as a means of incorporating them into a national legal system. Should there be a move toward recognition from the outset by national legal systems, with review no longer serving to admit awards but to exclude those that cannot be accepted? This presupposes a more ambitious perspective than that of ruling on the fate of the contested award. The supervisory authority's decision must be placed in the overall context of the international arbitration system of dispute settlement. As Professor A.-M. Slaughter points out, "[t]he emergence of global judicial relations is rooted in the pluralism of multiple legal systems, but driven by the expression of a deeper common identity" [124]. Without the awareness and the will to participate in a common objective, decisions originating in foreign legal systems, reduced to mere anecdotes, will at best only arouse condescending curiosity. In legal systems that do not recognize the precedential value of their own judicial decisions, it is paradoxical to prefer to give their own determinations a higher decision-making authority than foreign decisions while denying the international dimension of the rules to be applied and the problems to be solved. There is nothing impossible about this as exemplified in common law jurisdictions using foreign precedents to find the best solution for resolving a dispute [125]. Principles are a universal language, and their use should lead to foreign decisions being taken into consideration,

124. A. M. Slaughter, "A Global Community of Courts" (2003) 44 *Harvard International Law Journal*, No. 1, p. 191.

125. R. French, "The Globalisation of Public Law – A Quilting of Legalities", *Cambridge Public Law Conference*, 12 September 2016; Home Grown Laws in a Global Neighbourhood – Australia, the United States and the Rest, Albritton Lecture, University of Alabama School of Law, 18 January 2011.

regardless of the legal tradition to which the court of origin belongs [126]. It therefore takes a certain voluntarism to undertake a motivation that will resonate with others.

48. Not all supervisory bodies fulfill the desired conditions for the task. Only those that adopt a collaborative approach with arbitrators and other supervisory authorities can claim to regulate arbitral justice. Developing a coherent, global body of case law that is open to the influence of international law is easier when the supervisory courts do not work in a closed environment [127]. This is a mission that will remain devoid of purpose for many of them. There are two solutions for these. Remedy their shortcomings, which presupposes an awareness on the part of their public authorities. An outsourcing policy could then be advocated, delegating review to the courts best able to deal with the issues raised and which are willing to place their resources at the service of the international community [128]. If this international division of labor is not appropriate, it may be possible, without prejudice to the security of the system as a whole, insofar as, since review of awards is a volatile litigation because users can make the necessary corrections in

---

126. E. Gaillard, "Comparative Law in International Arbitration", *Jus Comparatum* 1 (2020), pp. 1-35 (International Academy of Comparative Law: *aidc-iacl.org*). See also G. Canivet, "L'influence de la comparaison des droits dans l'élaboration de la jurisprudence", Etudes Malinvaud, Litec, 2007, p. 133; "Le juge est-il un comparatiste ?", Ecole doctorale de l'Université Lyon III, Lecture of 15 December 2005; B. Markesinis, "Judicial Mentality: Mental Disposition or Outlook as a Factor Impeding Recourse to Foreign Law", *Tulane Law Review*, 2006, Vol. 80, No. 4, p. 1325. J. Allard and L. Van den Eynde, "Le dialogue des jurisprudences comme source du droit", in *Les sources du droit revisitées* (I. Hachez, Y. Cartuyvels, H. Dumont, Ph. Gérard, F. Ost and M. van de Kerchove (eds.)), Vol. 3, normativités concurrentes, Anthémis, Université St-Louis, 2012, p. 285; S. Cassese, "La fonction constitutionnelle des juges non nationaux. De l'espace juridique global à l'ordre juridique global", Conference at the Cour de cassation, 12 June 2007.

127. G. Canivet, Rôle et responsabilité des juridictions dans la mise en œuvre des principes de la gouvernance mondiale, Mélanges E. Zoller, Dalloz, 2018, p. 543:

> "[i]nternational judicial cooperation is examined from the perspective of governance, i.e. an institutional process, formal or informal, generating the authority necessary for the implementation of collective actions aimed not only at achieving objectives of universal value but also at legitimizing them before a wide audience" (No. 22);

M. Delmas-Marty, "Penser un monde juridique poreux", in *Porosités du droit*, V. Grosswald Curran (ed.), Société de Législation Comparée, Colloques, Vol. 45, 2020, p. 15.

128. S. Menon, "International Commercial Courts: Towards a Transnational System of Dispute Resolution" Opening Lecture for the DIFC Courts Lecture Series 2015. L. Reed, "International Dispute Resolution Courts: Retreat or Advance? 10th John E. C. Brierley Memorial Lecture", The McGill Dispute Resolution Journal, Vol. 4 (2017-2018), A. S. King and P. K. Bookman, Traveling Judges, *Am J. Intl. Law*, Vol. 116, Issue 3, July 2022, pp. 477-533.

the light of the performance of the reviewing courts by changing their choice of seat of arbitration or by concluding choice of court clauses for actions for annulment [129], to resolve to leave each institution on the road to evolution and to extrapolate on a comparison borrowed from the historian Yuval Noah Harari on the evolution of DNA between species, some at the speed of a cart pulled by an ox, others at supersonic speed [130] *.

129. CA Paris, *Le Parmentier, Miss francophonie* v. *Miss France*, Judgment of 17 June 2004, No. 2002/20314.

130. Y. N. Harari and Homo Deus, "A Brief History of Tomorrow", Random House, 2016; Sapiens, A Brief History of Humankind, Random House, 2014.

* I would also like to thank Professor S. Poillot-Peruzzetto, Conseiller en service extraordinaire at the Cour de cassation in France, for her comments during the preparation of this lecture, and my thanks also go to Mr J.-J. Arnaldez, former Deputy Registrar of the International Court of Justice, for his friendly proofreading.

BIOGRAPHICAL NOTE

Dominique Hascher, born on 22 May 1956, in Neuilly-sur-Seine (France).

Secondary education at Lycée Henri IV (Paris), law studies at the Universities of Paris II and Harvard (Fulbright Scholar). Joined the French judicial service in 1978, seconded to the International Court of Arbitration of the International Chamber of Commerce as General Counsel and Deputy Secretary General (1990-1998), Judge at the Court of Cassation in 2012, currently international judge at the Supreme Court of Singapore. President or member of *ad hoc* committees established under the Washington Convention of 18 March 1965 (ICSID). President of an international arbitral tribunal in Brussels (appointed by the co-arbitrators, judge at the International Court of Justice and professor of law). Appointing authority nominated by the Permanent Court of Arbitration in the case of *Pey Casado* v. *Chile*. Associate professor, University of Paris I (2001-2015); visiting professor, University College London (2005), University of Texas School of Law, Austin (2007). President of the Society of Comparative Legislation (2015-2019), member of the American Law Institute, of the Governing Board (Advisory Member) of the International Council Commercial Arbitration (ICCA), the International Arbitration Institute, the French committees on arbitration and private international law; Secretary General of the French branch of the International Law Association (1998-2006); member of the scientific committee of the Revue de l'arbitrage, editorial advisor to the Revue camerounaise de l'arbitrage. Knight of the National Order of the Legion of Honor (2005), the National Order of Merit (1998), Hon. Bencher of Gray's Inn, London (2004).

PRINCIPAL PUBLICATIONS

Les grandes décisions du droit de l'arbitrage commercial, Dalloz, 2019 (with I. Fadlallah).

Les représentations de l'arbitrage à travers la jurisprudence, Les Conférences de l'Académie sur l'héritage scientifique d'Emmanuel Gaillard, Brill, Nijhoff, 2023, p. 109.

"Principes et pratique de procédure dans l'arbitrage commercial international", *Recueil des cours*, Vol. 279 (2000), p. 50.

Articles, case law notes and bibliographic notices: *Journal du droit International, Revue de l'arbitrage, Revue critique de droit international privé, Travaux du comité français de droit international privé, Bulletin de la Cour internationale d'arbitrage de la CCI, Revue de règlement des différends de McGill, Bulletin ASA, Arbitration International, Yearbook Commercial Arbitration, Journal of Arab Arbitration, American Review of International Arbitration, Maritime and Commercial Law Quarterly*; chapters in various collective works.

PRIVATE INTERNATIONAL LAW AND INTERNATIONAL COMMERCIAL ARBITRATION

by

JEAN-MICHEL JACQUET

TABLE OF CONTENTS

INTRODUCTION

In this Mecca of private international law, the *Académie de droit international*, it may seem presumptuous to place private international law and international commercial arbitration on an equal footing, even if we have insisted on giving pride of place to private international law [1]. The traditions that delimit the scope of private international law are not the same everywhere, and, on that basis, for some, international arbitration can be regarded as a constituent chapter of private international law [2], while for others, it is situated at the frontiers of PIL, or even outside it altogether, either in splendid isolation [3] or as part of the expanding discipline of international commercial law [4]. The maturity it has acquired easily accommodates all configurations.

The most important point undoubtedly does not lie in examining the boundaries of academic disciplines. It lies in the fact that the disputes that form the backbone of international commercial arbitration are made up of a matter that, in itself, is indisputably a matter of private international law: international commercial relations, particularly contractual relations between private individuals, fall within the sphere of private international law when, by virtue of their internationality, they give rise to conflicts of law and raise problems of international jurisdiction of courts and of the international effect of judicial decisions. All the "hallmarks" of private international law are mobilised here.

---

1. It may also seem presumptuous to wish to revisit a subject that has recently been discussed at the Academy in a masterly fashion. Our lecture would like to encourage readers to refer to the resulting course: G. A. Bermann, "International Arbitration and Private International Law", *Recueil des cours*, Vol. 381, *Pocket Books of the Hague Academy of International Law*, Brill-Nijhoff, 2017.

2. See B. Audit and L. d'Avout. *Droit international privé*, 7th ed., Economica, 2013, p. 1005 *et seq.*

3. Cf. E. Loquin, *L'arbitrage du commerce international*, Joly, 2015; J. B. Racine, *Droit de l'arbitrage*, Thémis, Droit PUF, 2016; G. Kaufmann-Kohler and A. Rigozzi, *International Arbitration. Law and Practice in Switzerland*, Oxford University Press, 2015; G. Born, *International Commercial Arbitration*, Kluwer Law International, 3rd ed., 2020; M. De Boisséson, Cl. Fouchard and J. Madesclair, *Le droit français de l'arbitrage*, Lextenso, 2023; J. El Ahdab and D. Mainguy, *Droit de l'arbitrage, Théorie et pratique*, LexisNexis, 2021.

4. *Droit du commerce international*, J. Beguin and M. Menjucq (eds.), Traités LexisNexis, 2nd ed., 2011, p. 947 *et seq.*; M. Audit, S. Bollée and P. Callé, *Droit du commerce international et des investissements étrangers*, LGDJ, Lextenso ed., 3rd ed., 2019; C. Kessedjian and V. Pironon, *Droit du commerce international*, Thémis Droit PUF, 3rd ed., 2024, 2013, p. 457 *et seq.*; J. M. Jacquet, Ph. Delebecque and L. Usunier, *Droit du commerce international*, Dalloz, 4th ed., 2021, p. 997 *et seq.*

Ultimately, therefore, it would not be absurd to think of international arbitration being absorbed into private international law, and the problem of relationships would no longer arise.

But that would be to go astray. It would be as if arbitration were completely transparent. Now arbitration has become a veritable institution that acts as a screen between international trade operators and private international law, the rules of which would be applicable in the absence of arbitration. In other words, arbitration stands between the international legal situations that fall within its remit and the jurisdictions of the legal orders that would – in the absence of arbitration – be called upon to apply the rules of private international law that condition their jurisdiction and settle the conflicts of laws with which they are faced.

In these circumstances, it is not surprising that arbitration also appears to be a form of justice that differs from the State forms of justice that private international law usually organises. While these systems of justice are, for the most part, national, arbitration appears from the outset to be a transnational system of justice, which is further distinguished from State systems of justice by its private nature.

International arbitration poses the problem of the interface between private international law and the disputes governed by its rules. On the one hand, it is dependent on the rules that ensure its existence and preside over its operation; on the other hand, it will find itself confronted, like State courts, but as an *alternative form* of justice, with the assessment of its own jurisdiction, in the settlement of disputes that bring into play conflict of laws and conflict of jurisdiction rules.

From this dual perspective, arbitration can be viewed either as an institution (I) or as a jurisdiction (II). It is by following this thread that we will explore the complex links that cannot fail to be established between private international law and international arbitration.

I. International arbitration as an institution

The place currently occupied by international arbitration as a means of settling disputes in international economic relations leads us to regard it as a veritable institution. The use of this term may come as a surprise for a form of justice that is not institutionalised. Admittedly, international arbitration was neither conceived nor built as an institution. But it has become one under the impetus of its own resources and the favourable context in which it has evolved for more than sixty years. If we consider, according to the classic definition [5], that an institution corresponds to a *"socially established and legally sanctioned practice"*, arbitration is indeed an institution. It is established in a social field within which its very specific purpose is recognised and integrated by the legal systems with which it comes into contact.

In these circumstances, it is legitimate to expect private international law to play a certain role in the establishment of this institution. Yet the singularity of international arbitration has led private international law to favour its less usual methods (A), with more limited use of choice of law rules (B).

A) Conventional method and material rules

The operation of international arbitration is hampered by two obstacles that had to be overcome, otherwise its development would have been irretrievably compromised.

Since the jurisdiction of arbitral tribunals is based on an arbitration agreement concluded by the parties, arbitration has needed to benefit from international "recognition" of arbitration agreements. Only such recognition can bring about the withdrawal of State courts when they also have jurisdiction over a dispute entrusted to an arbitral tribunal. This was the aim of the Geneva Protocol of 23 September 1923 on arbitration clauses. The second obstacle arises as international arbitration needs to ensure a certain international effectiveness of any award made by the arbitral tribunal. This was the purpose of the Geneva Convention of 26 September 1927 on the Enforcement of Foreign Arbitral Awards.

The New York United Nations Convention of 10 June 1958 rendered these first two conventions obsolete [6]. The Convention on the Recognition and Enforcement of Foreign Arbitral Awards, as its title indicates, focuses on recognition and enforcement abroad. It sets out the agreement of the signatory States on the conditions for the international effectiveness of the award. But it should not be forgotten that Article II of this Convention is devoted to the recognition of arbitration agreements. In the final analysis, therefore, the Convention has superseded its two predecessors by encompassing their two objects, arbitration agreement and award. It has modernised the applicable rules

5. Definition provided by the *Larousse dictionary* (six volumes).

6. See *Guide to the Convention on the Recognition and Enforcement of Foreign Arbitral Awards New York 1958*, UNCITRAL Secretariat, E. Gaillard and G. A. Bermann (eds.), Pedone, Paris, 2017.

and given greater prominence to arbitration. Its success is considerable, as it has now been ratified by 159 countries. The European Convention of Geneva of 21 April 1961 has exerted much less influence, although it has tackled with great perspicacity certain issues that did not fall within the scope of the New York Convention.

The conventional route was therefore favoured. This has led to the predominant use of the substantive rules method. The international nature of "international arbitration" is matched by substantive rules providing the specific solutions that the authors of the conventions considered essential and best suited. However, none of these texts was intended to cover the entire field of "arbitration". Each one has been limited to its own subject and many important issues have been left aside.

It is hardly surprising, therefore, that the countries most interested in promoting arbitration have found it necessary to supplement the work initiated at international level with the adoption or modernisation of national legislation. Thus, for the last forty years or so, laws relating to arbitration, both domestic and international, have been added to the international conventions, which were left unchanged.

Is the proliferation of such laws likely to give rise to conflicts of law and thus compromise the harmonisation, or even unification, of international arbitration law? Doesn't the conflict shift to arbitration laws?

B) Conflicting arbitration laws?

Conflicts of arbitration laws are limited, essentially for two reasons.

a) The 1985 UNCITRAL Model Law on International Commercial Arbitration alone illustrates the first of these reasons. It was the instrument of an ambition perfectly suited to the needs of the time. Since international arbitration was booming, the world did not need to increase the diversity of regulations with enthusiasm or confusion, but on the contrary, it needed to achieve, if not their unification, at least their harmonisation. Without aiming for completeness or claiming perfection, because the aim was to find the most appropriate common denominator, the Model Law has fulfilled its mission successfully. The large number of countries that have now modelled their arbitration law on the Model Law bears witness to this. By standardising arbitration laws, the Model Law has reduced the number of "false conflicts", to use an American term, in international arbitration.

b) But there is a second reason why even false conflicts are rare. It has to do with the choice of connecting factor in the matter. It is generally asserted that the laws of States that are devoted to arbitration are applicable to the various arbitrations according to the place where the seat of the arbitration is established [7]. As each arbitration has a unique seat, this seat consequently determines the applicable arbitration law. The seat would thus act as a connecting factor in the eyes of a bilateral conflict rule, according to the dominant model in this area. Thus, each particular international arbitration procedure would be located at the seat of the arbitration, whose law is applicable to it.

This presentation is not in contradiction with observable reality but suffers from an approximation. The vast majority of arbitration laws applicable to international arbitration contain a substantive provision setting out their scope of application in the area [8]. To this end, they almost systematically refer to arbitration proceedings whose seat is located on the territory of the State that has issued the rules. These provisions constitute unilateral conflict rules which, in most cases, but not always, are identical, thus avoiding encroachment and therefore positive conflicts of laws in arbitration matters. We can, therefore, continue to assert, without too much fear of being contradicted, that, generally speaking, any arbitration procedure is subject to its own law, depending on its seat. But this saga of conflict [9] goes one step further: it forges the concept of *lex arbitrii*! Just as in matters of contracts, the conflict rule leads to the designation of the *lex contractus*, so, in matters of arbitration, the conflict rule leads to the consecration of the *lex arbitrii*! Is this just a taste for Latin formulae, a simple question of words? This picture, which appears relatively classical, is not as classical as it seems.

---

7. See J. F. Poudret and S. Besson, *Droit comparé de l'arbitrage international*, Bruylant, LGDJ, Schultess, 2002, p. 86 *et seq*. It should be noted that these authors have particularly emphasised the distinction, which is important from our perspective, between "the rules governing arbitration under the supervision of a national court and those governing arbitration proceedings" (*op. cit.*, No. 113, p. 84); G. Born, *International Arbitration: Law and Practice*, 2nd ed., Wolter Kluwer, 2016, p. 107 *et seq*.

8. Cf. J.-M. Jacquet, "La *lex arbitrii* dans l'arbitrage commercial international: mythe ou réalité?", *Unité et diversité du droit international, Ecrits en l'honneur du Professeur Pierre-Marie Dupuy*, Martinus Nijhoff Pub., 2014, p. 669 *et seq*.

9. In the words of P. Gothot, "Simples réflexions à propos de la saga des conflits de lois", *Mélanges en l'honneur de Paul Lagarde, Le droit international privé: esprit et méthodes*, Dalloz, 2005, p. 343 *et seq*.

C) The question of the lex arbitrii

The choice made by most national legislators to declare applicable the laws they have adopted in international arbitration matters on the basis of the seat of the arbitration should not lead to hasty conclusions. While the law of the seat, the *lex arbitrii*, has a role to play, it is a limited one and does not correspond exactly to the effect usually produced in private international law by the designation of the law applicable to a legal situation on the basis of a connecting factor.

First of all, it should be noted that international arbitration has never been regarded as a subject for regulation, leaving national legislators with a blank cheque. The role of international conventions, already mentioned, provides proof of this. It follows from the New York Convention that the law of international arbitration is clearly based, not on the determination of the national law to which each arbitration procedure will be subject but on a system favourable to the effectiveness of arbitration, the lines of force of which are traced by the substantive rules contained in the treaty [10].

The objective thus defined is that the functioning of international arbitration should be neither hindered by borders nor disrupted by the diversity, even relative, of national laws. The preferred means of meeting this objective is to set up an international system of co-ordination between the national legal systems with which each arbitration procedure comes into contact. For the New York Convention, this co-ordination takes place at two levels: the arbitration agreement that forms the basis for recourse to arbitration must be recognised internationally as soon as it has been drawn up in accordance with certain minimum rules (Art. II-I); the control exercised over awards when they are enforced must be substantially adequate and, as far as possible, identical, whatever the country whose courts are seised of the matter (Art. V).

So the primary task devoted to private international law is not to resolve conflicts of law. Rather, through its "treaty law" branch, it seeks to structure arbitration flexibly in its international configuration, rather than corset it under the sway of the law of one State. Conflicts of law are secondary in the eyes of the New York Convention. This movement implicitly recognises the fact that international commercial

10. Cf. E. Gaillard, "Observations sur la philosophie de l'arbitrage international", *Où va l'arbitrage international ? De la crise au renouveau*, F. Osman and A. C. Yildirim (eds.), Journées d'études méditerranéennes en l'honneur du professeur Ali Bencheneb, LexisNexis, 2017, p. 3 *et seq.*; G. Born, *op. cit.*, 2nd ed., p. 18.

arbitration is a genuine institution, capable to a large extent ensuring its own functioning, and whose relationship with the legal systems with which it inevitably comes into contact must be established in the best possible way. Thus, co-ordination does not only take place between potentially conflicting legal orders. It also takes place with the institution of arbitration itself, which seems only reductively capable of being assimilated to a simple legal relationship that can be located under the empire of a given law [11].

Rather than the exclusivity of the law of the seat, we are witnessing the multilocalisation of arbitration. There are two irreducible poles of attraction: the seat of the arbitration and the place of enforcement of the award [12]. It should also be noted that there has been a shift in the translation of the two crucial points of arbitration at the level of "connecting factors": the arbitration agreement gives way to the seat of arbitration; the award is referred to its place of enforcement under a reasoning that borrows more from the effect of foreign judgments than from the law of conflicts of laws.

In itself, the law of the seat of the arbitration has no particular basis being declared applicable to the arbitration agreement. But it does contain the rules for determining the law applicable to the arbitration agreement, as well as certain substantive rules relating to the operation of an arbitration proceeding. This is no mean achievement. Thus, the seat of arbitration, by designating the *lex arbitrii*, makes it possible above all to determine a governing law for the arbitration from the outset

As for the place of enforcement of the award, the New York Convention reiterates the irrevocable right of the country of enforcement to set the conditions for the effectiveness of the award. As soon as the award is recognised or enforced in a country other than that of the seat of the court, the role of the *lex arbitrii* diminishes inexorably in favour of the law in force (international convention or national law) at the place of enforcement. Moreover, once the award has been made, it is in the award that the arbitration is embodied. We can, therefore, consider that the multi-localisation of arbitration is not an accident, of course, as is generally the case for foreign elements. It is a structural component of international arbitration. It calls for the use of appropriate legal

---

11. See S. Lecuyer, *Appréciation critique du droit international privé conventionnel. Pour une autre approche de l'harmonisation des relations privées internationales*, preface by M.-N. Jobard-Bachellier, LGDJ, 2007, pp. 138-139.
12. This place can be multiple.

instruments. In this respect, the *lex arbitrii* is not the only law that can come into play. It must give way, at least in part, to other laws.

In fact, the strongest application of the *lex arbitrii* today lies in the jurisdiction it confers on the courts of the forum to apply the law of the forum to specific issues (supporting judge and constitution of the arbitral tribunal, provisional measures intended for the courts, annulment of an award, etc.).

This is to some extent what French international arbitration law expresses. The Decree of 13 January 2011 (like its predecessor) refuses to determine its scope in space. Its abstract applicability is triggered by the mere finding that an arbitration is international in nature within the meaning of Article 1504 CPC. Its concrete applicability depends on the referral of an international arbitration to a French court [13].

At this stage, the conclusion is clear: private international law has deployed the necessary means to deal with international arbitration, without abusing them. In the presence of an institution which has not always imposed itself without encountering resistance, but which has become inescapable, it has accompanied it more than it has sought to obtain its submission. This method of intervention has produced results that can truly be considered positive: the New York Convention has created the legal biotope that is essential for international arbitration to flourish. Conflicts of law, fortunately avoided, have left the field open to substantive rules derived from treaties as well as national laws, established in a spirit of collaboration and therefore universalist rather than nationalist. In this way, the institution can reveal an autonomy that seems indispensable to its function of transnational justice [14]. It should now be considered from the jurisdictional angle that corresponds to its function.

II. International arbitration as a jurisdiction

In the international legal order, the discontinuity of legal orders is accompanied by a discontinuity of jurisdictional systems. In private international law, the first question to be asked when a dispute arises is that of choosing the country before whose courts the case will be

13. On this reform, see Th. Clay (ed.), *Le nouveau droit français de l'arbitrage*, Université de Versailles, Lextenso ed., 2011.

14. On the autonomy of international arbitration, see A. T. von Mehren, "To What Extent Is International Commercial Arbitration Autonomous?", *Le droit des relations économiques internationales, Etudes offertes à B. Goldman*, Litec, 1982, p. 217 *et seq.*; J.-B. Racine, *Droit de l'arbitrage*, *op. cit.*, p. 45 *et seq.*

brought. If the case has significant points of contact with several countries, the plaintiff will often be able to choose between various jurisdictions with concurrent jurisdiction, for example, the courts of the defendant's habitual residence or of the place where the goods were delivered. Under certain conditions, private international law also accepts jurisdiction clauses, which allow the parties to choose, before the dispute arises, the specific national court before which the case shall be settled. In private international law, proceedings before the competent court will be governed solely by the law of the forum. A set of rules, established unilaterally or by agreement, will in principle determine in each State how foreign judgments are to be treated.

It is in relation to the system outlined above that arbitration must be situated. In practice, the issue is straightforward. Arbitration is a further option available to the parties, in addition to the solutions provided by private international law. Is it not then up to private international law to integrate this option within the general framework that it has already outlined? In order to answer this question, it is necessary to consider first the place of the arbitral tribunal in the concert of jurisdictions (A), then the position of the arbitral award in relation to the decisions that the courts of States may render in respect of it (B) and finally the problems raised by conflicts of law that may arise before an arbitral tribunal (C).

A) The integration of arbitration jurisdiction into the concert of jurisdictions

International arbitration is not just another jurisdiction to be added to the body of State courts before which a dispute could be brought; it is *another* jurisdiction. Its otherness derives both from its nature, since arbitration is a private form of justice, and from its system, since it is a form of justice based on contract, although not without a jurisdictional dimension [15]. The problem will then be to determine how the jurisdiction of the arbitral tribunal fits in with the jurisdiction of the State courts.

a) The basis of arbitral jurisdiction will not be of much interest to us as the issue is well known. It is based on the will of the parties as expressed in the arbitration agreement. It should be emphasised that this voluntarist basis is exclusive of any other. Unlike in the case of State justice, there is no objective ground of jurisdiction in favour of international arbitration. Here, the jurisdiction does not pre-exist the

15. See E. Loquin, *op. cit.*, p. 26 *et seq.*

dispute; on the contrary, it is the dispute that gives life to the jurisdiction. For this to happen, the consent of the parties is essential. This trend is amplified by the substantive rules that promote the effectiveness of the arbitration agreement, such as the autonomy of the arbitration clause from the main contract, a rule that is now almost universally accepted.

b) A more delicate issue is the practical relationship between arbitration proceedings and State proceedings when the parties disagree on jurisdiction. We know that, potentially, jurisdictions co-exist. In practice, a disagreement may arise between the parties over the existence, applicability (in the case of transfer, for example) or validity of an arbitration agreement invoked by one of them in support of arbitration proceedings. The question may be raised before the arbitral tribunal or before the national court. In either case, it calls for an answer that could be valid on both the arbitral tribunal and the State courts. We are thus on the borderline between arbitration law and private international law. How do we distinguish between them?

The answer given by the UNCITRAL Model Law in Article 16 (1) or the laws of the many States that have adopted the same solution is well known. It establishes the principle that the arbitral tribunal has jurisdiction to rule on its own jurisdiction. It is clearly situated on the side of arbitration law, but this solution nonetheless inevitably produces certain consequences at the level of private international law. As transposed into arbitration law, this principle can have two sides.

On the positive side, it gives the arbitral tribunal the power to rule on its own jurisdiction. This power seems perfectly justified. It is the prerogative of every judge, and the arbitrator exercises the function of a judge. Admittedly, by declaring itself competent, the arbitral tribunal probably neutralises the jurisdiction of a State court. But had this not already been removed by the arbitration agreement between the parties?

The *Kompetenz-Kompetenz* principle of jurisdiction also has a negative side. On the negative side, the principle of *Kompetenz-Kompetenz* of arbitrators extends its effect to the level of the court of the State seised by one of the parties, thus potentially depriving it of the right to rule itself on the disputed arbitral jurisdiction.

If the arbitral tribunal has not already been seised, the solution seems at first sight rather difficult to explain. Is it not up to the State court first seised to rule on the application of the arbitration clause, which could be the only obstacle to its jurisdiction? Why wait for a hypothetical constitution of the arbitral tribunal? These arguments carry a lot of weight. But often, bringing a case before a State court in the presence of an arbitration clause is a delaying tactic that must be avoided. Moreover, can a court's decision on an issue that is then in the nature of an incidental question be sufficient to constitute a definitive obstacle to arbitral jurisdiction [16]? This rule may be considered justified.

But the issue takes on a different dimension when the arbitral tribunal has already been constituted and seised of the case. This time, both tribunals are seised and able to rule more or less simultaneously on the same issue. The conflict is obvious. Admitting the negative effect of the principle of jurisdiction settles the problem by denying the court seised the possibility of ruling on the arbitration's jurisdiction. He must refer the question to the arbitral tribunal, whose decision will thus be binding – at least provisionally – on the parties and on the State court seised. This solution is not unanimous in comparative law, but it has been promoted in France and is gaining ground in other countries such as Switzerland [17].

In the context of the European Union, the Court of Justice, ruling on an English *anti-suit injunction* (protecting an arbitration agreement) likely to affect the jurisdiction of an Italian court, considered that the boundary between the two universes could prove problematic [18]. Regulation 44/2000, in force at the time, declared that it did not apply to arbitration, which seemed to simplify the problem. But the jurisdiction of arbitrators, which removed the jurisdiction of national courts, still had an impact on the latter. According to the CJEU, the judges of the countries of the Union should not be deprived of their power of appreciation, which is what the negative effect of *Kompetenz-Kompetenz* would have led to, in their view. They saw this as an infringement of the rights of a party challenging an arbitration clause, thus depriving it of the judicial protection to which it is entitled under the European Regulation. This case shows that a serious difficulty may arise if one refuses, as the Court does, to bring into play the negative effect of jurisdiction in the European context. The primacy given to

16. Moreover, does Article 8.2 of the Model Law not invite the arbitral tribunal to continue the proceedings and even to make an award pending the decision of the court of the State to which the objection is addressed?

17. For France, see Ch. Seraglini and J. Ortscheidt, *Droit de l'arbitrage interne et international*, Montchrestien Lextenso ed., 2nd ed., 2019, p. 559 *et seq.*; E. Loquin, *op. cit.*, p. 213 *et seq.*; for Switzerland, cf. G. Kaufmann-Kohler and A. Rigozzi, *op. cit.*, No. 5.06, p. 239 *et seq.*; *Commentaire romand*, A. Bucher (ed.), Helbing Lichtenhahn, 2011, p. 1626 *et seq.*, by P.-Y. Tschanz.

18. *Allianz SpA* v. *West Tankers Inc.*, ECJ, 10 February 2009, C-185-07, *JDI*, 2009, p. 1281, note B. Audit, *Rev. crit DIP*, 2009, p. 373, note H. Muir-Watt; *D.*, 2009, p. 981, note C. Kessedjian, *JCP G.*, 2009, No. 37, 227, note P. Callé.

State courts amounts to giving them a dual power of appreciation (arbitral jurisdiction as well as their own jurisdiction), while leaving none to arbitral tribunals, unless they agree to resist a decision that does not recognise their jurisdiction, which is sometimes recommended.

Private international law and the law of international arbitration can thus co-exist with difficulty. The problem mentioned above has not yet found a unanimous solution [19].

Could a similar difficulty arise with regard to the effect of the award? The architecture of the remedies will be revealing in this respect.

B) The architecture of the judicial review of the award

There is a system of judicial review of the awards. This is divided in two in a particular way: it oscillates between a direct recourse against the award, in which the action for annulment occupies the first place, and an indirect recourse in the context of the action for recognition or *exequatur* of the award. This has important consequences.

1) The rules governing the recognition or enforcement of arbitration awards are fairly similar to the rules governing the recognition or enforcement of foreign judgments. In the case of foreign judgments, the competent court in the country of enforcement must check that a certain number of conditions have been met. These focus on the jurisdiction of the court that gave the judgment and whether the judgment conflicts with international public policy. Within the European Union, this system is highly simplified and very conducive to efficiency.

In the case of arbitration awards, recognition or enforcement is sought at the place where recognition or enforcement are sought. The New York Convention sets out the rules for review. This review is not very different from the review of foreign judgments. It is, however, based on control principles adapted to arbitration matters. Verification of the validity of the arbitration agreement plays an essential role. Checking that the arbitral tribunal is properly constituted has no equivalent for judgments. But these specific features do not alter the purpose of the review: in both cases, the aim is to ensure that the decision of the foreign judges or arbitrators complies with the conditions laid down in the receiving legal system for the foreign judgment or arbitral award to

---

19. Cf. CJEU, *Gazprom*, Aff. C. 536/13, 13 May 2015, concl. Advocate General Wathelet (not followed by the Court); *High Court, Nori Holdings LTD & Ors* v. *Public Joint-Stock Company Bank Otkritie Financial Corporation* (2018) EWHC 1343 (Comm).

be effective. International arbitration law is strongly inspired by private international law. It might also be said that private international law has been adapted to arbitration. But annulment casts a shadow.

2) The annulment of a State court decision can only take place before a higher court of the legal system in which it was given. The annulled decision is deprived of all effect both in its original legal system and in any other legal system. This is a question of allocation of jurisdiction based on the sovereignty of States. It does not raise any difficulties and is followed without discussion

The same principles cannot be applied to arbitral awards. There is no transnational mechanism for setting aside arbitral awards (with the remarkable exception of ICSID arbitration). States have, therefore, come to confer jurisdiction on their courts to set aside arbitration awards made in international matters. In the vast majority of cases, the action to set aside the award is brought before the State court designated by the rules in force in the country in which the arbitration has its seat. The system that results *a priori* from this can be presented as follows [20]: the annulment decision acquires a specific systemic scope; the annulment judge in the country where the arbitration has its seat has exclusive jurisdiction and his decision produces *erga omnes* effects.

This system is based on a certain conception of the relationship between arbitration justice and State justice. This view is not in itself wrong. Firstly, in the absence of any other solution, there is nothing absurd about the validity of an arbitral award being reviewed by a State court. Secondly, it is not illogical to declare that an award set aside by a court recognised as having jurisdiction for that purpose is consequently deprived of existence. There is a broad consensus on this solution.

In recent years, however, this consensus has been broken in certain situations. On legal grounds that are not always identical, the courts of certain countries have refused to take into account the annulment of awards made abroad. French case law has played a particularly prominent role in this area [21]. This solution has led some courts to agree

20. Cf. W. M. Reismann and B. Richardson, "Tribunals and Courts :An Interpretation of the Architecture of International Commercial Arbitration", ICCA (2011), *ICCA Congress Series*, No. 16, The Next Fifty Years, 50th Anniversary Conference, p. 17 *et seq*.

21. Cf. Cass. Civ. 1, 9/10/1984, *Société Pablak Ticaret Sirketi* v. *Société Norsolor*, *Rev. arb.*, 1985, p. 431, note B. Goldman, *JDI*, 1085, p. 679, note Ph. Kahn, *Rev. crit Dip*, 1985, note B. Dutoit, *D.*, 1985, p. 101, note J. Robert; Cass. Civ. 1, 23/03/1994, *Société Hilmarton* v. *Société OTV*, *JDI*, 1994, p. 701, note E. Gaillard, *Rev. arb.*, 1994,

to grant *exequatur* to awards despite their annulment abroad, which they refuse to take into account.

There are two opposing rationales. One, which is considered satisfactory in international arbitration law but which is mainly based on private international law, is that the judgment setting aside the award has deprived it of any claim to international effect that would survive the setting aside [22]. A variant of this first solution, which is becoming increasingly popular, is to give effect to the foreign judgment setting aside the award insofar as the rules of private international law lead to the recognition of that judgment [23]. Refusal to give effect to the set aside award is no longer automatic. The other approach, based exclusively on the law of international arbitration, accepts the survival of an award whose setting aside is reduced to a purely local effect, with the real control of the award shifting to any country where its recognition or enforcement may be sought.

The second solution is not without its complications, since a new award, rendered as a result of the annulment of the first, may find itself competing with the initial award, the annulment of which is not recognised in certain countries. However, these complications do not seem insurmountable [24]. The main merit of this second solution is that it draws attention to the disadvantages of a system in which annulment by a court at the seat of the court would automatically have *erga omnes* international effect [25].

The New York Convention does not provide a definitive answer. In any case, it does not seem to oblige the enforcement judge to give effect to an annulment decided abroad. Above all, it seems to invite States whose courts are seised of enforcement to reason directly about the

p. 327, note Ch. Jarrosson; Cass. Civ. 9/06/2007, *Société PT Putrabali Adyamulia* v. *Soc. Rena Holding* et al., *Rev. arb.*, 2007, 507, report J.-P. Ancel and note E. Gaillard; Paris, 14/1/1997, *République arabe d'Egypte* v. *Société Chromalloy Aero Services*, *Rev. arb.*, 1997, p. 395, note Ph. Fouchard; Paris, 29 September 2005, *Direction générale de l'Aviation civile de l'Emirat de Dubai* v. *Soc Bechtel*, *Rev arb.*, 2006, p. 695, note H. Muir-Watt.

22. Cf. W. M. Reisman and B. Richardson, *op. cit.*

23. Cf. M. Scherer, "Les effets des jugements étrangers relatifs aux sentences arbitrales", *Travaux du Comité français de droit international privé*, années 2012-2014, p. 101 *et seq.*

24. Cf. the *Hilmarton* case cited above.

25. The jurisdiction of the seat of arbitration sometimes has only very tenuous links with the arbitration and, above all, with the merits of the case. Certain specific grounds for setting aside do not necessarily merit internationalisation, as Article IX of the European Convention on International Commercial Arbitration of 21 April 1961 has already acknowledged.

award by applying specific criteria to it, rather than seeking to give effect to a foreign court decision [26].

Finally, we need to consider the situation of arbitral tribunals when faced with problems of conflict of laws.

C) Settlement of conflicts of law

The question to be asked here is directly linked to the internationality of the subject matter of the dispute to be settled by the arbitrators. The internationality of the arbitration is not generally deduced from the internationality of the issues in dispute (except in French law, where it constitutes the criterion of the internationality of the arbitration), but it usually leads to it. Arbitrators, therefore, have to determine the law applicable to the substance of the dispute, which is a characteristic question of private international law. However, the way it is handled demonstrates a serious departure from the classic canons of private international law. This can be explained by two complementary considerations.

1) International arbitration is contract-based justice

The contractual basis of arbitration can be seen in the fundamental fact that arbitration is a form of justice that must be chosen by means of an agreement between the persons who have recourse to it. It also manifests itself in the contractual organisation of arbitration between the parties and the arbitrators or arbitration institution. It is, therefore, possible to conceive as an immediate consequence of this situation the universally widespread recourse to the principle of autonomy on the question of the law applicable to the merits of the dispute, as well as to the arbitration procedure.

It may nevertheless be argued that, since the principle of autonomy is the main conflict rule in contractual matters, it was to be expected that it would be retained in international arbitration insofar as the vast majority of disputes referred to arbitral tribunals are contractual in

26. Cf. E. Gaillard, "Observations sur la philosophie de l'arbitrage international", *supra*, "La vision américaine des sentences annulées au siège (Observations sur les arrêts *Pemex* et *Thai-Lao Lignite* de la Cour d'appel fédérale du 2e circuit du 2 août et 20 juillet 2017)", *Rev. arb.*, 2018, p. 1147; L. Radicati di Brozolo, "The Control System of Arbitral Awards: A Pro-Arbitration Critique of Michael Reisman's Normative Architecture of International Commercial Arbitration", *ICCA (2011), ICCA Congress Series No. 16, the Next Fifty Years, 15th Anniversary Conference*, p. 74 *et seq.*

nature. There is no reason why the principle of autonomy, an almost universally accepted conflict rule in contractual matters, should lose its *raison d'être* before an arbitral tribunal. Arbitrators will, therefore, refer first and foremost to the choice of law clauses that may be contained in the contracts they have to rule on.

But beyond the conflict of laws rule, in international arbitration, there is another reason to respect the choice of the parties. The parties' wishes influence the structure of the arbitral debate. The ability of the parties to designate the applicable law is also part of this perspective, which must be distinguished from the conflict rule [27]. The conflictual significance of the parties' agreement on the applicable law can thus be added to an agreement that is fundamentally an agreement under arbitration law. This agreement constitutes an element in the configuration of the arbitrators' mission [28]. The fact that the rule on applicable law is shaped by arbitration law rather than by private international law leads to the second consideration.

2) *International arbitration is a form of justice without* lex fori

A priori, there is no reason why arbitral tribunals should not have recourse to private international law when faced with conflicts of law. However, it is now widely accepted that international arbitral tribunals do not have a *lex fori* [29]. The *lex fori* of a State court is consubstantial with it. Established by a State, it dispenses justice on behalf of that State within the framework of that State's legal system. However, an arbitral tribunal does not dispense justice on behalf of a State. Moreover, its links with a particular legal system, including that of its seat, are too tenuous for it to be automatically subject to the conflict of laws rules in force there. Swiss international arbitration law makes this clear, even

27. Cf. P. Mayer, "Le choix de la loi dans la jurisprudence arbitrale", in S. Corneloup and N. Joubert (eds.), *Le Règlement communautaire "Rome I" et le choix de la loi dans les contrats internationaux*, Université de Bourgogne-CNRS, Travaux de recherche sur le droit des marchés et des investissements internationaux, Litec, 2011, Vol. 35, p. 423 *et seq.*

28. Cf. ICSID *Mine/Guinea* award of 6 January 1988, extracts, *JDI*, 1991, p. 166 *et seq.*, obs. E. Gaillard.

29. See A. Bucher, "La dimension sociale du droit international privé", *Recueil des cours*, tome 341 (2009), p. 268 *et seq.*, L. Chedly, "Où va le for arbitral? *Where Is International Arbitration Going? De la crise au renouveau*", *Journées d'études méditerranéennes en l'honneur du professeur Ali Bencheneb*, LexisNexis, 2017, p. 145 *et seq.*

though the concept of *lex arbitrii* is considered to be perfectly accepted in Switzerland [30].

The two considerations set out above complement each other. It is up to the law of international arbitration, in view of the conditions just mentioned, to provide arbitral tribunals with the appropriate rules for determining the law applicable to the substance of the dispute. The main consequences of this remain to be defined.

3) *Consequences*

These consequences must be considered both at the level of the content of the rule and at the level of the general mechanisms of private international law.

a) *The content of the rule*

1. *Choice made by the parties*

This is where the principle of autonomy comes into its own. Given the particular context to which we have just referred, it is understandable that the principle of autonomy should appear to have been purged of the particular determinations it acquires as a rule of conflict in a particular legal order. The field of autonomy is thus opened up more widely. This is the case when arbitration law (and not private international law) allows the parties to designate not only the law of a State, taken as a whole, but also "rules of law", whether State or non-State [31].

2. *Absence of choice by the parties*

It goes without saying that the option given to the parties to determine the applicable law may not have been exercised. In this case, a subsidiary rule, which is much less elaborate than the conflict rules in force in national legal systems, gives arbitrators the power to determine the applicable law themselves. Arbitration practice has thus developed within the very flexible framework defined by the subsidiary rule. It is rich in solutions based on a variety of methods [32]. Some of

30. See P. Lalive, J.-F. Poudret and C. Reymond, *Le droit de l'arbitrage interne et international en Suisse*, Payot, Lausanne, 1989, p. 387 *et seq.*
31. For example, cf. Article 1511 of the French Code of Civil Procedure, Article 187 of the Swiss Private International Law Act.
32. Cf. G. A. Bermann, *op. cit.*, p. 329 *et seq.*

them do not exclude recourse to conflict rules drawn from outside arbitration law. These may be drawn from a single legal system, chosen by the arbitrators on the basis of what they consider to be a special link with their arbitration. In most cases, this will be the law of the seat of the arbitration. However, the arbitrators may also draw up a conflict rule based on the common body of rules of the States with which the arbitration body has certain links (law of the seat and law of the parties' habitual residence or registered office). They may also consider the existence of general principles of private international law which they prefer to apply. Finally, where the *lex arbitrii* or the arbitration rules chosen by the parties so authorise, the arbitrators may choose the applicable law or rules of law on the basis of the criteria they consider most appropriate, without reference to a conflict rule.

b) *At the level of the general mechanisms of private international law*

The private international law resulting from international arbitration law, or intended for it [33], may appear insufficiently developed or even rudimentary. We have seen that it is made up of rules that do not belong to a national conflict of laws system. However, a conflict of laws system includes not only conflict rules but also rules relating to the general mechanisms of private international law. Can this lack of "arbitral private international law" be without disadvantages?

The question arises on at least three levels: the question of qualifications, the determination of the content of foreign law and international public policy. It should be noted immediately that the absence of a *lex fori* for the arbitral tribunal has an impact on the three questions mentioned [34].

The absence of a *lex fori* prevents the usual reasoning on *lege fori* qualification before the national courts. Instead, the arbitrator must find other solutions [35].

---

33. According to an admittedly somewhat schematic distinction, it is possible to consider that private international law resulting from arbitration will rather result from arbitration rules, whereas law intended for arbitration will result from international conventions and arbitration laws.

34. Cf. B. Goldman, "Les conflits de lois en matière d'arbitrage international de droit privé", *Recueil des cours*, Vol. 109 (1963), p. 351 *et seq.*

35. Cf. M. de Boisseson, "L'arbitre international et le problème de la qualification", *Liber Amicorum Claude Reymond, Autour de l'arbitrage*, Litec, 2004, p. 29 *et seq.*; C. Reymond, "Conflits de lois en matière de responsabilité délictuelle devant l'arbitre international", *Travaux du Comité français de droit international privé 1988-1989*

Similarly, the problem of the status of foreign law before the court of the forum does not arise as such in arbitration, where the distinction between forum law and foreign law is irrelevant. The problem of determining the content of foreign law nevertheless remains in relation to laws that all become "foreign" to the arbitral tribunal [36]. It therefore appears that the principle of *jura novit curia*, applied with many variations before national courts, cannot simply be transposed to arbitration [37].

Finally, the international public policy that an arbitral tribunal ruling on an international matter must respect should not be assimilated to that of a State. The arbitral tribunal may nonetheless take account of the international public policy of the place of arbitration or the place of enforcement of the award, in order to protect the award against a ground for nullity or refusal of enforcement [38]. However, rationally speaking, the only public policy to which it can have recourse should be transnational or "truly international" public policy [39].

Ultimately, the private international law applied by the arbitrator is exposed to serious distortions. The extent to which private international law, as we usually consider it, is dependent on the presence of the State, and its justice system becomes clearer. At the level of transnational justice represented by arbitration, private international law appears to have no backbone, to be decentralised without the presence of a State legal order of reference. This almost invincibly gives rise to the idea of a substitute arbitral forum or an arbitral legal order for the boldest minds [40].

---

et 1989-1990, p. 97 *et seq.*; G. Kaufmann-Kohler, "La qualification en droit international privé", *Travaux du Comité français de droit international privé*, 2010-2012, p. 30 *et seq.*

36. See "Recommandations de l'Association de droit international sur la détermination du contenu du droit applicable en matière d'arbitrage commercial international", presentation by D. Bensaude, *Rev. arb.*, 2009, p. 445 *et seq.*

37. See Iura Novit Curia *In International Arbitration*, F. Ferrari and G. Cordero-Moss (eds.), Juris Arbitration Law, 2018.

38. On the role of public policy and overriding mandatory rules, see *Recommendations of the International Law Association on Recourse to Public Policy as a Ground for Refusing to Recognise or Enforce International Arbitral Awards*, *Rev. Arb.*, 2002, p. 1066 *et seq.*, presentation by P. Mayer.

39. Cf. G. A. Bermann, *op. cit.*, p. 572 *et seq.*; J.-B. Racine, *Droit de l'arbitrage*, *op. cit.*, p. 593 *et seq.*

40. Cf. E. Gaillard, "Aspects philosophiques du droit de l'arbitrage international", Martinus Nijhoff, 2008; "Souveraineté et autonomie : réflexions sur les représentations de l'arbitrage international", *JDI*, 2007, p. 1163 *et seq.*; L. Chedly, *op. cit.*, p. 154 *et seq.*; D. Bentolila, *Arbitrators as Lawmakers*, Wolters Kluwer, 2017, p. 246 *et seq.*

BIOGRAPHICAL NOTE

Jean-Michel Jacquet, born on 17 November 1945 in Montbéliard, France.

Bachelor's and Doctorate in Law from the University Robert-Schuman of Strasbourg; advanced studies diploma from the University of Paris II Panthéon-Assas; tenured professor of law faculties; seconded professor at Cheikh-Anta-Diop University in Dakar (1983-1990); professor at the University of Social Sciences of Toulouse, director of the University Center of Albi (1990-1994); professor at the Graduate Institute of International and Development Studies (Geneva), director of the Institute (2002-2004); honorary professor since 2012, teaching at MIDS (Master of International Dispute Settlement, Geneva); director of the *Journal international* (Clunet) from 2003 to 2018; delegate of France to the UNCITRAL Working Group from 1992 to 2021 (United Nations Commission on International Trade Law) since 1992; member of the French Committee of Private International Law; member of the French branch of the International Law Association.

PRINCIPAL PUBLICATIONS

Books

Principe d'autonomie et droit applicable aux contrats internationaux, Foreword by J.-M. Bischoff, Paris, Economica, 1983.

Le contrat international, Paris, Dalloz, Connaissance du droit, 1st ed., 1992, 2nd ed., 1998.

Droit du commerce international, with Ph. Delebecque, Paris, Dalloz, Cours, 1st ed., 1997, 2nd ed., 1999, 3rd ed. 2002.

Droit du commerce international, avec Ph. Delebecque and S. Corneloup, Paris, Dalloz, Précis, 1st ed., 2007, 2nd ed., 2010, 3rd ed., 2014.

Articles, monographs

"Réflexions sur la spécificité du juridique", *Revue sénégalaise de philosophie*, 1985, No. 7/8, pp. 175-183.

"La norme juridique extraterritoriale dans le commerce international", *JDI*, 1985, pp. 327-405.

"L'Etat, opérateur du commerce international", *JDI*, 1989, pp. 621-690.

"La Cour suprême du Sénégal et le droit international", *Les Cours suprêmes d'Afrique*, Paris, Economica, (1989).

"L'incorporation de la loi dans le contrat", Comité français de droit international privé, Travaux du Comité français de droit international privé, 1993-1994, Paris, Pedone, 1996, p. 23 *et seq.*

"Aperçu de l'œuvre de la Conférence de La Haye de droit international privé dans le domaine économique", *JDI*, 1994, pp. 5-58.

"La loi de l'Etat contractant", in *Mélanges dédiés à Louis Boyer*, Presses universitaires des sciences sociales de Toulouse, 1996, pp. 283-295.

"Contrat", *Encyclopédie juridique Dalloz, Répertoire de droit international*, 1998.

"Le droit de la vente internationale de marchandises : le mélange des sources", in *Mélanges en l'honneur de Philippe Khan*, Litec, 2000, p. 75 *et seq.*

"Réflexions sur les sources du droit du commerce international", *Droit et patrimoine*, 2000, No. 82, pp. 39-49.

"Sociabilité et droit du commerce international", in V. Gowlland-Debbas and L. Boisson de Chazournes (eds.), *The International Legal System in Quest of Equity and Universality/L'Ordre juridique international, un système en quête d'équité et d'universalité, Liber Amicorum Georges Abi-Saab*, Martinus Nijhoff, 2001, p. 251 *et seq.*

"La fonction supranationale de la règle de conflits de lois", *Recueil des cours*, Vol. 292 (2002), pp. 151-248.

"Rapport de synthèse – Les Etats dans le contentieux économique international", *Revue de l'arbitrage, Comité français de l'arbitrage*, 2003, Vol. 2003, No. 3, pp. 1071-1088.

"La loi type de la CNUDCI du 24 juin 2002 sur la conciliation commerciale internationale", *Revue de l'arbitrage, Comité français de l'arbitrage*, 2004, Vol. 2004, No. 1, pp. 63-75.

"Law Governing the Merits of the Dispute", *UNCTAD, Course on Dispute Settlement, International Commercial Arbitration*, Geneva, 2005, pp. 1-36.

"Voici venu le temps des traités ! (quelques réflexions sur l'évolution du droit des contrats d'Etat)", in *Promoting Justice, Human Rights and Conflict Resolution Through International Law/La promotion de la justice, des droits de l'homme et du règlement des conflits par le droit international : Liber Amicorum Lucius Caflisch*, Martinus Nijhoff, Leiden, 2007, pp. 1121-1131.

"Le droit français des contrats et les principes UNIDROIT", *Uniform Law Review*, Vol. XIII, 2008, p. 179 *et seq.*

"Le principe d'autonomie entre consolidation et évolution, Vers de nouveaux équilibres entre ordres juridiques", in *Mélanges en l'honneur de H. Gaudemet- Tallon*, Paris, Dalloz, 2008, p. 727 *et seq.*

"Le contrat international: l'originalité des méthodes", *Journal des sociétés*, 2009, No. 66, p. 16 *et seq.*

"L'émergence du droit souple ou 'le droit réel' dépassé par son double", in *Etudes à la mémoire du Professeur B. Oppetit*, Paris, Litec, 2009, p. 331 *et seq.*

"Avons-nous besoin de jurisprudence arbitrale?", *Revue de l'arbitrage*, 2010, p. 445 *et seq.*

"La *lex arbitrii* dans l'arbitrage commercial international: mythe ou réalité?", in *Unité et diversité du droit international, Ecrits en l'honneur du professeur Pierre-Marie-Dupuy*, Martinus Nijhoff, 2014, p. 669 *et seq.*

"Les libertés de l'arbitre", in *Mélanges en l'honneur du professeur Pierre Mayer*, LGDJ-Lextenso, 2015, p. 311 *et seq.*

"Les lois de l'arbitrage", *JDI*, 2015, p. 3 *et seq.*

"Contrat d'Etat", in D. Bentolila, *Jurisclasseur droit international*, 2018, fasc. 571/90.

"Le droit à l'épreuve des siècles et des frontières", in *Mélanges en l'honneur du professeur Bertrand Ancel*, LGDJ-Iprolex, Paris, Madrid, 2018, pp. 905-927.

"Sur l'exercice de la fonction normative de la Commission des Nations Unies pour le droit commercial international (CNUDCI)", in *Mélanges en l'honneur du professeur Claude Witz*, LexisNexis, 2018, pp. 361-375.

INDEPENDENCE AND IMPARTIALITY OF JUDGES AND ARBITRATORS IN INVESTOR-STATE DISPUTES

by

GABRIELLE KAUFMANN-KOHLER

TABLE OF CONTENTS

ABBREVIATIONS

Burgh House Principles	Burgh House Principles on the Independence of the International Judiciary
CAS	Court of Arbitration for Sport
CETA	Canada-European Union Comprehensive Economic and Trade Agreement
CIDS	Center for International Dispute Settlement of the Faculty of Law of the University of Geneva and the Graduate Institute of International and Development Studies
CJEU	Court of Justice of the European Union
CPTPP	Comprehensive and Progressive Trans-Pacific Partnership Agreement
ECHR	European Convention for the Protection of Human Rights and Fundamental Freedoms
ECtHR	European Court of Human Rights
IBA Guidelines	IBA Guidelines on Conflicts of Interest in International Arbitration
ICC	International Criminal Court
ICJ	International Court of Justice
ICSID	International Centre for Settlement of Investment Disputes
ICTY	Criminal Tribunal for the former Yugoslavia
IOC	International Olympic Committee
PCA	Permanent Court of Arbitration
UDHR	Universal Declaration of Human Rights
UNCITRAL	United Nations Commission on International Trade Law
UNGA	United Nations General Assembly
WTO	World Trade Organization

CHAPTER I

INTRODUCTION: A TOPIC AT THE HEART OF INTERNATIONAL LITIGATION

This inaugural lecture* is devoted to a topic that lies at the heart of international justice: the independence and impartiality of the judge and the arbitrator. When it is not necessary to distinguish one from the other, I will use the term "adjudicator" [1].

Independence and impartiality are so fundamental that, without them, there can be no justice or, in the words of the International Court of Justice (ICJ):

> "[T]he Court . . . acts only on the basis of law, independently of all outside influence or intervention whatsoever . . . A court functioning as a court of law can act in no other way." [2]

Not surprisingly, access to an impartial and independent tribunal features prominently among human rights, for example, in the Universal Declaration of Human Rights and the European Convention on Human Rights [3]. Nor is it surprising to find that a court's legitimacy largely depends on its independence and impartiality [4].

As an arbitrator and academic teaching arbitration law, the independence and impartiality of the arbitrator are long time fellow

---

* The author would like to thank Laura Zinnerman of LKK Arbitration for her help in researching and finalizing the footnotes.

This article is an English translation of *Indépendance et impartialité du juge et de l'arbitre dans le règlement des différends entre investisseurs et Etats*, originally published in French in *Recueil des Cours de l'Académie de droit international de La Haye/Collected Courses of the Hague Academy of International Law*, Vol. 427, Brill, 2022, pp. 9-50. In this version, all quotations originally in a language other than English have also been translated.

1. In French, where the English term "adjudicator" has no equivalent, the term *"tiers"* is used to refer both to the judge and the arbitrator.

2. ICJ, *Legal Consequences for States of the Continued Presence of South Africa in Namibia (South West Africa) notwithstanding Security Council Resolution 276 (1970)*, Advisory Opinion, *ICJ Reports 1971*, p. 23, para. 29.

3. UDHR, Article 10; ECHR, Article 6, para. 1.

4. UNCITRAL, 36th session of Working Group III, A/CN.9/964 (6 November 2018), para. 67; C. Giorgetti *et al.*, "Independence and Impartiality in Investment Dispute Settlement: Assessing Challenges and Reform Options", *Journal of World Investment & Trade*, 2020, pp. 442-443; T. Squatrito, "A Comparative Analysis of Formal Independence", in R. Howse *et al.* (eds.), *The Legitimacy of International Trade Courts and Tribunals*, Cambridge, Cambridge University Press, 2018, pp. 407-409.

travelers, both in theory and practice. It was in the context of the reform of investment arbitration and of the idea of creating a multilateral investment court that I was led to focus on the impact that the transition from *ad hoc* to permanent justice may have on the independence and impartiality of the adjudicator [5]. Arbitral justice is called *ad hoc* because tribunals are constituted to resolve a single dispute and then cease to exist.

The question of the impact of the form of justice on the seemingly monolithic notions of independence and impartiality has also arisen in the context of the criticisms of the current investor-State dispute settlement regime. These criticisms are well known [6]. Some, perhaps the most important, concern the arbitrators themselves, specifically their real *or apparent* lack of independence and impartiality [7]. I stress the word "apparent" because impartiality and independence are judged by the appearance they create in the eyes of a reasonable third party [8]. Criticism is leveled above all at the close proximity between arbitrators and parties or counsel and the multiple roles that the same individual can play in different arbitrations at the same time, arbitrator in one and counsel or expert in another [9]. The solutions envisaged to remedy these criticisms are also well known: improving the current system of *ad hoc* tribunals or replacing the current regime with a permanent court; there are also discussions about setting up a permanent appeals body to be superimposed on the existing arbitral system [10]. I will not dwell on the

5. G. Kaufmann-Kohler and M. Potestà, *The Composition of a Multilateral Investment Court and of an Appeal Mechanism for Investment Awards*, CIDS Report 2017, available on the UNCITRAL and CIDS websites.

6. UNCITRAL, 34th session of Working Group III, A/CN.9/930/Add.1/Rev.1 (26 February 2018), part two; UNCITRAL, 34th session of Working Group III, A/CN.9/930/Rev.1 (19 December 2017), part one; UNCITRAL, 34th session of Working Group III, Note by the Secretariat, *Possible Reform of Investor-State Dispute Settlement (ISDS)*, A/CN.9/WG.III/WP.142 (18 September 2017); UNCITRAL, 49th session, Note by the Secretariat, *Settlement of Commercial Disputes: Presentation of a Study on the Mauritius Convention on Transparency in Treaty-Based Investor-State Arbitration as a Possible Model for Further Reforms of Investor-State Dispute Settlement,* A/CN.9/890 (24 May 2016).

7. S. Ratner, "International Investment Law Through the Lens of Global Justice", *Journal of International Economic Law*, 2017, pp. 768-770.

8. Instead of numerous references to national and international law, see IBA Guidelines (General Rule 2) and Burgh House Principles (Recitals and Principle 14.2), which reflect a consensus.

9. UNCITRAL, 36th session of Working Group III, A/CN.964 (6 November 2018), paras. 64-108.

10. See generally on appeals: UNCITRAL, 40th session of Working Group III, Note by the Secretariat, *Possible Reform of Investor-State Dispute Settlement (ISDS) – Issues relating to the Operation of an Appeal Mechanism and the Enforcement of*

appeal mechanism, as most of the comments on the court equally apply to the appeal mechanism.

Some treaties have already implemented solutions, for example, by adopting a code of conduct for arbitrators, such as the Code of Conduct for Arbitrators under the Trans-Pacific Partnership Agreement, better known under the acronym of CPTPP [11]. Other treaties set up semi-permanent courts, such as the Comprehensive Economic and Trade Agreement between Canada and the European Union (CETA) [12]. The bulk of the reform initiatives to improve the existing system and create new structures, however, is currently being developed by UNCITRAL Working Group III [13]. It is on this work that the present lecture will focus.

The aim of the lecture is to suggest measures to better ensure the independence and impartiality of investment arbitrators and to guarantee that a future multilateral investment court dispenses independent and impartial justice. Comparing how impartiality and independence are deployed in an *ad hoc* environment and in a permanent context will enable us to better perceive the weak points of both mechanisms. On that basis, we will be able to analyze how the weaknesses can be remedied. What are the differences between the two forms of justice in terms of independence and impartiality? What are the main risks to the independence and impartiality of judges, as opposed to arbitrators? And

---

Its Decisions, A/CN.9/WG.III/WP.202 (12 November 2020); id./WG.III/WP.202 (12 November 2020); *idem*, 38th session of Working Group III, Note by the Secretariat, *Appeal Mechanism and Multilateral Jurisdictional Mechanism*, A/CN.9/WG.III/WP.185 (29 November 2019); M. Bungenberg and A. Reinisch, *From Bilateral Arbitral Tribunals and Investment Courts to a Multilateral Investment Court – Options regarding the Institutionalization of Investor-State Dispute Settlement*, 2nd ed., Springer Open, 2020; A.-J., van den Berg, "Appeal Mechanism for ISDS Awards: Interaction with the New York and ICSID Conventions", *ICSID Review – Foreign Investment Law Journal*, 2019, p.156; G. Kaufmann-Kohler and M. Potestà, *op. cit. supra* note 5 and for a comparison, International Investment Law Centre Cologne, *Comparative Report of the IILCC Study Group on ISDS Reform on the Creation and Implementation of a Multilateral Investment Court*, Research Paper Series of the International Investment Law Centre Cologne, 2020, available at iilcc.uni-koeln.de/sites/iilcc/reports/IILCC_Study_Group_on_ISDS_Reform_-_MIC_Report_-01-2020.pdf (accessed 29 June 2022).

11. CPTPP, Code of Conduct for Investor-State Dispute Settlement in accordance with Chapter 9 Section B (investor-State dispute settlement). See also CETA, Annex 29-B, Code of Conduct for Arbitrators and Mediators.

12. CETA, Chapter 8: Investment, Section F, Settlement of investment disputes between investors and States.

13. See e.g. UNCITRAL, 42nd session of Working Group III, A/CN.9/1092 (23 March 2022); UNCITRAL, *op. cit. supra* note 4; UNCITRAL, 35th session of Working Group III, A/CN.9/935 (14 May 2018).

finally, what are the solutions that could eliminate or at least reduce these risks?

To answer these questions, I will begin by defining the concepts at issue: independence and impartiality. I will then add a reference to the related concepts of neutrality and accountability. Second, I will seek to highlight the elements that distinguish the independence and impartiality of a judge from that of an arbitrator. This review will reveal the respective vulnerabilities of the two regimes. Third and last, I will scrutinize certain measures likely to improve the independence and impartiality of arbitrators sitting on *ad hoc* tribunals, on the one hand, and of judges who may one day be members of a multilateral investment court, on the other hand.

CHAPTER II

NOTIONS: INDEPENDENCE, IMPARTIALITY, NEUTRALITY AND ACCOUNTABILITY

While our topic focuses on the settlement of disputes by international tribunals, both permanent and *ad hoc*, the imperative of independence and impartiality applies to all forms of binding administration of justice, including national litigation and commercial arbitration [14]. In all these methods of dispute resolution, the requirement for independence and impartiality is firmly anchored. As James Crawford put it, "the critical issue is not *whether* the principles of judicial independence and impartiality apply, but rather *what* those principles demand" [15].

It is true that relevant texts do not always expressly name the two requirements. For example, the ICJ Statute or the ICSID Convention speak only of independence, while the Rome Statute of the International Criminal Court (ICC) requires only impartiality as a qualification for judges [16]. It is also true that, in the abundant case law and doctrine on the subject, the perceptive reader will discern all kinds of nuances regarding the content and boundaries of the two notions [17]. Despite these variations, the different notions can be circumscribed as follows.

---

14. C. Kessedjian, "Le tiers impartial et indépendant en droit international : Juge, arbitre, médiateur, conciliateur", *Recueil des cours*, tome 403 (2020), paras. 54, 424.

15. J. Crawford and J. McIntyre, "The Independence and Impartiality of the International Judiciary", in S. Shetreet and C. Forsyth (eds.), *The Culture of Judicial Independence: Conceptual Foundations and Practical Challenges*, Leiden, Martinus Nijhoff, 2012, p. 191.

16. ICJ Statute, Article 2; ICSID Convention, Article 14, para. 1; ICC Statute, Article 36, para. 3 *(a)*; Article 41.2 *(a)* of the ICC Statute on grounds for disqualification is also limited to lack of impartiality. However, Article 40 requires judges to exercise their functions independently.

17. See e.g. *Raiffeisen Bank International AG and Raiffeisenbank Austria dd* v. *Republic of Croatia*, ICSID, Decision on the Proposal to Disqualify Stanimir Alexandrov, 17 May 2018, para. 82; G. Kaufmann-Kohler and M. Potestà, *op. cit. supra* note 5, para. 69; A. Torres Pérez, "From Judicial Independence to Interdependence in the International Sphere", *Maastricht Journal of European and Comparative Law*, 2017, p. 467.

A. *Impartiality*

Impartiality implies the exercise of a judgment that is not influenced by elements that are not in the record of the case, including prejudice against one of the parties to the dispute [18]. Impartiality is subjective in nature; it essentially depends on the judge's state of mind [19]. It is measured by appearance for the good reason that state of mind is difficult, if not impossible, to prove [20].

B. *Independence*

Independence, on the other hand, is more factual or objective in nature; it focuses on measuring the distance between the adjudicator and possible sources of influence [21]. As such, it is rather a means of arriving at an impartial judgment. It is narrower than impartiality, since it seeks to counteract influences exerted by external factors, but it has no hold on preconceived ideas in the absence of such influences. In other words, the two notions are close and overlap to some extent but are nevertheless distinct.

There are two aspects to independence: the structural aspect, also known as institutional, and the individual aspect [22], also known as personal. Personal or individual independence refers to the absence of links between the person of the adjudicator and the parties or the dispute. Institutional or structural independence refers to the absence

---

18. For example, D. Caron, "Editorial Comment: The Independence and Impartiality of Legal Systems", *World Arbitration & Mediation Review*, 2011, pp. 268-269.

19. J. Malenovský, "L'indépendance des juges internationaux", *Recueil des cours*, Vol. 349 (2011), p. 29.

20. G. Kaufmann-Kohler and A. Rigozzi, *International Arbitration: Law and Practice in Switzerland*, Oxford, Oxford University Press, 2015, para. 4.112.

21. T. Squatrito, *op. cit. supra* note 4, pp. 406-407; M. Lachs, "A Few Thoughts on the Independence of Judges of the International Court of Justice", *Columbia Journal of Transnational Law*, 1986-1987, p. 599; ECtHR, *Le Compte, van Leuven and de Meyere* v. *Belgium*, 23 June 1981, § 55, Series A, No. 43.

22. R. Gulati, "Judicial Independence at International Courts and Tribunals: Lessons Drawn from the Experiences of the International Court of Justice and the Appellate Body of the World Trade Organization", in E. de Brabandere (ed.), *International Procedure in Interstate Litigation and Arbitration, A Comparative Approach*, Cambridge, Cambridge University Press, 2021, pp. 55-57; CJEU, Opinion of 30 April 2019, C-1/17, ECLI:EU:C:2019:341, paras. 202-203; S. Shetreet, "Creating a Culture of Judicial Independence: The Practical Challenge and the Conceptual and Constitutional Infrastructure", in S. Shetreet and C. Forsyth (eds.), *The Culture of Judicial Independence: Conceptual Foundations and Practical Challenges*, Leiden, Martinus Nijhoff, 2012, p. 44.

of external influence on the institution providing dispute settlement as such [23].

More specifically, institutional independence requires that the members of a judicial body be protected from interference that may jeopardize the exercise of their function, irrespective of a specific dispute [24]. The institution must be able to dispense justice "free from direct or indirect interference or influence by any person or entity", in the words of the Burgh House Principles, a text on the independence of international tribunals drawn up by the International Law Association [25]. This independence is intimately linked to the very essence of the jurisdictional function. Without it, a decision-making body is not a real court [26].

In contrast, personal independence means that an arbitrator or judge as an individual cannot have a relationship with a party to the dispute, whether financial, professional or personal [27]. The requirement extends to counsel for the parties, to other participants in the proceedings, such as witnesses or experts, and to the dispute itself [28]. There could, for instance, be a connection with the dispute if an arbitrator had given a legal opinion on it [29]. The obvious risk is that the existence of such a connection or relationship will affect the adjudicator's judgment. Individual independence is akin to impartiality in its component related to the absence of bias in favor of or against one of the parties. The difference is that impartiality relates to the adjudicator's state of mind – indeed, one could say that impartiality is independence of mind – whereas individual independence relates to the relationship existing between the adjudicator and the parties or the dispute [30].

---

23. H. Ruiz Fabri, "Conflicts of Interests: Navigating in the Fog", *American Journal of International Law*, 2019, pp. 308-309; UNCITRAL, 36th session of Working Group III, Note by the Secretariat, *Possible Reform of Investor-State Dispute Settlement (ISDS) – Ensuring the Independence and Impartiality of Arbitrators and Decision-Makers in ISDS*, A/CN.9/WG.III/WP.151 (30 August 2018), para. 14. See also C. Giorgetti *et al. op. cit. supra* note 4, pp. 444-445.

24. J. Crawford and J. McIntyre, *op. cit. supra* note 15, p. 201.

25. Burgh House Principles, Principle 1.1.

26. As the ICJ stated succinctly in the Advisory Opinion cited *supra* in note 2, p. 16, para. 29.

27. See in general G. Born, *International Commercial Arbitration*, 3rd ed., The Hague, Kluwer Law International, 2021, pp. 1908-1909.

28. C. Giorgetti *et al., op. cit. supra* note 4, pp. 445-446.

29. See, for example, General Rule 2.1 (red list subject to renunciation) of the IBA Guidelines.

30. G. Kaufmann-Kohler and M. Potestà, *op. cit. supra* note 5, para. 73.

C. Neutrality

Some authors add to these notions neutrality or disinterestedness *(désintéressement)* [31]. Catherine Kessedjian, in her general course on the independent third party in international law, is an eminent example with regard to neutrality, which she defines as "the distance that the third party must maintain from each of the parties, from the interests and stakes that are theirs, in the sense . . . of the right distance to separate the parties and pacify their relationship" [32]. Considering the definitions of impartiality and independence that we have just adopted, the content of neutrality as described here is subsumed in the other two notions, so that reference to neutrality seems superfluous.

That said, the neutrality of arbitrators in investment arbitration is mainly discussed in the context of the polarization of the pool of arbitrators [33]. Faced with the growing polarization between pro-investor and pro-State arbitrators, some stand out for their lack of inclination toward one position or the other, in other words, for their neutrality. Rather than introducing a new category, one should inquire whether polarization is not a perversion of the system, which is contrary to the principle of impartiality, a question to which we will return [34].

D. Accountability

Another notion worth mentioning is accountability, meaning being answerable to someone for one's actions. Critics of the current regime complain that arbitrators lack accountability because they are neither elected nor chosen in a democratic governance process [35]. Accountability is not the same as independence. There is a clear tension between judicial independence and accountability [36]. Despite this conflict, accountability is seen as a necessary counterweight to curb the

---

31. C. Kessedjian, *op. cit. supra* note 14, paras.. 439, 454; T. Clay, *L'arbitre*, Dalloz, Paris, 2001, pp. 268-269.
32. C. Kessedjian, *id.* at para. 454.
33. UNCITRAL, 36th session of Working Group III, A/CN.9/964 (6 November 2018), para. 71.
34. See Section IV.b (2) below.
35. J. Jemielniak, "Commercial Stakeholders in International Economic Dispute Resolution and the Issue of Adjudicatory Independence", *Maastricht Journal of European and Comparative Law*, 2017, p. 592.
36. A. Follesdal, "Survey Article: The Legitimacy of International Courts", *Journal of Political Philosophy*, 2020, p. 484; G. Kaufmann-Kohler, "Accountability in International Investment Arbitration", *Les Cahiers de l'Arbitrage*, 2016, pp. 583-587.

excesses of independence [37]. Like independence and impartiality, it thus helps to ensure the legitimacy of the judicial function [38].

E. Adjudicator personality and collegiality

Finally, when discussing the impartiality of judges and arbitrators, it would be wrong to ignore the fact that an individual's judgment – whether conscious or part of unconscious bias – is conditioned by his or her origins, education, environment, political opinions, understanding of the role of law, vision of human relationships, of society, of the world, and other factors [39]. In other words, absolute impartiality does not exist. In reality, it would probably not be desirable, as it would be akin to indifference, when one would prefer adjudicators capable of empathy. The aim of the principle of impartiality is not to erase the adjudicator's personality but to prevent concrete circumstances or predispositions from altering his or her judgment. That said, the dividing line between a person's strong views and lack of impartiality can sometimes be difficult to draw.

This is where the idea of collegiality comes in, to mitigate the effects of overly strong individual opinions. The more diverse the composition of the tribunal, the greater its impact. Diversity is essential to legitimacy and still has not been given its rightful place [40]. It helps to balance points of view by taking into account a variety of perspectives and sensitivities [41].

---

37. D. Guilfoyle, "Lacking Conviction: Is the International Criminal Court Broken? An Organisational Failure Analysis", *Melbourne Journal of International Law*, 2019, p. 42; G. van Harten and P. Křístková, "Comments on Judicial Independence and Impartiality in ISDS: A Paper Prepared for the UNCITRAL Working Group III", *All Papers*, 2018, para. 18, available at https://digitalcommons.osgoode.yorku.ca/all_papers/327/ (accessed 29 June 2022); D. Cardamone, "Independence of International Courts", in P. de Albuquerque and K. Wojtyczek (eds.), *Judicial Power in a Globalized World*, Cham, Springer, 2019, pp. 99-100.
38. D. Cardamone, *op. cit. supra* note 37.
39. C. Kessedjian, *op. cit. supra* note 14, para. 390.
40. N. Torbisco-Casals, "The Legitimacy of International Courts: The Challenge of Diversity", *Journal of Social Philosophy*, 2021, pp. 501-503; UNCITRAL, 36th session of Working Group III, A/CN.9/964 (6 November 2018), paras. 91-96.
41. C. Kessedjian, *op. cit. supra* note 14, para. 391, quoting Lady Hale, President of the UK Supreme Court between 2017 and 2020, on the issue of gender (see Lady Hale of Richmond, "How Diverse Are Judges?", in J. Cooper (ed.), *Being a Judge in the Modern World*, Oxford, Oxford University Press, 2017, p. 184):

> "I take the view that 'difference' is important in judging and that gender diversity, along with many other dimensions of diversity, is a good, indeed a necessary, thing for several reasons. The principal reason is democratic legitimacy – the judiciary should reflect the whole community, not just a small section of it; the

CHAPTER III

DIFFERENCES AND WEAKNESSES: INDIVIDUAL AND STRUCTURAL INDEPENDENCE

This part of the lecture looks at the differences between arbitrators and judges in terms of independence and impartiality and identifies the weaknesses within each system. It then seeks to establish whether the introduction of a permanent investment court would lead to changes in terms of impartiality and independence.

A. *Impartiality*

Let us start with impartiality. Whether arbitrator or judge, the adjudicator must exercise a judgment free from outside influences, bias or preconceived opinions. It is, therefore, hard to see how a judge would be different from an arbitrator when it comes to the exercise of impartial judgment. That said, as we have seen, impartiality partly overlaps with individual independence. From this perspective, there are indeed differences between judges and arbitrators. I will deal with these in the context of individual independence, which will be addressed below.

B. *Independence*

For the time being, let us move on to independence. Here, one identifies two significant differences between arbitration and permanent judicial body. First, while it is true that both components of independence – structural and individual – are required in both systems, their respective weighting varies depending on the system in question. In an *ad hoc* mechanism, it is above all individual independence that is relevant. This stems from the fact that an *ad hoc* tribunal is set up for a single case and ceases to exist as soon as that case is resolved; that the arbitral institution, if there is one, has a limited role; that the arbitrator

public should be able to feel that the courts are their courts, that their cases are being decided and the law is being developed by people like them, not by alien beings from another planet; and this should enhance rather than undermine public confidence in the law and the legal system".

is appointed by the parties; and that he or she necessarily has other activities susceptible to creating links with the parties or the dispute [42].

This prevalence of individual independence in arbitration does not mean that the structural counterpart is nonexistent [43]. When arbitration takes place under the aegis of an arbitral institution, such as ICSID or the PCA, the institution must be designed in such a way as to guarantee structural independence, failing which the award will not be recognized as such. The Court of Arbitration for Sport (CAS), which is not a court but an arbitral institution, provides an illustration. On several occasions, the Swiss [44] and German [45] national courts and the European Court of Human Rights (ECtHR) [46] have scrutinized the organic and financial links between sports organizations and CAS. An initial Swiss ruling criticizing CAS's lack of institutional independence from the International Olympic Committee (IOC) prompted structural reform [47]. Subsequently, while German courts and a number of authors had deemed that CAS was still too close to the sports governing bodies [48], the German and Swiss courts of last resort and the ECtHR confirmed its structural independence [49].

42. In this respect, see, for example, the distinctions between the panel system and the Appellate Body in the WTO dispute settlement model: J. Jemielniak, *op. cit. supra* note 35, pp. 588-589. Some proposals to create a permanent investment tribunal address precisely one or more of these aspects (F. Dias Simões, "Can Investment Dispute Settlement Ever Be Depoliticized?", *Cardozo International and Comparative Law Review*, 2021, pp. 515-516). See also UNCITRAL, 36th session of Working Group III, Note by the Secretariat, *Possible Reform of Investor-State Dispute Settlement (ISDS) – Ensuring the Independence and Impartiality of Arbitrators and Decision-Makers in ISDS*, A/CN.9/WG.III/WP.151 (30 August 2018), para. 15.

43. D. Hascher, "A Comparison between the Independence of State Justice and the Independence of Arbitration", *ICC International Court of Arbitration Bulletin – Special Supplement 2007*, 2008, pp. 78-81.

44. Swiss Federal Court, ATF 119 II 271, *Gundel* v. *Fédération Equestre Internationale*, Judgment of 15 March 1993.

45. Landesgericht Munich, Az. 37 O 28331/12, *Claudia Pechstein* v. *International Skating Union*, Decision of 26 February 2014; Oberlandesgericht Munich, Az. U 1110/14 Kart, *Claudia Pechstein* v. *International Skating Union*, Decision of 15 January 2015.

46. ECtHR, *Mutu and Pechstein* v. *Switzerland*, Judgment of 2 October 2018.

47. It was the *Gundel* ruling, cited in note 44, that triggered the structural reform implemented by the 1994 edition of the Code of Sports-related Arbitration; for further explanation, see G. Kaufmann-Kohler and A. Rigozzi, *op. cit. supra* note 20, para. 1.126-1.127.

48. Among others, A. Vaitiekunas, *The Court of Arbitration for Sport: Law-Making and the Question of Independence*, Bern, Stämpfli, 2014, pp. 138-139; A. Rigozzi, "L'importance du droit suisse de l'arbitrage dans la résolution des litiges sportifs internationaux", *Revue de droit suisse*, 2013, pp. 304-308.

49. *Mutu and Pechstein* v. *Switzerland* Judgment, cited in note 46; see also German Bundesgerichtshof, Az. KZR 6/15, *Pechstein* v. *International Skating Union*,

It is no coincidence that these questions about structural independence have arisen in connection with CAS. Unlike most arbitration institutions, CAS plays an important part in the resolution of the dispute. Moreover, for many athletes, CAS arbitration is forced arbitration. For these reasons, the structural component of independence carries more weight than in other arbitral institutions, where independence is primarily protected by the individual element [50].

Unlike *ad hoc* tribunals, where individual independence matters most, in permanent courts, it is the structural component of independence that comes to the fore, precisely because of their permanent nature. What is more, permanent members of a judicial institution are less likely to be exposed to individual conflicts of interest, especially if they perform their duties on a full-time basis, with the result that personal independence becomes less relevant [51].

This same difference in the weight of the components of independence is visible if we seek to determine the areas of vulnerability of each system. In arbitration, the main weakness lies in the risk that an arbitrator may have contacts or predispositions that contaminate his or her judgment [52]. In a permanent court, the vulnerability lies elsewhere: it lies above all in risk of undue influence or interference that could be exerted by the States that have set up the court and control its composition [53]. This fragility is common to all international judicial bodies. The blockage of the appointment of new members of the WTO's Appellate Body by the United States, albeit under a slightly different system, is a sad illustration of this vulnerability.

The second difference between *ad hoc* and permanent regimes lies in the method of implementing structural independence. In an *ad hoc* mechanism, structural independence is first and foremost ensured

---

Judgment of 7 June 2016; Swiss Federal Tribunal, ATF 129 III 445, *Lazutina* v. *Comité International Olympique*, Judgment of 27 May 2003.

50. A. Rigozzi, "Sports Arbitration and the European Convention of Human Rights – Pechstein and beyond", in C. Müller *et al.* (eds.), *New Developments in International Commercial Arbitration 2020*, Bern, Stämpfli, 2020, pp. 97-98.

51. For example, concerning the individual independence of ICJ judges: G. Hernández, "Impartiality and Bias at the International Court of Justice", *Cambridge Journal of International and Comparative Law*, 2012, pp. 189-190.

52. See in particular J. Crawford, "The Ideal Arbitrator: Does One Size Fit All?", *American University International Law Review*, 2018, pp. 1011-1012.

53. A. Carcano, "On the Exercise of the Judicial Function at the International Criminal Court: Issues of Credibility and Structural Design", *Questions of International Law*, 2020, pp. 17-20; A. Smith, "Judicial Nationalism in International Law: National Identity and Judicial Autonomy at the ICJ", *Texas International Law Journal*, 2005, pp. 204-210.

by the equality of the parties in the constitution of the tribunal [54]. In a permanent court resolving disputes between a State and a private individual, such as an investment or human rights court, there is no equality in the constitution, since only the defendant-State and not the private person who acts as plaintiff participates in the formation of the court [55]. It is true that the defendant-State contributes to the court's constitution not as a party to the dispute, but because it has created the court with other States. This does not alter the fact that the asymmetry is real and that structural independence must therefore be guaranteed by means other than participation in the constitution of the tribunal.

After impartiality and structural independence, the next step is to consider the differences between *ad hoc* and permanent mechanisms from the angle of individual independence. As we have already seen, situations affecting individual independence are by nature less frequent for a permanent judge than for an arbitrator. However, they are not entirely excluded; their frequency will be reduced if judges are employed full-time and subject to strict rules of incompatibility, particularly in respect of mandates external to the work of the court [56]. In any event, like arbitrators, judges must be able to be challenged if there are legitimate doubts about their independence.

---

54. V. Ferreres Comella, *The Constitution of Arbitration*, Cambridge, Cambridge University Press, 2021, pp. 87-89.

55. A. Torres Pérez, *op. cit. supra* note 17, pp. 465, 467.

56. See, for example, R. MacKenzie and P. Sands, "International Courts and Tribunals and the Independence of the International Judge", *Harvard International Law Journal*, 2003, pp. 271-285. The limitation of judges' external mandates was central to Judge Yusuf's statements before the UNGA and to the compilation of decisions adopted by the ICJ concerning the external activities of its members (UNGA, 73rd session, *Address by H. E. Mr. Abdulqawi A. Yusuf, President of the International Court of Justice, on the occasion of the seventy-third session of the General Assembly of the United Nations*, 25 October 2018, available at icj-cij.org/public/files/press-releases/0/000-20181025-PRE-02-00-EN.pdf (accessed 29 June 2022), pp. 12-13; ICJ, *Compilation of Decisions Adopted by the ICJ concerning the External Activities of Its Members*, 2020, available at icj-cij.org/en/autres-textes/compilation-decisions (accessed 29 June 2022)).

CHAPTER IV

MEASURES: FROM THE SELECTION OF JUDGES TO THE APPOINTMENT OF ARBITRATORS AND OTHER SOLUTIONS

We have now defined the concepts and delineated the differences in the application of the principles of independence and impartiality between *ad hoc* tribunals and permanent courts. This has enabled us to identify the weak points of each system: individual independence for arbitration and structural independence for permanent courts. Next, we should review how to remedy these weaknesses.

A. Permanent court

Starting with the institutional or structural independence of a future permanent investment court, what measures should be taken to avoid or mitigate the weaknesses identified? To answer this question, we must first recognize the risks and threats, or put differently, the sources of potential interference. It follows from the foregoing considerations that, among the potential sources, one finds first and foremost the States that have set up the court and are at the same time subject to its jurisdiction. If the court is placed under the aegis of an international organization, there would also be the organs of that organization. In addition, the court must also be independent of non-State actors, such as business associations, civil society groups and other interest groups that could exert pressure on judges [57].

Having identified the sources of undue influence, the next step is to take stock of the means to safeguard the structural independence essential to a permanent court. The ECtHR lists such means in the following terms:

> "In order to establish whether a body can be considered 'independent', regard must be had, *inter alia*, to the manner of appointment of its members and their term of office, to the existence

57. D. Cardamone, *op. cit. supra* note 37, pp. 96-98; A. Torres Pérez, *op. cit. supra* note 17, pp. 468-469.

of guarantees against outside pressures and to the question whether the body presents an appearance of independence." [58]

Drawing on the elements cited by the ECtHR, adding findings from judicial independence and various texts such as the Burgh House Principles of the International Law Association and the Oslo Resolution of the Brandeis Institute, and drawing lessons from the practice of existing international courts, especially the ICC and the ECtHR, five main measures emerge. Within the confines of this lecture, I will merely brush them with broad strokes [59].

1. The first measure refers to the method of selecting judges. Since it has a direct impact on independence, it must be designed to ensure that judges are chosen for their competence, integrity and diversity and not by virtue of political considerations, horse trading between States or the desire to reward a deserving personality or other inappropriate contingencies [60]. Setting precise criteria, inviting applications, consulting widely with all stakeholders, vetting candidates by an independent commission, and ensuring the transparency of the selection process, are all measures that should make it possible to achieve this objective [61].
2. The second means relates to security of tenure, which implies the irremovability of the judge during his or her term of office, except on specific grounds invoked within a predetermined procedure. With security of tenue should also come financial security, i.e. the guarantee of appropriate remuneration [62]. In this context, a single long-term mandate with no possibility of renewal seems preferable to several short-term ones, as the absence of possible renewal protects against the temptation or pressure to rule in ways that would ensure reelection [63]. Similarly, privileges and immunities are

58. ECtHR, *Langborger* v. *Sweden*, 22 June 1989, para. 32, Series A No. 155.

59. For more details, see G. Kaufmann-Kohler and M. Potestà, *op. cit. supra* note 5.

60. R. Gulati, *op. cit. supra* note 22, pp. 63-66; A. Torres Pérez, "Can Judicial Selection Secure Judicial Independence? Constraining State Governments in Selecting International Judges", in M. Bobek (ed.), *Selecting Europe's Judges: A Critical Review of the Appointment Procedures to the European Court*, Oxford, Oxford University Press, 2015, p. 189.

61. See e.g. Burgh House Principles, Principle 2.3; Brandeis Institute for International Judges, *Oslo Recommendations for Enhancing the Legitimacy of International Courts*, Recommendation A, available at brandeis.edu/ethics/international-justice/past-projects/biij/2018-oslo-recommendations.html (accessed 29 June 2022).

62. Burgh House Principles, Principle 3.1.

63. E. Voeten, "The Politics of International Judicial Appointments", *Chicago Journal of International Law*, 2009, p. 400.

meant to guarantee that judges perform their duties without being influenced by fears for their security [64].

3. The third factor is the availability of adequate resources. What applies to individual members also applies to the institution. The availability of sufficient financial and human resources must not be allowed to become a means of pressure compromising judicial independence [65].
4. The fourth measure consists in setting rules on incompatibility of functions designed to ensure that independence is not jeopardized by outside activities, which could also undermine the institution's legitimacy in the eyes of the public [66].
5. Fifth and last, a well-designed method of allocating cases within the court is another way of promoting independence. The aim is to avoid the risk of manipulation so that a given case is assigned to one judge rather than another [67].

How these measures of protection are actually implemented will, of course, depend on the characteristics of the court being set up. How many judges would there be? Could each State appoint a judge, or would there be fewer judges than constituent States (which seems likely)? How would geographical diversity – this term covering levels of development in particular – and gender diversity be ensured? Would there be any nationality restrictions? Would judges work full-time, which seems desirable, or part-time? Would cases be judged by pre-constituted chambers? All these elements will have to be taken into consideration when shaping the arrangements protecting the structural independence of a permanent court [68].

---

64. J. Crawford and J. McIntyre, *op. cit. supra* note 15, p. 211.

65. D. Cardamone, *op. cit. supra* note 37, p. 95; D. Shelton, "Legal Norms to Promote the Independence and Impartiality of International Tribunals", *The Law and Practice of International Courts and Tribunals*, 2003, p. 40.

66. K. Oellers-Frahm, "International Courts and Tribunals, Judges and Arbitrators", *Max Planck Encyclopedias of International Law*, 2019, para. 19, available at opil.ouplaw.com/view/10.1093/law:epil/9780199231690/law-9780199231690-e45 (accessed 29 June 2022); S. Voigt, "The Independence of International Courts – Making Reputation Work", *Maastricht Journal of European and Comparative Law*, 2017, p. 526.

67. G. van Harten and P. Křístková, *op. cit. supra* note 37, pp. 9-13; M. Fabri and P. Langbroek, "Is There a Right Judge for Each Case? A Comparative Study of Case Assignment in Six European Countries", *European Journal of Legal Studies*, 2007, p. 292; K. Malleson, "Safeguarding Judicial Impartiality", *Legal Studies*, 2002, pp. 67-69.

68. See in particular M. Bungenberg and A. Reinisch, *Draft Statute of the Multilateral Investment Court*, Baden-Baden, Nomos, 2021; International Investment

B. Ad hoc *tribunals*

What measures may improve the existing *ad hoc* arbitration system? As you will recall, the fragility here lies in the risk that an arbitrator lacks individual independence. In addition to the *ad hoc* nature of the tribunals, the mechanism is characterized by the fact that arbitrators are generally appointed by the parties. The appointment of arbitrators by the parties is a strength and a weakness at the same time. It is a strength because, thanks to the equality of the parties in the constitution of the tribunal, the current arbitration system avoids problems of structural independence. It is a weakness because it is the source of many difficulties associated with individual independence and impartiality [69]. As a result, the appointment of arbitrators by the parties contributes significantly to the lack of legitimacy of investment arbitration. Whether this lack of legitimacy is perceived or real is of little importance, as the result is the same: the rejection of this form of dispute settlement by many States, a segment of public opinion and other stakeholders.

Three circumstances are often cited as grounds for challenging an investment arbitrator and form the basis of much criticism of the current system: repeated appointments, polarization of arbitrators and issue conflict.

1. Repeat appointments occur when the same party or counsel appoints the same arbitrator repeatedly [70]. This practice is open to criticism because repeated appointments can create affinities or the hope of new appointments depending on the outcome of the dispute, which can influence the arbitrator's judgment or at least give this impression [71]. It is true that case law holds that the sheer number of appointments by the same person is not in and of itself a ground

---

Law Centre Cologne, *op. cit. supra* note 10; G. Kaufmann-Kohler and M. Potestà, *op. cit. supra* note 5.

69. This dichotomy between strength and weakness is well illustrated by C. Giorgetti *et al. op. cit. supra* note 4, pp. 453-455. For a critical perspective on this method of appointing arbitrators, G. Kahale, "Rethinking ISDS", *Brooklyn Journal of International Law*, 2018, pp. 23-27; J. Paulsson, "Moral Hazard in International Dispute Resolution", *ICSID Review - Foreign Investment Law Journal*, 2010, pp. 351-355.

70. See generally C. Giorgetti *et al.*, *idem*, pp. 457-458; D. Behn *et al.*, "Empirical Perspectives on Investment Arbitration: What Do We Know? Does It Matter?", *Journal of World Investment & Trade*, 2020, pp. 242-245; W. Wilson Koh, "Think Quality Not Quantity: Repeat Appointments and Arbitrator Challenges", *Journal of International Arbitration*, 2017, pp. 719-729; F. Slaoui, "The Rising Issue of 'Repeat Arbitrators': A Call for Clarification", *Arbitration International*, 2009, pp. 103-119.

71. W. Wilson Koh, *id.* at 712-713.

for challenge; objective circumstances are required to demonstrate that successive appointments affect the impartial judgment of the arbitrator [72]. Nevertheless, the appearance thus created is not conducive to inspiring confidence, and the practice undermines the perception of the system as legitimate [73].

As a remedy, one could imagine limiting the number of appointments by the same party or the same counsel. That said, the code of conduct for arbitrators and judges currently being drafted by UNCITRAL does not limit repeat appointments [74]. It simply requires that arbitrators' mandates be disclosed [75]. Given existing case law, this will hardly improve the negative perception.

Another option, also under discussion, would be for arbitrators to be appointed by an institution rather than by the parties, possibly in consultation with the parties [76]. This option, which is provided in the Dutch model treaty [77], would be more effective. Initial discussions on the subject within UNCITRAL Working Group III suggest, however, that it has few supporters, the objection being that it would deprive the disputing parties of the opportunity to choose an arbitrator.

---

72. For example, *VM Solar Jerez GmbH* v. *Kingdom of Spain*, ICSID, Decision on the Proposal to Disqualify Prof. Dr Guido Santiago Tawil, 24 July 2020, para. 92; *Ayat Nizar Raja Sumrain* v. *Kuwait*, ICSID, Decision on the Claimants' Proposal to Disqualify Prof. Zachary Douglas and Mr V. V. Veeder, 2 January 2020, para. 125; *Raiffeisen* v. *Croatia*, *op. cit.* V. V. Veeder, 2 January 2020, para. 125; *Raiffeisen* v. *Croatia*, *op. cit. supra* note 17, paras. 87-89; *Compañía de Aguas del Aconquija SA and Vivendi Universal SA* v. *Argentine Republic*, ICSID, Decision on the Challenge to the President of the Committee, 3 October 2001, para. 25. See also M. Kinnear and F. Nitschke, "Disqualification of Arbitrators under the ICSID Convention and Rules", in C. Giorgetti (ed.), *Challenges and Recusals of Judges and Arbitrators in International Courts and Tribunals*, Leiden, Brill, 2015, pp. 57-59.

73. W. Wilson Koh, *op. cit. supra* note 70, pp. 737-738.

74. For an overview of the code of conduct, see C. Giorgetti and J. Dunoff, "*Ex Pluribus Unum?* On the Form and Shape of a Common Code of Ethics in International Litigation", *American Journal of International Law*, 2019, pp. 312-316.

75. UNCITRAL, 42nd session of Working Group III, *Possible Reform of Investor-State Dispute Settlement (ISDS) – Revised Version of the Draft Code of Conduct*, A/CN.9/WG.III/XLII/CRP.2 (1 February 2022), Article 10; UNCITRAL, 41st session of Working Group III, Note by the Secretariat, *Possible Reform of Investor-State Dispute Settlement (ISDS) – Draft Code of Conduct*, A/CN.9/WG.III/WP.209 (15 September 2021), paras. 56-63; ICSID, "Repeat Appointments", *Code of Conduct – Background Papers*, 2021, available at icsid.worldbank.org/sites/default/files/Background_Papers_Repeat_Appointments_final_25.2.2021.pdf (accessed 29 June 2022).

76. UNCITRAL, 40th session of Working Group III, Note by the Secretariat, *Possible Reform of Investor-State Dispute Settlement (ISDS) – Selection and Appointment of Members of ISDS Tribunals*, A/CN.9/WG.III/WP.203 (16 November 2020), paras. 21-27.

77. Dutch Model Bilateral Investment Treaty 2019, Article 20, al. 5.

The creation of a permanent body would obviously do away with this concern [78]. If the body were only semipermanent [79], and the disputing parties were to choose an adjudicator from a roster of preselected persons, the risk of repeated appointments would persist. In fact, it may even be exacerbated, as the choice would be more limited than at present. The problem would also continue to some lesser extent in the case of a permanent court if the rules on incompatibilities allowed judges to accept arbitral appointments in disputes not subject to the jurisdiction of the court [80].

2. The polarization of the pool of arbitrators between those appointed by investors and those appointed by States is linked to a particular form of repeat appointments. These are not repeat appointments by the same party but by the same *category of party*, investor or State [81], each looking to appoint a like-minded arbitrator. In the best-case scenario, a balanced decision emerges from the opposition of pro-investor and pro-State views. When this is not so, polarization seems problematic. One possibility is that the contributions of the co-arbitrators neutralize each other, which places a disproportionate responsibility on the shoulders of the chair and is not compatible with the notion of collegiality. Another possibility is that polarization exposes a weak chair to the influence of the most convincing of the co-arbitrators [82], which risks tilting the balance in a direction that does not correspond to an impartial judgment. Whether these risks materialize or not, their mere existence is likely to adversely affect

78. G. Kaufmann-Kohler and M. Potestà, *op. cit. supra* note 5, para. 96.

79. UNCITRAL, 40th session of Working Group III, Note by the Secretariat, *Possible Reform of Investor-State Dispute Settlement (ISDS) – Selection and Appointment of Members of ISDS Tribunals*, A/CN.9/WG.III/WP.203 (16 November 2020), paras. 28-39.

80. G. Kaufmann-Kohler and M. Potestà, *op. cit. supra* note 5, para. 97. On rules of incompatibility in general, see S. Shetreet, "Standards of Conduct of International Judges: Outside Activities", *The Law and Practice of International Courts and Tribunals*, 2003, pp. 127-161; and more specifically on our subject, see in particular N. Bernasconi-Osterwalder and M. Dietrich Brauch, "Is 'Moonlighting' a Problem? The Role of ICJ Judges in ISDS", *International Institute for Sustainable Development*, 2017, available at iisd.org/system/files/publications/icj-judges-isds-commentary.pdf (accessed 29 June 2022); C. Giorgetti, "The Challenge and Recusal of Judges of the International Court of Justice", in C. Giorgetti (ed.), *Challenges and Recusals of Judges and Arbitrators in International Courts and Tribunals*, Leiden, Brill, 2015, pp. 7-13.

81. V. Ferreres Comella, *op. cit. supra* note 54, p. 140; UNCITRAL, 36th session of Working Group III, A/CN.9/964 (6 November 2018), para. 71.

82. UNCITRAL, 35th session of Working Group III, A/CN.9/935 (14 May 2018), para. 54.

the perception of arbitration as a legitimate mechanism of dispute settlement [83].

3. Another circumstance often criticized in the current system is that of issue conflict. This term refers to a situation in which the arbitrator has formed an opinion on a question of law arising in connection with the dispute he or she is called upon to decide, through previous activity as counsel, expert, arbitrator or author of scientific publications [84]. That prior opinion can have been formed in two main ways: in the course of double hatting or in the context of a position expressed in a decision or publication.

   The first, double hatting, is the more preoccupying one in terms of the appearance of impartiality. It refers to the situation where the arbitrator simultaneously assumes the role of counsel or expert in another arbitration [85]. Investment law disputes frequently raise identical or similar legal issues. It is, therefore, arguable that an arbitrator might wish to set a precedent in support of a legal solution that he or she supports as counsel [86]. Even if that fear seems overrated, it is understandable that this blurring of boundaries does not inspire confidence. And while some arbitrators refrain from taking on multiple roles, empirical data shows that combining roles is not uncommon [87]. The ICSID-UNCITRAL code of conduct currently being drafted could prohibit or restrict double hatting, for example, by limiting the prohibition to proceedings involving the same State

83. *Ibid.*; A. Roberts, "Incremental, Systemic, and Paradigmatic Reform of Investor-State Arbitration", *American Journal of International Law*, 2018, p. 416.

84. American Society of International Law and International Council for Commercial Arbitration, *Report of the ASIL-ICCA Joint Task Force on Issue Conflicts in Investor-State Arbitration,* ICCA Reports No. 3, 2016, para. 2; C. Giorgetti *et al.*, *op. cit. supra* note 4, pp. 458-459; F. Marisi, "Independence and Impartiality: The Role of Soft Law in International Arbitration", *Arbitration*, 2019, p. 334; ICSID, "Issue Conflict", *Code of Conduct – Background Papers*, 2021, paras. 2-3, 6, available at icsid.worldbank.org/sites/default/files/Background_Papers_Issue_Conflict_Final_2.26.2021.pdf (accessed 29 June 2022); J. Brubaker, "The Judge Who Knew Too Much: Issue Conflicts in International Adjudication", *Berkeley Journal of International Law*, 2008, pp. 111-114.

85. ICSID, "Double-Hatting", *Code of Conduct – Background Papers*, 2021, para. 1, available at icsid.worldbank.org/sites/default/files/Background_Papers_Double-Hatting_(final)_2021.02.25.pdf (accessed 29 June 2022).

86. For an illustration, see the decision annulling an ICSID award in *Eiser Infrastructure Limited and Energía Solar Luxembourg Sàrl* v. *Kingdom of Spain*, Decision on the Kingdom of Spain's Application for Annulment, 11 June 2020, paras. 218-219, where, as counsel in two other arbitrations, one of the arbitrators had worked in collaboration with the claimant's expert, a circumstance which the arbitrator had not disclosed.

87. M. Langford *et al.*, "The Revolving Door in International Investment Arbitration", *Journal of International Economic Law*, 2017, pp. 301-331.

measures or the same treaty. It is true that strict prohibition would hinder the expansion of the pool of arbitrators, as junior arbitrators often act in parallel as counsel until their workload is sufficient to accept only arbitrator appointments [88]. Despite this admittedly serious disadvantage, a ban on arbitrators acting simultaneously as counsel or experts in other proceedings, or the requirement that the parties to the dispute consent to these multiple functions, seem to better guarantee the appearance of impartiality, which is essential for the legitimacy of a dispute settlement resolution method [89]. This is also why the ban on multiple roles prevails in sports arbitration [90], where recurring legal issues are also frequent. Such a prohibition is also provided in several recent investment treaties [91]. The same ban should apply to a semipermanent system, or else the credibility of the institution risks being undermined [92]. Contrary to the *ad hoc* system, in a permanent structure, it is unlikely that a judge would act as counsel or expert, even in proceedings "external" to his or her court [93].

As part of issue conflicts, one also counts the situation in which the adjudicator has taken a position on a legal issue in the context of an award or a scientific publication [94]. The concern expressed is that the adjudicator will not have an open mind when it comes to deciding in the arbitration the very issue on which he or she has already expressed a view elsewhere. Under the current system, previous decisions or writings are not considered to affect impartiality [95]. This comes as no surprise, given

88. *Id.* at 322-323.
89. C. Giorgetti *et al.*, *op. cit. supra* note 4, pp. 459-460, 466-467.
90. CAS, Code of Sports-related Arbitration, S18.
91. CETA, cited *supra* note 12, Article 8.30 (1); CPTPP, cited *supra* note 11, Article 3 *(d)*; Investment Protection Agreement between the European Union and Its Member States, of the one part, and the Socialist Republic of Vietnam, of the other part, Chapter 3: Dispute Settlement, Article 3.40; Dutch Model Bilateral Investment Treaty, cited *supra* note 77.
92. In this context, see the regulation of the double hatting of *ad hoc* judges at the ICJ, whose situation is comparable to that of an arbitrator due to the method of appointment and the nonpermanent nature of the role: ICJ, *Instructions de procédure*, Instruction VII, available at icj-cij.org/en/instructions-de-procedure (accessed 29 June 2022). The binding nature of this instrument is open to debate (see S. Talmon, "Article 43", in A. Zimmermann *et al.* (eds.), *The Statute of the International Court of Justice: A Commentary*, 3rd ed., Oxford, Oxford University Press, 2012, p. 1096).
93. ICJ, Compilation of Decisions, *supra* note 56, Section A.
94. M. Kinnear and F. Nitschke, *op. cit. supra* note 72, pp. 55-57.
95. IBA Guidelines, General Rule 4.1.1 (green list); among other decisions, see *Vattenfall AB* et al. v. *Federal Republic of Germany II*, PCA and ICSID, Recommendation pursuant to the request by ICSID dated 8 May 2020 on the Respondent's Proposal to Disqualify All Members of the Arbitral Tribunal dated 16 April 2020, 6 July 2020,

that expertise and experience are criteria for the selection of arbitrators and judges. As the Appeals Chamber of the Criminal Tribunal for the former Yugoslavia put it,

> "the possession of [experience] is a statutory requirement for Judges to be elected to this Tribunal. It would be an odd result if the operation of an eligibility requirement were to lead to an inference of bias" [96].

If positions taken in previous awards are sometimes still perceived as a conflict, this is mainly due to the way in which arbitrators are appointed. This perception results from the fact that, for the parties, one of the criteria for selecting an arbitrator lies precisely in the content of the decisions he or she has handed down in the past. With the establishment of a permanent court, i.e. a body whose constitution does not depend on the disputing parties, this perception would fall away. This is all the more true given that the need for consistency in jurisprudence is one of the driving forces behind the reform and the creation of an investment court. And, to achieve consistency, one would expect judges to largely rule following their prior decisions, which obviously would not rule out a shift in case law.

paras. 112, 116; *Urbaser SA* et al. v. *Argentine Republic*, ICSID, Decision on Claimants' Proposal to Disqualify Professor Campbell McLachlan, Arbitrator, 12 August 2010, paras. 45-49.

96. ICTY, Appeals Chamber, *Prosecutor* v. *Furundžija*, Judgment of 21 July 2000, para. 205.

CONCLUSION

FOR AN INDEPENDENT AND IMPARTIAL JUSTICE SYSTEM THAT IS PERCEIVED AS SUCH

It is time to reach a conclusion. To sum up, in terms of independence and impartiality, the current investment arbitration regime and the mechanism of a permanent court each have their weak points, individual independence for the former and structural independence for the latter. Remedies are available to improve the former and fine-tune the latter to guarantee independent and impartial justice. Ongoing reform work is addressing both and is likely to result in a menu of dispute resolution options for States.

In conjunction with other characteristics such as diversity, independence and impartiality shape the legitimacy of a dispute resolution method, legitimacy in the sociological, Weberian sense of the term, i.e. the acceptance of authority by the addressees of a decision. Is legitimacy, and hence justice, better served by an *ad hoc* tribunal or by a permanent body? This is a matter of legal policy that will be up to the States to decide. Whether they choose one or the other, it will be incumbent on them to do the utmost to guarantee the effectiveness and appearance of independence and impartiality, in the interest of a well-functioning justice system.

BIBLIOGRAPHY

Texts and other documents

American Society of International Law and International Council for Commercial Arbitration, Report of the ASIL-ICCA Joint Task Force on Issue Conflicts in Investor-State Arbitration, ICCA Reports No. 3, 2016.

Brandeis Institute for International Judges, *Oslo Recommendations for Enhancing the Legitimacy of International Courts*, available at brandeis.edu/ethics/international-justice/past-projects/biij/2018-oslo-recommendations.html (accessed 29 June 2022).

Burgh House Principles on the Independence of the International Judiciary (adopted in 2004).

Code of Sports-Related Arbitration of the Court of Arbitration for Sport (current version in force since 1 July 2020).

Comprehensive and Progressive Trans-Pacific Partnership Agreement (CPTPP) (entered into force 30 December 2018).

Comprehensive Economic and Trade Agreement between Canada and the European Union (CETA) provisionally entered into force on 21 September 2017).

Convention for the Protection of Human Rights and Fundamental Freedoms (entry into force 3 September 1953).

Convention on the Settlement of Investment Disputes between States and Nationals of Other States (ICSID Convention) (entry into force 14 October 1966).

Dutch Model Bilateral Investment Treaty, 2019.

IBA Guidelines on Conflicts of Interest in International Arbitration (adopted 23 October 2014).

ICJ, *Compilation of Decisions Adopted by the ICJ concerning the External Activities of Its Members*, 2020, available at icj-cij.org/en/autres-textes/compilation-decisions (accessed 29 June 2022).

ICJ, *Instructions de procédure*, available at icj-cij.org/en/instructions-de-procedure (accessed 29 June 2022).

ICSID, "Double-Hatting", Code of Conduct – Background Papers, 2021, available at icsid.worldbank.org/sites/default/files/Background_Papers_Double-Hatting_(final)_2021.02.25.pdf (accessed 29 June 2022).

ICSID, "Issue Conflict", Code of Conduct – Background Papers, 2021, available at icsid.worldbank.org/sites/default/files/Background_Papers_Issue_Conflict_Final_2.26.2021.pdf (accessed 29 June 2022).

ICSID, "Repeat Appointments", Code of Conduct – Background Papers, 2021, available at icsid.worldbank.org/sites/default/files/Background_Papers_Repeat_Appointments_final_25.2.2021.pdf (accessed 29 June 2022).

Investment Protection Agreement between the European Union and Its Member States, of the one part, and the Socialist Republic of Vietnam, of the other part (signed on 30 June 2019).

Rome Statute of the International Criminal Court (entered into force 1 July 2002).

Statute of the International Court of Justice (entered into force 24 October 1945).

UNCITRAL, 34th session of Working Group III, A/CN.9/930/Add.1/Rev.1 (26 February 2018), part two.

UNCITRAL, 34th session of Working Group III, A/CN.9/930/Rev.1 (19 December 2017), part one.

UNCITRAL, 34th session of Working Group III, Note by the Secretariat, *Possible Reform of Investor-State Dispute Settlement (ISDS)*, A/CN.9/WG.III/WP.142 (18 September 2017).

UNCITRAL, 35th session of Working Group III, A/CN.9/935 (14 May 2018).

UNCITRAL, 36th session of Working Group III, A/CN.9/964 (6 November 2018).

UNCITRAL, 36th session of Working Group III, Note by the Secretariat, *Possible Reform of Investor-State Dispute Settlement (ISDS) – Ensuring the Independence and Impartiality of Arbitrators and Decision Makers in ISDS*, A/CN.9/WG.III/WP.151 (30 August 2018).
UNCITRAL, 38th session of Working Group III, Note by the Secretariat, *Appeal mechanism and multilateral jurisdictional mechanism*, A/CN.9/WG.III/WP.185 (29 November 2019).
UNCITRAL, 40th session of Working Group III, Note by the Secretariat, *Possible Reform of Investor-State Dispute Settlement (ISDS) – Issues relating to the Operation of an Appeal Mechanism and the Enforcement of Its Decisions*, A/CN.9/WG.III/WP.202 (12 November 2020).
UNCITRAL, 40th session of Working Group III, Note by the Secretariat, *Possible Reform of Investor-State Dispute Settlement (ISDS) – Selection and Appointment of Members of ISDS Tribunals*, A/CN.9/WG.III/WP.203 (16 November 2020).
UNCITRAL, 41st session of Working Group III, Note by the Secretariat, *Possible Reform of Investor-State Dispute Settlement (ISDS) – Draft Code of Conduct*, A/CN.9/WG.III/WP.209 (15 September 2021).
UNCITRAL, 42nd session of Working Group III, A/CN.9/1092 (23 March 2022).
UNCITRAL, 42nd session of Working Group III, *Possible Reform of Investor-State Dispute Settlement (ISDS) – Revised Version of the Draft Code of Conduct*, A/CN.9/WG.III/XLII/CRP.2 (1 February 2022).
UNCITRAL, 49th Session, Note by the Secretariat, *Settlement of Commercial Disputes: Presentation of a Study on the Mauritius Convention on Transparency in Treaty-Based Investor-State Arbitration as a Possible Model for Further Reforms of Investor-State Dispute Settlement*, A/CN.9/890 (24 May 2016).
UNGA, 73rd session, *Address by H. E. Mr Abdulqawi A. Yusuf, President of the International Court of Justice, on the occasion of the seventy-third session of the United Nations General Assembly*, 25 October 2018, available at icj-cij.org/public/files/press-releases/0/000-20181025-PRE-02-00-EN.pdf (accessed 29 June 2022).
Universal Declaration of Human Rights (adopted 10 December 1948).

Judicial and arbitral decisions

CJEU, Opinion of 30 April 2019, Opinion 1/17 of the Court (Full Court), C-1/17, ECLI:EU:C:2019:341.
ECtHR, *Langborger* v. *Sweden*, 22 June 1989, Series A No. 155.
ECtHR, *Le Compte, van Leuven and de Meyere* v. *Belgium*, 23 June 1981, Series A No. 43.
ECtHR, *Mutu and Pechstein* v. *Switzerland*, No. 40575/10 and 67474/10, 2 October 2018.
German Bundesgerichtshof, Az. KZR 6/15, *Pechstein* v. *International Skating Union*, Judgment of 7 June 2016.
ICJ, *Legal Consequences for States of the Continued Presence of South Africa in Namibia (South West Africa) notwithstanding Security Council Resolution 276 (1970)*, Advisory Opinion, *ICJ Reports 1971*.
ICSID, *Ayat Nizar Raja Sumrain* v. *Kuwait*, Decision on the Claimants' Proposal to Disqualify Prof. Zachary Douglas and Mr V. V. Veeder, 2 January 2020.
ICSID, *Compañía de Aguas del Aconquija SA and Vivendi Universal SA* v. *Argentine Republic*, Decision on the Challenge to the President of the Committee, 3 October 2001.
ICSID, *Eiser Infrastructure Limited and Energía Solar Luxembourg Sàrl* v. *Kingdom of Spain*, Decision on the Kingdom of Spain's Application for Annulment, 11 June 2020.
ICSID, *Raiffeisen Bank International AG and Raiffeisenbank Austria dd* v. *Republic of Croatia*, Decision on the Proposal to Disqualify Stanimir Alexandrov, 17 May 2018.
ICSID, *Urbaser SA* et al. v. *Argentine Republic*, Decision on Claimants' Proposal to

Disqualify Professor Campbell McLachlan, Arbitrator, 12 August 2010.
ICSID, *VM Solar Jerez GmbH* v. *Kingdom of Spain*, Decision on the Proposal to Disqualify Prof. Dr Guido Santiago Tawil, 24 July 2020.
ICTY, Appeals Chamber, *Prosecutor* v. *Furundžija*, Judgment of 21 July 2000.
Landesgericht Munich, Az. 37 O 28331/12, *Claudia Pechstein* v. *International Skating Union*, Decision of 26 February 2014.
Oberlandesgericht Munich, Az. U 1110/14 Kart, *Claudia Pechstein* v. *International Skating Union*, Decision of 15 January 2015.
PCA and ICSID, *Vattenfall AB* et al. v. *Federal Republic of Germany II*, Recommendation Pursuant to the Request by ICSID dated 8 May 2020 on the Respondent's Proposal to Disqualify All Members of the Arbitral Tribunal dated 16 April 2020, 6 July 2020.
Swiss Federal Court, ATF 119 II 271, *Gundel* v. *Fédération Equestre Internationale*, Judgment of 15 March 1993.
Swiss Federal Tribunal, ATF 129 III 445, *Lazutina* v. *Comité International Olympique*, Judgment of 27 May 2003.

Publications

Abtahi, H. *et al.*, "The Composition of Judicial Benches, Disqualification and Excusal of Judges at the International Criminal Court: A Survey", *Journal of International Criminal Justice*, Vol. 11, 2013, pp. 379-398.
Alemanno, A., "How Transparent Is Transparent Enough? Balancing Access to Information Against Privacy in European Judicial Selections", in M. Bobek (ed.), *Selecting Europe's Judges: A Critical Review of the Appointment Procedures to the European Court*, Oxford, Oxford University Press, 2013, pp. 203-222.
Appleton, A. E., "Judging the Judges or Judging the Members? Pathways and Pitfalls in the Appellate Body Appointment Process", in L. Choukroune (ed.), *Judging the State in International Trade and Investment Law*, Cham, Springer, 2016, pp. 11-32.
Behn, D. *et al.*, "Empirical Perspectives on Investment Arbitration: What Do We Know? Does It Matter?", *Journal of World Investment & Trade*, 2020, pp. 188-250.
Bernasconi-Osterwalder, N., and M. Dietrich Brauch, "Is 'Moonlighting' a Problem? The Role of ICJ Judges in ISDS", *International Institute for Sustainable Development*, 2017, available at iisd.org/system/files/publications/icj-judges-isds-commentary.pdf (accessed 29 June 2022).
Bjorklund, A. K. *et al.*, "The Diversity Deficit in International Investment Arbitration", *Journal of World Investment & Trade*, 2020, pp. 410-440.
Bobek, M., "Prologue: The Changing Nature of Selection Procedures to the European Courts", in M. Bobek (ed.), *Selecting Europe's Judges: A Critical Review of the Appointment Procedures to the European Court*, Oxford, Oxford University Press, 2015, pp. 1-24.
Born, G., *International Commercial Arbitration*, 3rd ed., The Hague, Kluwer Law International, 2021.
Brower, C. N., and C. B. Rosenberg, "The Death of the Two-Headed Nightingale: Why the Paulsson-van den Berg Presumption that Party-Appointed Arbitrators are Untrustworthy Is Wrongheaded", *Arbitration International*, 2013, pp. 7-44.
Brubaker, J., "The Judge Who Knew Too Much: Issue Conflicts in International Adjudication", *Berkeley Journal of International Law*, 2008, pp. 111-152.
Bungenberg, M., and A. Reinisch, *Draft Statute of the Multilateral Investment Court*, Baden-Baden, Nomos, 2021.
Bungenberg, M., and A. Reinisch, *From Bilateral Arbitral Tribunals and Investment Courts to a Multilateral Investment Court – Options regarding the Institutionalization of Investor-State Dispute Settlement*, 2nd ed., Springer Open, 2020.
Carcano, A., "On the Exercise of the Judicial Function at the International Criminal

Court: Issues of Credibility and Structural Design", *Questions of International Law*, 2020, pp. 3-23.
Cardamone, D., "Independence of International Courts", in P. de Albuquerque and K. Wojtyczek (eds.), *Judicial Power in a Globalized World*, Cham, Springer, 2019, pp. 91-104.
Caron, D., "Editorial Comment: The Independence and Impartiality of Legal Systems", *World Arbitration & Mediation Review*, 2011, pp. 255-270.
Clay, T., *L'arbitre*, Dalloz, Paris, 2001.
Cleis, M. N., "The Independence and Impartiality of ICSID, Arbitrators: Current Case Law Alternative Approaches, and Improvement Suggestions", Leiden, Brill Nijhoff, 2017, pp. 32-53.
Crawford, J., "The Ideal Arbitrator: Does One Size Fit All?", *American University International Law Review*, 2018, pp. 1003-1022.
Crawford, J., and J. McIntyre, "The Independence and Impartiality of the International Judiciary", in S. Shetreet and C. Forsyth (eds.), *The Culture of Judicial Independence: Conceptual Foundations and Practical Challenges*, Leiden, Martinus Nijhoff, 2012, pp. 189-214.
Dias Simões, F., "Can Investment Dispute Settlement Ever Be Depoliticized?", *Cardozo International and Comparative Law Review*, 2021, pp. 507-537.
Dimitropoulos, G., "Measuring Judicial Independence in International Law: Putting Together the Pieces of the Puzzle", *Maastricht Journal of European and Comparative Law*, 2017, pp. 531-551.
Eldar, O., "Vote-Trading in International Institutions", *European Journal of International Law*, 2008, pp. 3-41.
Elsig, M., and M. Pollack, "Agents, Trustees, and International Courts: The Politics of Judicial Appointment at the World Trade Organization", *European Journal of International Relations*, 2014, pp. 391-415.
Fabri, M., and P. Langbroek, "Is There a Right Judge for Each Case? A Comparative Study of Case Assignment in Six European Countries", *European Journal of Legal Studies*, 2007, pp. 292-315.
Fach Gómez, K., *Key Duties of International Investment Arbitrators, A Transnational Study of Legal and Ethical Dilemmas*, Springer Open, 2019.
Ferreres Comella, V., *The Constitution of Arbitration*, Cambridge, Cambridge University Press, 2021.
Follesdal, A., "Survey Article: The Legitimacy of International Courts", *Journal of Political Philosophy*, 2020, pp. 476-499.
Fontanelli, F. *et al.*, "Lights and Shadows of the WTO-Inspired International Court System of Investor-State Dispute Settlement", *European Investment Law and Arbitration Review*, Vol. I, 2016, pp. 191-266.
Franck, S. D., "Development and Outcomes of Investment Treaty Arbitration", *Harvard International Law Journal*, Vol. 50 (2), 2009, pp. 435-490.
–, "The Legitimacy Crisis in Investment Treaty Arbitration: Privatizing Public International Law Through Inconsistent Decisions", *Fordham Law Review*, 2005, pp. 1521-1625.
Giorgetti, C., "Who Decides Who Decides in International Investment Arbitration", *University of Pennsylvania Journal of International Law*, 2014, pp. 431-486.
–, "The Challenge and Recusal of Judges of the International Court of Justice", in C. Giorgetti (ed.), *Challenges and Recusals of Judges and Arbitrators in International Courts and Tribunals*, Leiden, Brill, 2015, pp. 3-33.
Giorgetti, C. *et al.*, "Independence and Impartiality in Investment Dispute Settlement: Assessing Challenges and Reform Options", *Journal of World Investment & Trade*, 2020, pp. 441-474.
Giorgetti, C., and J. Dunoff, "*Ex Pluribus Unum?* On The Form and Shape of a Common Code of Ethics in International Litigation", *American Journal of International Law*, 2019, pp. 312-316.
Guilfoyle, D., "Lacking Conviction: Is the International Criminal Court Broken?

An Organisational Failure Analysis", *Melbourne Journal of International Law*, 2019, pp. 1-52.

Gulati, R., "Judicial Independence at International Courts and Tribunals: Lessons Drawn from the Experiences of the International Court of Justice and the Appellate Body of the World Trade Organization", in E. de Brabandere (ed.), *International Procedure in Interstate Litigation and Arbitration, A Comparative Approach*, Cambridge, Cambridge University Press, 2021, pp. 51-88.

Helfer, L. R., and A.-M. Slaughter, "Why States Create International Tribunals: A Response to Professors Posner and Yoo", *California Law Review*, 2005, pp. 899-956.

Hernández, G., "Impartiality and Bias at the International Court of Justice", *Cambridge Journal of International and Comparative Law*, 2012, pp. 183-207.

Hascher, D., "A Comparison between the Independence of State Justice and the Independence of Arbitration", *ICC International Court of Arbitration Bulletin – Special Supplement 2007*, 2008, pp. 77-89.

International Investment Law Centre Cologne, *Comparative Report of the IILCC Study Group on ISDS Reform on the Creation and Implementation of a Multilateral Investment Court*, Research Paper Series of the International Investment Law Centre Cologne, 2020, available at iilcc.uni-koeln.de/sites/iilcc/reports/IILCC_Study_Group_on_ISDS_Reform_-_MIC_Report_-01-2020.pdf (accessed 29 June 2022).

Jemielniak, J., "Commercial Stakeholders in International Economic Dispute Resolution and the Issue of Adjudicatory Independence", *Maastricht Journal of European and Comparative Law*, 2017, pp. 582-601.

Jones, J. R. W. D., "Composition of the Court", in A. Cassese *et al.* (eds.), *The Rome Statute of the International Criminal Court: A Commentary*, Vol. I, Oxford University Press, 2002, pp. 235-267.

Kahale, G., "Rethinking ISDS", *Brooklyn Journal of International Law*, 2018, pp. 11-50.

Kaufmann-Kohler, G., "Accountability in International Investment Arbitration", *Les Cahiers de l'Arbitrage*, 2016, pp. 581-589.

Kaufmann-Kohler, G., and M. Potestà, *The Composition of a Multilateral Investment Court and of an Appeal Mechanism for Investment Awards*, CIDS Report 2017, available on the UNCITRAL and CIDS websites.

Kaufmann-Kohler, G., and A. Rigozzi, *International Arbitration: Law and Practice in Switzerland*, Oxford, Oxford University Press, 2015.

Keith, K. J., "Challenges to the Independence of the International Judiciary: Reflections on the International Court of Justice", *Leiden Journal of International Law*, 2017, pp. 137-154.

Kelemen, R. D., "Selection, Appointment, and Legitimacy. A Political Perspective", in M. Bobek (ed.), *Selecting Europe's Judges: A Critical Review of the Appointment Procedure to the European Court*, 2015, pp. 245-259.

Kessedjian, C., "Le tiers impartial et indépendant en droit international : Juge, arbitre, médiateur, conciliateur", *Recueil des cours*, tome 403 (2020).

Kinnear, M., and F. Nitschke, "Disqualification of Arbitrators under the ICSID Convention and Rules", in C. Giorgetti (ed.), *Challenges and Recusals of Judges and Arbitrators in International Courts and Tribunals*, Leiden, Brill, 2015, pp. 34-79.

Lachs, M., "A Few Thoughts on the Independence of Judges of the International Court of Justice", *Columbia Journal of Transnational Law*, 1986-1987, pp. 593-600.

Lady Hale of Richmond, "How Diverse Are Judges?", in J. Cooper (ed.), *Being a Judge in the Modern World*, Oxford, Oxford University Press, 2017.

Langford, M. *et al.*, "The Revolving Door in International Investment Arbitration", *Journal of International Economic Law*, 2017, pp. 301-331.

Mackenzie, R. *et al.*, "Selecting International Judges: Principle, Process, and Politics", Oxford, Oxford University Press, 2010.

Mackenzie, R., and P. Sands, "International Courts and Tribunals and the Independence of the International Judge", *Harvard International Law Journal*, 2003, pp. 271-285.

Malacrida, R., "WTO Panel Composition: Searching Far and Wide for Administrators of World Trade Justice", in G. Marceau (ed.), *A History of Law and Lawyers in the GATT/WTO: The Development of the Rule of Law in the Multilateral Trading System*, Cambridge, Cambridge University Press, 2015.

Malenovský, J., "L'indépendance des juges internationaux", *Recueil des cours*, Vol. 349 (2011).

Malintoppi, L., "Independence, Impartiality, and Duty of Disclosure of Arbitrators", in P. Muchlinski *et al.* (eds.), *The Oxford Handbook of International Investment Law*, 2012, pp. 789-829.

Malleson, K., "Safeguarding Judicial Impartiality", *Legal Studies*, 2002, pp. 53-70.

Marisi, F., "Independence and Impartiality: The Role of Soft Law in International Arbitration", *Arbitration*, 2019, pp. 326-345.

Meron, T., "Judicial Independence and Impartiality in International Criminal Tribunals", *American Journal of International Law*, 2005, pp. 359-369.

Oellers-Frahm, K., "International Courts and Tribunals, Judges and Arbitrators", *Max Planck Encyclopedias of International Law*, 2019, available at opil.ouplaw.com/view/10.1093/law:epil/9780199231690/law-9780199231690-e45 (accessed 29 June 2022).

Paulsson, J., "Moral Hazard in International Dispute Resolution", *ICSID Review – Foreign Investment Law Journal*, 2010, pp. 339-355.

Popova, I., and J. L. Polebaum, "Emerging Expectations for Arbitrators: 'Issue Conflict' in Investor-State Arbitration and beyond", *Fordham International Law Journal*, 2018, pp. 937-952.

Posner, E. A., and J. C. Yoo, "Judicial Independence in International Tribunals", *California Law Review*, 2005, pp. 1-74.

–, "Reply to Helfer and Slaughter", Berkeley, *California Law Review*, 2005, pp. 957-974.

Posner, E. A., and M. F. P. de Figueiredo, "Is the International Court of Justice Biased?", *John M. Olin Program in Law and Economics*, Working Paper No. 234, 2004, pp. 2-36.

Ratner, S., "International Investment Law Through the Lens of Global Justice", *Journal of International Economic Law*, 2017, pp. 747-775.

Rigozzi, A., "L'importance du droit suisse de l'arbitrage dans la résolution des litiges sportifs internationaux", *Revue de droit suisse*, 2013, pp. 301-325.

–, "Sports Arbitration and the European Convention of Human Rights – Pechstein and beyond", in C. Müller *et al.* (eds.), *New Developments in International Commercial Arbitration 2020*, Bern, Stämpfli, 2020, pp. 77-130.

Roberts, A., "Incremental, Systemic, and Paradigmatic Reform of Investor-State Arbitration", *American Journal of International Law*, 2018, pp. 410-432.

–, "Would a Multilateral Investment Court Be Biased? Shifting to a Treaty Party Framework of Analysis Arbitration", *EJIL:Talk!*, 2017, available at https://www.ejiltalk.org/would-a-multilateral-investment-court-be-biased-shifting-to-a-treaty-party-framework-of-analysis/ (accessed 29 June 2022).

Rogers, C. A., "The Politics of International Investment Arbitrators", *Santa Clara International Law Review*, 2013, pp. 223-262.

Ruiz Fabri, H., "Conflicts of Interests: Navigating in the Fog", *American Journal of International Law*, 2019, pp. 307-311.

Sands, P. *et al.*, "The Burgh House Principles on the Independence of the International Judiciary", *The Law and Practice of International Courts and Tribunals*, 2005, pp. 247-260.

Sands, P., "The Independence of the International Judiciary: Some Introductory Thoughts", S. Charnovitz *et al.* (eds.), *Law in the Service of Human Dignity: Essays in Honour of Florentino Feliciano*, Cambridge, Cambridge University Press, 2005, pp. 313-322.

Sauvé, J. M., "Selecting the European Union's Judges: The Practice of the Article 255 Panel", M. Bobek (ed.), *Selecting Europe's Judges: A Critical Review of the Appointment Procedure to the European Court*, 2015, pp. 79-86.
Schabas, W. A., "The International Criminal Court: A Commentary on the Rome Statute", Oxford, *Oxford University Press*, 2016, pp. 253-254.
Scheu, J. (ed.), *Creation and Implementation of a Multilateral Investment Court*, Nomos, 2022.
Shelton, D., "Legal Norms to Promote the Independence and Impartiality of International Tribunals", *The Law and Practice of International Courts and Tribunals*, 2003, pp. 27-62.
Shetreet, S., "Creating a Culture of Judicial Independence: The Practical Challenge and the Conceptual and Constitutional Infrastructure", in S. Shetreet and C. Forsyth (eds.), *The Culture of Judicial Independence: Conceptual Foundations and Practical Challenges*, Leiden, Martinus Nijhoff, 2012, pp. 17-67.
Shetreet, S., "Standards of Conduct of International Judges: Outside Activities", *The Law and Practice of International Courts and Tribunals*, 2003, pp. 127-161.
Slaoui, F., "The Rising Issue of 'Repeat Arbitrators': A Call for Clarification", *Arbitration International*, 2009, pp. 103-119.
Smith, A., "Judicial Nationalism in International Law: National Identity and Judicial Autonomy at the ICJ", *Texas International Law Journal*, 2005, pp. 197-232.
Squatrito, T., "A Comparative Analysis of Formal Independence", in R. Howse *et al.* (eds.), *The Legitimacy of International Trade Courts and Tribunals*, Cambridge, Cambridge University Press, 2018, pp. 405-431.
Talmon, S., "Article 43", in A. Zimmermann *et al.* (eds.), *The Statute of the International Court of Justice: A Commentary*, 3rd ed., Oxford, Oxford University Press, 2012, pp. 1088-1171.
Torbisco-Casals, N., "The Legitimacy of International Courts: The Challenge of Diversity", *Journal of Social Philosophy*, 2021, pp. 491-515.
Torres Pérez, A., "Can Judicial Selection Secure Judicial Independence? Constraining State Governments in Selecting International Judges", in M. Bobek (ed.), *Selecting Europe's Judges: A Critical Review of the Appointment Procedures to the European Court*, Oxford, Oxford University Press, 2015, pp. 182-201.
Torres Pérez, A., "From Judicial Independence to Interdependence in the International Sphere", *Maastricht Journal of European and Comparative Law*, 2017, pp. 462-483.
van den Berg, A.-J., "Appeal Mechanism for ISDS Awards: Interaction with the New York and ICSID Conventions", *ICSID Review – Foreign Investment Law Journal*, 2019, pp. 156-189.
–, "Charles Brower's Problem with 100 Per Cent – Dissenting Opinions by Party-Appointed Arbitrators in Investment Arbitration", *Arbitration International*, 2015, pp. 381-391.
–, "Dissenting Opinions by Party-Appointed Arbitrators in Investment Arbitration", in M. Arsanjani *et al.* (eds.), *Looking to the Future: Essays on International Law in Honor of W. Michael Reisman*, Leiden, Brill Nijhoff, 2010, pp. 821-843.
van Harten, G., and P. Křístková, "Comments on Judicial Independence and Impartiality in ISDS: A Paper Prepared for the UNCITRAL Working Group III", *All Papers*, 2018, available at https://digitalcommons.osgoode.yorku.ca/all_papers/327/ (accessed 29 June 2022).
Vaitiekunas, A., *The Court of Arbitration for Sport: Law-Making and the Question of Independence*, Bern, Stämpfli, 2014.
Van Vechten Veeder, "The Historical Keystone to International Arbitration: The Party-Appointed Arbitrator – From Miami to Geneva", in D. D. Caron *et al.* (eds.), *Practising Virtue: Inside International Arbitration*, Oxford, Oxford University Press, 2015, pp. 128-149.
Voeten, E., "The Politics of International Judicial Appointments", *Chicago Journal of International Law*, 2009, pp. 387-405.

Voigt, S., "The Independence of International Courts – Making Reputation Work", *Maastricht Journal of European and Comparative Law*, 2017, pp. 511-530.

de Waele, H., "Not Quite the Bed That Procrustes Built: Dissecting the System for Selecting Judges at the Court of Justice of the European Union", in M. Bobek (ed.), *Selecting Europe's Judges: A Critical Review of the Appointment Procedure to the European Court*, 2015, pp. 25-51.

Waibel, M., and Y. Wu, *Are Arbitrators Political? Evidence from International Investment Arbitration*, January 2017, available at http://www.yanhuiwu.com/documents/arbitrator.pdf (accessed 29 June 2022).

Wilson Koh, W., "Think Quality Not Quantity: Repeat Appointments and Arbitrator Challenges", *Journal of International Arbitration*, 2017, pp. 711-740.

Wood, M., "The Selection of Candidates for International Judicial Office: Recent Practice Challenges", in T. M. Ndiaye and W. Rüdiger (eds.), *Law of the Sea, Environmental Law and Settlement of Disputes: Liber Amicorum Judge Thomas A. Mensah*, Leiden, Brill Nijhoff, 2007, pp. 357-368.

Zimmermann, D., *The Independence of International Courts*, Nomos, 2014.

BIOGRAPHICAL NOTE

Gabrielle Kaufmann-Kohler, born 2 November 1952 in Mulhouse, France.

Professor Emerita at the Law School of the University of Geneva, where she taught from 1993 to 2018, founded and directed the Geneva LL.M. in International Dispute Settlement (MIDS), a joint project of the Graduate Institute of International and Development Studies and the University of Geneva, headed the Law School's Department of Private International Law and codirected the Center for International Dispute Settlement (CIDS), whose Board she currently chairs. She is also or has been a visiting professor at the National University of Singapore (from 2019), Sciences Po Paris (from 2020), Tsinghua University, Beijing (2019), Georgetown University (2019-2021) and MIDS Geneva (from 2018). She has taught private international law, then international arbitration law and directed research projects in the latter field.

An international arbitrator, she is active in investment and commercial arbitration and in the past in sports arbitration, with over 240 arbitrations, mainly as chair of the tribunal; a study published in 2016 named her "most influential arbitrator" in investment arbitration. Admitted to the Geneva and New York bars, she is a partner in LKK Arbitration, which she cofounded in 2008, after having been a partner in Schellenberg Wittmer from 1996 to 2007 and in Baker & McKenzie from 1985 to 1995 and an associate in Baker & McKenzie Geneva and New York from 1981 to 1985.

Among other responsibilities in arbitration institutions and organizations, she is Honorary President of the International Council for Commercial Arbitration (ICCA), of which she was President from 2018 to 2020; Honorary President of the Swiss Arbitration Association (ASA), which she chaired from 2001 to 2005; and cofounder of the Foundation for International Arbitration Advocacy (FIAA). She is also an expert with the Swiss delegation to UNCITRAL Working Group III on the reform of investment dispute settlement, coauthor of two CIDS reports to UNCITRAL on the reform and cofounder of the Academic Forum on the Reform of Investor-State Dispute Settlement, which she directed in its early days.

PRINCIPAL PUBLICATIONS

Books

Investor-State Dispute Settlement and National Courts – Current Framework and Reform Options, Springer Open, 2020 (coauthor M. Potestà).

The Composition of a Multilateral Investment Court and of an Appeal Mechanism for Investment Awards, CIDS Report 2017, available on the UNCITRAL and Geneva Center for International Dispute Settlement (CIDS) websites (coauthor M. Potestà).

Can the Mauritius Convention Serve as a Model for the Reform of Investor-State Arbitration in Connection with the Introduction of a Permanent Investment Tribunal or an Appeal Mechanism?, CIDS Report 2016, available on the UNCITRAL and Geneva Center for International Dispute Settlement (CIDS) websites (coauthor M. Potestà).

International Arbitration: Law and Practice in Switzerland, Oxford, Oxford University Press, 2015 (coauthor A. Rigozzi).

Arbitrage international: Droit et pratique à la lumière de la LDIP, 2nd ed., Bern, Weblaw, 2010 (coauthor A. Rigozzi).

Online Dispute Resolution – New Challenges for Contemporary Justice, The Hague and Zurich, Kluwer/Schulthess, 2004 (coauthor T. Schultz).

Arbitration at the Olympics – Issues of Fast-Track Dispute Resolution and Sports Law, The Hague, Kluwer, 2001.

La clause d'élection de for dans les contrats internationaux, Basel, Helbing & Lichtenhahn, 1980.

Articles and book chapters

"Commercial Arbitration before International Courts and Tribunals – Reviewing Abusive Conduct of Domestic Courts", *Arbitration International*, 2013, p. 153.

"The Transnationalization of National Contract Law by the International Arbitrator", in M. Kohen and D. Bentolila (eds.), *Liber Amicorum Jean-Michel Jacquet*, Paris, LexisNexis, 2013, p. 107.

"Soft Law in International Arbitration – Codification and Normativity", *Journal of International Dispute Settlement*, 2010, p. 283.

"When Arbitrators Facilitate Settlement: Amiable Imposition or Actual Solution?", *Arbitration International*, 2009, p. 187.

"Integrating Mediation into Arbitration: Why It Works in China", *Journal of International Arbitration*, 2008, p. 479 (coauthor Fan Kun).

"Arbitral Precedent: Dream, Necessity, or Excuse?", *Arbitration International*, 2007, p. 357.

"The Governing Law: Fact or Law? – A Transnational Rule on Establishing Its Content", in M. Wirth (ed.), *Best Practices in International Arbitration, ASA Special Series No. 26*, 2006, p. 79.

"Consolidation of Proceedings in Investment Arbitration: How Can Multiple Proceedings arising from the Same or Related Situations Be Handled Efficiently?", *ICSID Review – Foreign Investment Law Journal*, 2006 (coauthors L. Boisson de Chazournes, V. Bonnin and M. M. Mbengue), p. 59.

"The Arbitrator and the Law: Does He/She Know It? Apply It? How? And a Few More Questions", *Arbitration International*, 2005, p. 631.

"Globalization of Arbitral Proceedings", *Vanderbilt Journal of Transnational Law*, 2003, p. 1314.

"Discovery in International Arbitration: How Much Is Too Much?", *SchiedsVZ*, 2004 (coauthor P. Bärtsch), p. 13.

"Global Implications of the FAA: The Role of Legislation in International Arbitration", *ICSID Review – Foreign Investment Law Journal*, 2005, p. 339.

"Online Dispute Resolution and Its Significance for International Commercial Arbitration", in G. Aksen *et al.* (eds.), *Global Reflections on International Law, Commerce and Dispute Resolution, Liber Amicorum in Honor of Robert Briner*, Paris, 2005, p. 437.

"Qui contrôle l'arbitrage? Autonomie des parties, pouvoirs des arbitres et principe d'efficacité", in *Liber Amicorum Claude Reymond – Autour de l'arbitrage*, Paris, Litec, 2004, p. 153.

"Annulment of ICSID Awards in Contract and Treaty Arbitrations: Are There Differences?", in E. Gaillard and Y. Banifatemi (eds.), *Annulment of ICSID Awards: The Foundation of a New Investment Protection Regime in Treaty Arbitration*, Huntington, Juris Publishing, 2004, p. 189.

"Arbitration Procedure: Identifying and Applying the Law Governing the Arbitration Procedure", in A. van den Berg (ed.), *The Role of the Law of the Place of Arbitration in Improving the Efficiency of Arbitration Agreements and Awards: 40 Years of Application of the New York Convention, ICCA Congress Series No. 9*, 1999, p. 336.

"Internet: mondialisation de la communication – mondialisation de la resolution des litiges?", in K. Boele-Woelki and C. Kessedjian (eds.), *Internet, Which Court Decides? Which Law Applies?*, 1998, p. 89.

"Le lieu de l'arbitrage à l'aune de la mondialisation – Réflexions à propos de deux formes récentes d'arbitrage", *Revue de l'arbitrage*, 1998, p. 517.

"La prestation caractéristique en droit international privé des contrats: l'influence de la Suisse", in *Essays on the Occasion of the 75th Anniversary of the Swiss Association for International Law, Annuaire suisse de droit international*, Zurich, Polygraphischer Verlag, 1989, p. 195.

"Conflits en matière d'obtention de preuves à l'étranger", *Annuaire suisse de droit international*, 1985, p. 110.

"Compétence internationale et bouleversements politiques", in C. Reymond and E. Bucher (eds.), *Mélanges Frank Vischer*, Zurich, Schulthess, 1983, p. 16.

THE LEGITIMACY OF ARBITRATION

by

ALEXIS MOURRE

TABLE OF CONTENTS

ARBITRATION, LEGITIMACY, LEGITIMATION: PRODUCTION OF DISCOURSE AND CITIZEN PERCEPTIONS

To speak of the legitimacy of arbitration is to speak of its place in society, of the way in which society perceives it and ultimately of the political and social role that society assigns to it at a given time in history. It is, therefore, a question not of its legality in the normative sense, which is established by the legal system that governs it, but of the extent to which this legal system is accepted by society, of the reasons for this acceptance, and therefore of the social and political forces that ultimately determine the evolution of the arbitration system. Although the two questions are ultimately linked, this lecture will, therefore, focus on the process by which arbitration is legitimised rather than on the legal conditions of the legitimacy of the institution itself.

Legitimacy is the capacity of an authority or institution to be accepted by those over whom it exercises power. Stacie Strong defines it as "a psychological property of an authority, institution, or social arrangement that leads those connected to it to believe that it is appropriate, proper and just" [1]; it is immediately clear that legitimacy cannot result from the inherent qualities of the institution alone but is essentially established by the way in which the social body regards it. Legitimacy, in its broadest sense, would thus be what underpins society's belief in the rightness of an institution or authority, a belief that is necessary for the acceptance of a given power relationship. As Weber put it, "the basis of all domination, and therefore of all docility, is belief" [2]. In the particular context of arbitration, it concerns the belief in the rightness of the possibility given to certain individuals to have their disputes judged by private tribunals. The legitimacy of arbitration is thus based on a fundamental belief in the usefulness of the resulting relations of domination: acceptance of the authority of the arbitrators, renunciation of the right to have recourse to the State judge, obligation to enforce the award. In fact, this was the subject of a very just observation

1. S. Strong, "Truth in a Post-Truth Society: How Sticky Defaults, Status Quo Bias, and the Sovereign Prerogative Influence the Perceived Legitimacy of International Arbitration", *University of Illinois Law Review*, 2018, p. 543, citing T. R. Tyler, "Psychological Perspectives on Legitimacy and Legitimation", 57 *Ann. Rev. Psychol.* 375, 375, 2006.
2. *Op. cit.*, p. 345.

by Emmanuel Gaillard, who, despite his well-known positivism, concludes at the end of his lecture on the representations of arbitration that his vision of the arbitral legal order, like any other representation of arbitration, ultimately pertains to "the realm of belief, if not faith" [3]. Yet all beliefs are the product of the historical and social relations within which they are embedded; but what is the underlying dialectic that powers its genesis and development and, hence, the legitimisation or delegitimisation of arbitration?

It is only recently that legal authors have taken a real interest in the legitimacy of arbitration in domestic and international relations, and the fact that it has been called into question in the field of investment protection is certainly not unrelated to this interest. Over the last fifteen years or so, numerous studies have been devoted to its real or supposed crisis, both in commercial relations and when the public interest is at stake, but these have generally focused on the content of arbitration law, its merits and supposed shortcomings, as well as the reforms that should be brought, rather than on a broader historical and political reflection on the processes by which arbitration is legitimised or delegitimised [4].

Nevertheless, as mentioned in the introduction, the legitimacy of arbitration must be distinguished from its legality and efficiency, just as it must be from its legitimisation, in that the former concept is static and concerns the conditions of acceptance of the institution at a given historical time, while the latter concept concerns the historical, political and social process that leads to its acceptance or rejection. Admittedly, legitimacy, legality, efficiency and legitimisation are connected, because

3. E. Gaillard, *Aspects philosophiques du droit de l'arbitrage international*, Livres de poche de l'Académie, 2008, p. 209. E. Silva Romero, for his part, uses the concept of legal fiction in a similar way as an "assumption that something is true even if it may be untrue", "Les 'fictions juridiques', dans le langage du droit français de l'arbitrage international", *Revue de l'arbitrage*, 2021, p. 345, and his forthcoming lecture at the Academy on the same subject.

4. In addition to the above-mentioned course by E. Gaillard, we refer to the study by D. Fernandez Arroyo, "The Legitimacy and Public Accountability of Global Litigation: The Particular Case of Transnational Arbitration", and the doctrine cited, *The Transformation of Enforcement, European Economic Law in Global Perspective*, H.-W. Micklitz and A. Wechsler (eds.), Hart Publishing, 2016, and by the same author, "Nothing is for Free: The Prices to Pay for Arbitrabilizing Legal Disputes, Privatizing Dispute Resolution, Trends and Limits", L. Cadiet, B. Hess and M. Requejo Isidro (eds.), *Studies of the Max Planck Institute Luxembourg for International, European and Regulatory Procedural Law, No. 18*, with A. Senegacnik, "Global Governance's Inescapable Legitimacy Conundrum: A Call to Reform International Commercial Arbitration", A. Bjorklund, S. Kroll and F. Ferrari (eds.), *The Cambridge Compendium on International Arbitration*, Cambridge University Press, Chapter 59, pp. 1802-1824, forthcoming; A. Stone Sweet and F. Grisel, *The Evolution of International Arbitration, Judicialization, Governance, Legitimacy*, OUP, 2017; M. Schinazi, The *Three Ages of International Commercial Arbitration*, Cambridge University Press, 2022.

inefficiency leads to a loss of legitimacy, and any loss of legitimacy is, in turn, likely to affect the legality of arbitration, whether in the form of a decrease of its field of application or a tightening of its regulatory and legal framework; but the acceptance of arbitration is not just an objective fact, and there are numerous examples of perfectly functional institutions that have been rejected for symbolic or political reasons. On the other hand, the processes by which arbitration is legitimised or delegitimised are based on historical, political, sociological and ideological factors that have as much to do with the dynamic relationship between the social body and the values on which it is founded as with society's reception of the discourse that arbitration constructs about itself. As one author put it by referring to a well-known Bourdieusian category [5], it is ultimately a matter of defining the political space *(champ politique)* in which legitimisation operates.

It is, therefore, by placing them in this dialectical process (1) that it will be possible to study the driving forces behind the process of legitimising arbitration (2) and then analyse the conditions of legitimacy that are the product of this process (3).

1. The dialectic of legitimacy

Stephan Schill must be credited for being the first, in a paper presented at the ICCA Congress in Miami in 2014 [6], to systematically study the relationship between legality and legitimacy in the field of arbitration, not only from a technical perspective but by focusing on the social relations on which the institution is founded. Schill's study, which will be discussed further on, has the merit of having departed from a self-centred analysis to address the dialogue arbitration maintains with society, not from the perception that arbitration has of itself but of the view that society has of it. The author concludes that arbitration has evolved from a dyadic mechanism, based essentially on the interaction of the parties and the arbitrators, to become a genuine system of transnational governance that requires it to abandon its illusions of self-sufficiency; the author thus studies the factors that contribute to the acceptability of arbitration from the point of view of society as a whole. It is to this study of the complex relationship between party

5. O. Corten, *Réflexions épistémologiques et méthodologiques sur les spécificités d'une étude politologique de la légitimité*, Cahiers européens de Bruxelles, 2000, No. 1, p. 9.

6. S. Schill, *Developing a Framework for the Legitimacy of International Arbitration*, ICCA Congress Series, 2015, p. 789.

autonomy, the institutionalisation of arbitration and the political and social acceptability that we will devote our attention in the reflections that follow.

The question of the relationship between legitimacy and legality is, of course, far from new in political philosophy. In *Economy and Society*, Max Weber developed his well-known theory of the three types of legitimacy: charismatic, traditional and rational. The first two are archaic forms of legitimacy, and the third is based on law, which is often confused with legality, the modern source of the legitimate exercise of power [7]. In a completely different vein, we recall how Carl Schmitt existentially justified the constitutional *coup d'état* that ended the Weimar Republic in 1932 on the grounds of the legitimacy of the political struggle and the claims of German nationalism [8]. Schmitt thus marked a divorce between legality and legitimacy, comparable in some respects to Marxism's questioning of bourgeois law. Beyond the gulf that separates the two authors, for Weber as for Schmitt, the question of legitimacy was embedded in a social relationship and a historical context.

Of course, the Weberian idea of charismatic domination applies poorly to arbitration, which has never had a leader, and even less disciples moved by a strong feeling of obedience. Traditional legitimacy, which is based on the perpetuation of sacralised practices, could to some extent be applied to arbitration, but only insofar as this method of dispute resolution would be seen as based on custom, which is no longer the case since a long time [9]; it should be noted, however, that Weber, describing the processes of conventionalisation of customary practices, gives the example of "the contemporary international arbitral courts" [10], which shows what arbitration owes to ancient forms of traditional domination. As for rational legitimacy, as we have said, it is for Weber confused with legality [11].

---

7. M. Weber, *Economie et société*, Plon, 1995, Vol. 1, p. 289 *et seq.*
8. Schmitt describes a State based on extra-legal legitimacy:

> "At the opposite extreme from legislative state is the governmental state, whose characteristic expression is the personified sovereign will and the authoritarian command of the head of state or government. The governmental state is animated less by an ethos than by a great pathos";

C. Schmitt, *Légalité et légitimité*, Les presses de l'Université de Montréal, 2015.

9. F. Gélinas, *Trade Usages and Implied Terms in the Age of Arbitration*, Oxford University Press, 2016.
10. *Op. cit.*, 2, p. 29.
11. *Op. cit.*, 1, p. 289.

It was not until the post-war period and the 1960s that studies in political sociology, in a move that challenged positivism, restored its autonomy to the notion of legitimacy. Norberto Bobbio developed the idea that the three characteristics of legal norms are justice, validity and effectiveness, and that effectiveness includes the requirement that the rule corresponds to the needs and aspirations of citizens [12]. Without opposing legality and legitimacy, Bobbio considers the relationship between the two concepts dialectically:

> "Order is not a body at rest, but a process: it moves and develops over time. The movement that manifests itself, firstly at the level of efficiency, produces the partial or total erosion, slowly or suddenly, of established rules or blocks of rules, and is inspired by new demands and new ideals, that is to say ultimately by the change in individual, group and society-wide evaluations of what is just and unjust." [13]

This was to say that norms evolve and die under the pressure exerted on them by social relationships; if power – in this case, the power of arbitrators – is legitimate because it is based on the agreement of the parties and on the rule of law that bestows binding force on that agreement, the sustainability of this legitimacy depends on other presuppositions of a historical, political and sociological nature; as Jean Carbonnier said by paraphrasing Herder, "le droit, comme toutes les choses, est roulé par les vagues du devenir universel" [14]. Arbitration, in the ever-changing historical, political and social context in which it is embedded, is in constant dialogue with society, thus developing representations of itself, or discourses of legitimization, whose ability to resonate with dominant values determines its evolution and durability.

The question raised is thus not only that of the legality of arbitration but also of society's adherence to it and the conditions of this adherence. Once again, we are talking about the creation of a belief that may, in some respects, escape any juridicity. However, this observation does not necessarily lead us to oppose legitimacy and legality, as Schmitt did; the positivist postulate linking legitimacy and legality

---

12. N. Bobbio, *Sur le principe de légitimité*, L'idée de légitimité, Annales de philosophie politique, PUF, 1967, p. 47 *et seq.*
13. *Op. cit.*, p. 59.
14. J. Carbonnier, *Flexible droit*, LGDJ, Paris, 1983, p. 13 ("Law, like all things, is carried by the waves of universal becoming").

remains true in certain respects, insofar as the latter contributes to the former, but it is reductive and does not really answer the question of the dialogue between society and arbitration and of the processes of legitimising arbitration. The foundations of legitimacy are not only legal (legality) but also, and perhaps above all, extra-legal, since on the one hand, arbitration is a living reality that evolves with the societies in which it takes place, and, on the other hand, the community's support for arbitration depends on the compatibility between arbitration and values that may be ethical or political in nature, foremost among which is a society's conception of the State at a given point in its history.

In order to provide a proper framework for our subject, it is important to remember the obvious: arbitration is a form of justice. Even though arbitration, particularly in international relations, has very specific features that distinguish it from ordinary justice, arbitral justice and State justice have the same function, which is to settle disputes by applying the law; society's dialogue with arbitration, therefore, necessarily rests on a counterpoint with State justice; i.e. a balance in which society draws the boundaries between the two institutions and their respective roles. Society's perception of arbitration is thus of a reflexive nature: its judgment on arbitration will be determined, at least in part, by its perception of ordinary justice and the extent to which the State intends to exercise its control over the law. The preference for arbitration will thus sometimes be driven by the public's distrust of the State, just as the restrictions that may be placed on it may result from centralising and statist aspirations; we have thus seen how, in recent times, the rejection of globalisation has turned entire parts of the public opinion against an institution that is wrongly or rightly perceived as the paradigm of a necessarily ultra-liberal and dangerous form of globalisation. Calvo's main idea, which had numerous and still vigorous ramifications in the field of investment law, was that everyone, nationals and foreigners alike, should agree to submit to the courts of the State [15]. Society's assessment of arbitration is therefore often about something else than arbitration.

This is not to suggest that there is an inherent hostility to arbitration on the part of the courts. Derek Roebuk has shown the falsity of

---

15. A. Mourre, "Perspectives of International Arbitration in Latin America", *The American Review of International Arbitration*, 2006, p. 598; H. Grigera-Naón, "Arbitration and Latin America: Progress and Setbacks", 21 *Arb. Int'l.* 27, 2005, p. 134; G. Tawil, "On the Internationalization of Administrative Contracts, Arbitration and the Calvo Doctrine", *ICCA Congress Series*, Vol. 15, pp. 328-331.

such an assumption, at least if it is expressed in a general way [16]. On the contrary, throughout history, from antiquity to the present day, arbitration has remained a permanent feature, showing that the institution's very foundations have never been really called into question. Bruno Oppetit has also rightly demonstrated the extent to which the harmonious relationship maintained throughout history – at least in recent times – between State courts and the institution of arbitration has helped to establish the legitimacy of the latter [17]. Without the support of States and their courts, arbitration could not function effectively and therefore could not claim to be a legitimate dispute resolution system. But such an observation can easily be reversed: if arbitration ceased to be perceived as a legitimate institution, would the support it currently receives from States and their courts be withdrawn? And might we not think that the basis of the social and political support given to arbitration is precisely the idea, or the belief, that arbitration is a *better* way of resolving certain disputes than litigation, either because the latter is unsuitable or because the State intends to optimise its resources by withdrawing certain disputes from the judicial system? But there is more than opportunism in these decisions: as we shall now see, it is the very concept of justice as a regalian function, and therefore of the powers of the State, as well as society's concept of the right to access to justice, that arbitration calls into question. In the Middle Ages, arbitration was widely used, upheld as it was by the uncertainties that existed at the time as to the respective jurisdictions of rival and neighbouring seigneurial powers, as much as by the scepticism on the neutrality of judges and the possibility of enforcing their decisions [18]. Arbitration was, therefore, permitted in almost all areas, including in matters of public law and domain [19]. If, during the High Middle Ages, arbitrators were obliged

---

16. D. Roebuk, "The Myth of Judicial Jealousy", Arbitration International, Vol. 10, No. 4, p. 395.

17. B. Oppetit, *Théorie de l'arbitrage*, PUF, Paris, 1998, p. 118.

18. H. Janeau, "L'arbitrage en Dauphiné au Moyen-Age : Contribution à l'histoire des institutions de paix", *Revue historique de droit français et étranger*, Vol. 24 (1946-1947), pp. 229-271.

19. "In the first centuries of the Middle Ages, it sometimes happened that there was no competent court for a given case, or more often that, through ignorance, independence or a desire to avoid the vexations of the lord or his people, litigants stayed away from the feudal courts. If we assume that jurisdiction is admitted, or imposed, and that the judge is willing to sit, his jurisdiction will often prove to be impotent",

H. Janeau, *op. cit.*, p. 235. J.-F. Poudret also shows that arbitration was used in matters concerning land ownership, demarcation, neighbourly relations, grazing land, rangeland

to comply with the rules of procedure followed by judges, later practice freed them from this constraint by introducing the notion of *amiable compositeur* and the distinction between arbitrator and *"arbitrateur"* [20]. The arbitration agreement was generally accompanied by an oath of the parties to enforce the award, and many charters and municipal statutes from the thirteenth and fourteenth centuries included a penalty clause in the event of non-enforcement. In addition, the award could not be appealed, based on the Roman law principle that: *A sententia arbitri non potest appellari, a sententia judicis appelatur* [21].

Three centuries later, with the advent of modern State, the institution changed profoundly. In France, a country of centralism and absolutism, it was no longer solely based on the sacred value of one's given word, but on the guarantee of the sovereign as the ultimate source of all legitimacy. Arbitration became institutionalised with the expansion of the royal power's legislative activities; it was thus encouraged and simultaneously regulated: rules were established to govern the procedure, enforcement was introduced, a sign that the award was worth nothing without the judge's approval, while at the same time making it compulsory in certain cases [22]. Despite the royal power having re-established the right to appeal against awards in 1510, thus putting an end to the old principle of Roman law prohibiting appeals [23], the Edict of Fontainebleau abolished this right in commercial matters in 1560, thus illustrating that the power had acquired sufficient confidence in an institution that was now constrained to strict regulation. The extent to which the monarchy favoured arbitration was thus proportional to the degree to which it had become part of the justice system. One author perfectly describes how the changes in the favour shown by monarchical France to arbitration illustrate the subtle dialectic that governs the relationship between arbitration and power:

---

rights, real estate guarantees, possessory actions such as spoliation, inheritance, public matters concerning royalties, duties towards the lord, confiscations, personal capacity and tax immunities, matrimonial causes, etc.; J.-F. Poudret, "Deux aspects de l'arbitrage dans les pays romands au Moyen Age : l'arbitrabilité et le juge-arbitre", *Revue de l'arbitrage*, 1999, p. 3.

20. A. Lefebvre-Teillard, *L'arbitrage de l'histoire*, archives de philosophie du droit, 52, 2009, p. 5.

21. H. Janeau, *op. cit.*, No. 18, p. 263.

22. Edict of Fontainebleau of August 1560; ordinances of 1673 on land trade and 1681 for the navy; *op. cit.*, pp. 192-195.

23. J. Hilaire, "L'arbitrage dans la période moderne (XVIe-XVIIIe siècle)", *Rev. arb.*, 2000, p. 192.

> "qu'il soit vu avec faveur ou avec défiance, l'arbitrage se trouve, en raison de sa nature particulière, au coeur des relations de pouvoir entre l'organe de gouvernement et la justice étatique. Favorisé par le premier, il peut être perçu comme une insupportable concurrence pour le deuxième, alors que lorsqu'il est considéré avec une plus grande méfiance, il peut au contraire de par son rejet renforcer l'alliance du pouvoir et des juges" [24].

In Elizabethan England, on the other hand, where arbitration had become the normal method of resolving disputes in both the private and public spheres, it continued to enjoy a very high degree of liberalism [25]. But the situation changed in the post-Elizabethan era of James I. In 1609, the Council handed down the *Vynior* judgment, which admitted the revocability of the arbitration agreement and which, according to a distinguished scholar, "for 300 years, limited the development of arbitration in commercial disputes, particularly in the United States" [26]; English case law took more than two centuries to re-establish the binding nature of arbitration agreements [27]. Can we entirely rule out the possibility that this paradigm shift was, to some extent at least, linked to the accession to the throne of a Calvinist monarch with strong absolutist views [28] yet allied with Puritans anxious to assert the predominance of the common law – a national law opposed to civil law of foreign

24. C. Jallamion, *Arbitrage et pouvoir politique en France du XVIIe au XIXe siècle*, *Rev. arb.*, 2005, pp. 3-62: "whether seen with favour or distrust, arbitration finds itself, as a consequence of its particular nature, at the heart of the power relationships between government and justice. If favoured by the former, it can be perceived as an intolerable competition, whereas if considered with more wariness, this rejection can reinforce the alliance between the power and the judiciary".

25. On arbitration in sixteenth-century England, D. Roebuk, *The Golden Age of Arbitration, Dispute Resolution under Elizabeth I*, Holo Books, 2015.

26. *The Myth of Judicial Jealousy, op. cit.*, p. 402; for a study defending the doctrine of the revocability of the arbitration agreement in the presence of a weaker party, P. D. Carrington and P. Y. Castle, "The Revocability of Contract Provisions Controlling Resolution of Future Disputes between the Parties", *Law and Contemporary Problems*, Vol. 67, 2004, p. 207, http://www.law.duke.edu/journals/67LCPCarrington.

27. *Scott* v. *Avery*, 5 HL Cas 811, 1856.

28. In 1598, James I published a treatise entitled *The Trew Law of Free Monarchies*, in which he based the king's power on divine right. On the political and religious context in England between the two centuries, cf. the classic work by L. Stone, *The Causes of the English Revolution (1529-1542)*, Routledge & Kegan, London, 1972, and in particular, concerning the role of the Puritans and the conflict between *common law* and civil law, pp. 97-98 and 103-105; cf. also Alexis Mourre, *Alberico Gentili (1552-1608) aux sources du droit international, Liber Amicorum Guy Horsmans*, Bruylant, 2004, pp. 802-803.

origins whose Roman roots placed it under suspicion of paganism – whereas arbitral tribunals generally applied *equity* [29]? This shows how the different political, cultural and social conditions that prevail in one country or another can lead arbitration down different paths.

Let us look at another example of this balancing act. In March 1790, the French Constituent Assembly had just broken down the parliaments and the provincial States, and the Revolution was now attacking what Mirabeau had called the "Palace industry" *(industrie du Palais)*, which public opinion associated with the corruption and arbitrariness of the Old Regime. Adrien Duport, who along with Antoine Barnave and Alexandre de Lameth was part of the left-wing triumvirate that dominated the Jacobin club for a time, was tasked with proposing a reform of the justice system. This movement could only lead to a more liberal system of arbitration. Indeed, in his speech to the Assembly on 29 March 1790, Duport concluded that arbitration should be favoured as long as the arbitration awards "conviennent à des hommes libres, puisqu'[elles] n'ont de force sur eux que par l'effet de leur confiance et de leur volonté" and that they "raffermissent dans le coeur de l'homme les notions primitives de la morale et de l'équité" [30]. This policy led to the adoption, alongside the law of 16 August 1790, of a provision bestowing constitutional value upon the right to arbitration:

> "l'arbitrage étant le moyen le plus raisonnable de terminer les contestations entre les citoyens, les législatures ne pourront faire

29. D. Roebuck, *The Golden Age of Arbitration, Dispute Resolution under Elizabeth I*, Holo Books, 2015, spec. 34 *et seq*. As Lawrence Stone shows (*supra* note), one of the forms that the conflict between Parliament and the King took at the time was a clash between civil and common law lawyers. Civil lawyers had historically been closer to the royal government because, in addition to matrimonial matters and inheritance – matters governed by the old canon law – they were called upon to deal with administrative matters and public affairs, while common lawyers were responsible for private law matters and contracts between individuals. The conflict became particularly acute in the early years of James I's reign, with the common law courts attacking the jurisdiction of the civil law courts when private interests were at stake, as was the case, for example, in matters of succession. The Archbishop of Canterbury asked the King to intervene personally to put an end to the practice of writs of prohibition – the forerunners of our anti-suit injunctions – which the common law courts frequently issued against the jurisdiction of the civil law courts. This conflict was settled in 1615 by the Earl of Oxford ruling of the Court of Chancery in favour of Equity, a solution confirmed by the King the following year on the advice of Francis Bacon.

30. Principes et plan sur l'établissement de l'ordre judiciaire by M. Duport, appended to the session of 29 March 1790, *Archives parlementaires de la Révolution française*, 1881, 12, p. 421. As long as arbitration awards "suit free men because they are only binding upon them by way of their trust and their free will" and that they "reinforce in their hearts the ancient notions of morals and equity".

aucune disposition qui tiendrait à diminuer, soit la faveur, soit l'efficacité des compromis"[31].

In the same Rousseauist vein, on 16 December 1809, the Paris Court of Appeal, acting upon the requisitions of public prosecutor Grégoire Mourre, handed down a ruling concerning the enforcement in France of an English arbitration award, affirming the universal nature of the right to be judged by arbitrators[32]; the Court confirmed that the English arbitrators had not exercised any territorial jurisdiction and that, as their authority was based on the *ius gentium*, their decisions should be *"reconnues chez tous les peuples"* ("recognizes by all peoples"). More than two centuries ago, it anticipated the *Hilmarton* and *Putrabali* decisions and affirmed a vision of arbitration based on the *ius gentium*, which, as we know, is the ancestor of international law.

However, other voices had been reclaiming the exclusive rights of the State over the administration of justice. Robespierre delivered a speech to the Assembly on 5 August 1790, barely a week after the formation of the first coalition of European powers against France, in which he described arbitration as an institution that contained all the seeds of partiality and where "les jugements ne seraient plus rendus suivant la justice, mais suivant l'affection des juges pour les parties"[33], and it is doubtful that the Arras revolutionary intended in his diatribe to distinguish between international or domestic, civil or commercial arbitration. Michelet states in his *Histoire de la Révolution française* that the Revolution then emerged from the age of innocence[34]; it was also, and for a long time, the harbinger of a retreat from the values of freedom that had led to the birth of democracy at the same time as to the rise of arbitration: with the war and the birth of modern class struggle[35], the time of liberalism was no longer ripe. Thus, when the Montagnard Convention introduced, in June 1793, a forced arbitration procedure applicable to the apportionment of communal property, it did so within a strict regulatory framework, which removed all freedom from the

---

31. Laws of 16 and 24 August 1790 on judicial organisation, title I, Article 1: "As arbitration is the most reasonable means of resolving disputes between citizens, legislatures are precluded from adopting any measure that would diminish either the favour or the effectiveness of arbitration agreements".

32. *Les Cahiers de l'Arbitrage*, 2019, 1, 49, note B. De Loynes de Fumichon.

33. 5 August 1790, AP, 1st Series, tome XVII, p. 621; where "judgments would no longer be made according to justice, but depending on the judges' inclination in favour of a party".

34. *Pléiade*, Vol. 1, p. 426.

35. For more information, see D. Guérin, *La lutte des classes sous la première République, Bourgeois et bras nus (1793-1797)*, Gallimard, 1968.

arbitrators and the parties [36] and once again transformed the arbitration tribunals into substitutes for State justice. Arbitrators would in effect be referred to by the 24 June 1793 Constitution as public arbitrators [37]; the Convention, having abolished the Old Regime judiciary, made of arbitrators new State judges, whose number and powers were regulated by the legislature [38], which would however not prevent the Constitution to proclaim, somewhat hypocritically, that "ne peut être porté aucune atteinte au droit qu'ont les citoyens de faire prononcer sur leurs différends par des arbitres de leur choix" [39].

Duport's *"arbitrage libre"*, which was born out of the Revolution's efforts to dismantle the justice of the Old Regime, thus gave way to a different institution, as a result of the affirmation of a new judicial order and of Napoleon's codification. The preparatory work for the 1806 French Code of Civil Procedure, which introduced the ban on arbitration in matters concerning public order, the State, public property and municipalities [40], justified to ban arbitration on the grounds that no matter how well educated they might be, arbitrators would never offer society the same guarantees of independence as judges vested by law [41], an idea that is still very much present in the French political imagination. What followed is well known: the *Prunier* ruling of 1843, which required the conclusion of an arbitration compromise *(compromis d'arbitrage)* identifying the subject matter of the dispute and the identity of the arbitrators, thus reducing the arbitration agreement to a mere non-binding promise [42]. The spirit of the times could not be better described than by quoting Troplong, for whom arbitration was a justice *"si défectueuse, si dépourvue de garanties"* that it was absolutely necessary to leave the parties free to repudiate it whenever necessary [43]: only the State can offer genuine guarantees of justice [44].

---

36. Jallamion, *Revue de l'arbitrage*, 2015, 10.
37. Article 9.
38. Article 90.
39. Article 86: "There shall be no limitation to the citizens' right to resolve their disputes through arbitrators of their choice".
40. Articles 86 and 1004.
41. J.-G. Locré, *Esprit du Code de procédure civile, ou Conférence du Code de procédure avec les discussions du Conseil, les observations du Tribunat, les exposés des motifs, les discours des orateurs du Tribunat*, P. Didot l'Aîné, Paris, 1816, Vol. 4, pp. 359-360.
42. I. Fadlallah and D. Hascher, *Les grandes décisions de droit de l'arbitrage commercial*, Dalloz, Paris, 2019, p. 3 *et seq*.
43. *Op. cit.*, p. 6. ("So defective, so devoid of guarantees.)
44. G. Born aptly likens the *Prunier* judgment to the view expressed by the American judge Joseph Story in an 1843 case, according to which:

It took France eighty years to rid itself of the legacy of the *Prunier* ruling, which is still reflected in the former Article 2061 of the French Civil Code prohibiting arbitration agreements, which was only reformed in a more liberal way in 2001. In the meantime, the needs of trade had made it possible to partially restore the effectiveness of arbitration, first in international matters by means of the conflict-of-laws rule designating a law other than French law [45], then in commercial matters by the 31 December 1925 law. France, as we know, ended up establishing one of the most favourable regimes for the validity and effectiveness of arbitration agreements, laying down a substantive rule of validity, unique in the world, only subject to the will of the parties [46]. This development calls for two observations.

On the one hand, the political acceptance of arbitration still finds its limits when the interests of the public authorities are at stake and even more so when the dispute has a political dimension. The pro-arbitration policy adopted by France in the second half of the last century, which seemed to be very solidly established, did not prevent the *Tapie* case from giving rise to an unprecedented political and media uproar, associating arbitration with the idea of a presumed fraud in which the former President of the Republic, who had just been defeated, was suspected of having participated. Everything in the political and journalistic commentaries tended to cast suspicion not only on the arbitration procedure to which Tapie had been a party, but on the arbitration itself: the possibility for the parties to choose their own arbitrators became a source of collusion; the existence of contacts between an arbitrator and one of the counsel proof of the partiality of the tribunal as a whole; and above all, the fact that the public interest was at state, in circumstances where Tapie himself had been close to the government at the time the arbitration compromise was signed, justified in the eyes of the detractors of arbitration to exclude this

> "Now we all know, that arbitrators at the common law, possess no authority whatsoever, even to administer an oath, or to compel the attendance of witnesses. They cannot compel the production of documents, and papers and books of account, or insist upon a discovery of facts from the parties under oath. They are not ordinarily well enough acquainted with the principles of law or equity, to administer either effectually, in complicated cases; and hence it has often been said, that the judgment of arbitrators is but *rusticum judicium*",

Tobey v. *County of Bristol*, 23 F Cas. 1313, 1321-23 (CCD Mass, 1845), quoted in "The Right to Arbitrate, Historical and Contemporary Perspectives", *Asian Dispute Review*, 2015, Vol. 17, No. 2, pp. 56-60.

45. DP 1879.1.56, S. 1878.1.1429, JDI 1879.285, GA No. 7.

46. Cass. Civ. 1re, 4 July 1972, *Hecht*; Cass. Civ. 1re, 20 December 1993, *Dalico*; Cass. Civ. 1re, 5 January 1999, *Zanzi*.

mean of dispute resolution [47]. Still, the most interesting aspect of the anti-arbitration campaign to which the *Tapie* case gave rise was the intense curiosity that it suscitated in the French public. For the first time, arbitration ceased to be a matter for specialists and became a matter of general interest, and anyone could be surprised to read in the daily press about the amount – undoubtedly extraordinarily high in the eyes of the uninitiated – of the arbitrators' remuneration, and the lack of transparency in the conditions of their appointment [48]. Among the manifestations of anti-arbitration scepticism that have recently taken hold in France when the public interest is at stake, we should also mention, of course, the aftermath of the INSERM judgment and the creation of a special system for reviewing awards having applied administrative law, even in international commercial matters [49].

On the other hand, in France and elsewhere, the scope of contemporary arbitration has become significantly more limited than it was during the Middle Ages. Whereas, in the thirteenth and fourteenth centuries, arbitration had been the common method of settling disputes in all areas, ranging from the capacity to inherit to tax and matrimonial matters, the revival of modern arbitration unfolded whithin a broader movement of specialization that brought it back into the domain of commercial relations. The development of arbitration since the 1960s has been closely linked to the growth of international trade and globalisation. At the same time, although arbitration remains available in consumer matters, particularly in the United States, and to a certain extent in employment relations [50], the scope of arbitrability in disputes involving a weaker party has receded [51], a sign that the legitimacy

47. Concerning the case as a whole and the reactions it provoked, see L. Mauduit, *Sous le Tapie*, Stock, 2008.

48. If, as Emile Durkheim said, public anger can be a source of law (*De la division du travail social*, PUF, 2013, pp. 70-71), we can see that it can also act upon it as a powerful regressive force.

49. B. Audit, "Le nouveau régime de l'arbitrage des contrats administratifs internationaux (à la suite de l'arrêt rendu par le Tribunal des conflits dans l'affaire INSERM)", *Revue de l'arbitrage*, 2010, p. 253; M. Laazouzi, "L'impérativité, l'arbitrage international des contrats administratifs et le conflit de loi", *RCDIP*, 1999, p. 654.

50. In consumer matters, see *Allied-Bruce Terminix Cos* v. *Dobson*, 513 US 265 (1995), US Supreme Court; see also *Jaguar*, Cass. Civ. 1re, 21 May 1997 – *Rev. arb.*, 1997, p. 538, note E. Gaillard; Section 91 of the English Arbitration Act 1996; Section 1031 (5) of the German Code of Civil Procedure and Section 13 German Civil Code. In labour relations, see *Steelworkers* v. *Enterprise Car*, 363 US 593 (1960), US Supreme Court; *BGE 136 III 467* (2010), Swiss Federal Court, relating to Article 177 (1) Swiss PILA.

51. See Arrêt *PWC*, Cass. Civ. 1re, 30 September 2020, No. 18-19.241; Ch. Seraglini, *Eclaircie pour la protection du consommateur dans l'arbitrage international* (à propos

of arbitration was becoming closely linked to the professional and international nature of the disputes to which it was intended to apply.

It was at the very time during which arbitration seemed to be most established, in the middle of the first decade of this century, that questions relating to arbitration in matters of investment protection began to attract increasingly critical interest from the public and the media. The idea gradually took hold that the benefits of the great globalisation movement which began in the early 1980s, of which China's accession to the WTO in 2001 was one of the high points, had not been shared in a sufficiently even manner. This idea was amplified by a strong feeling of downgrading among the middle classes in the most advanced countries following the crisis of 2008 and the increase in inequalities that followed. Western Europe and North America's leasers felt necessary to give the impression that national States could regain control of their destinies by limiting the effects of globalisation. Arbitration, by virtue of its global nature and its autonomy from national legal systems, was the natural victim of this movement. The process of delegitimising arbitration within the field of investment protection has developed over a long period, which is the sign of a profound trend. It began when, between 1995 and 1997, the OECD countries secretly negotiated the Multilateral Agreement on Investment, which they were forced to abandon in 1998 under pressure from non-governmental organisations and left-wing associations [52], and continued until its repudiation by the European Union twenty years later, with the imposition of a multilateral investment court in the CETA, the *Achmea* ruling and the end of intra-EU investment protection treaties [53]. The forces working against arbitration are clearly identifiable: the aspiration for greater transparency in the governance of public affairs, which stems from

---

de l'arrêt Cass. Civ. 1re, 30 septembre 2020); *BGHZ 145 (2020), German Federal Court of Justice; Martin Bank* v. *Worldcom*, 2002 NY Slip Op 40009(U); *Green Tree Fin. Corp-Ala.* v. *Randolph*, 531 US 79 (2000), US Supreme Court.

52. OECD, *The Multilateral Agreement on Investment, Consolidated Draft Text*, DAFFE/MAI(98)7/REV1, 24 April 1998, https://www.oecd.org/fr/investissement/accordssurlinvestissementinternational/accordmultilateralsurlinvestissement.htm. See Yoshi Kodama, "Dispute Settlement under the Draft Multilateral Agreement on Investment – The Quest for an Effective Investment Dispute Settlement Mechanism and Its Failure", *Journal of International Arbitration*, 1999, pp. 45-88.

53. P. Pinsolle and I. Michou, *Arbitrage : l'arrêt Achmea, la fin des traités d'investissements intra-UE ?*, Dalloz, Paris, 2018; E. Triantafilou and D. Pusztai, "Achmea, Investment Treaty Arbitration, Public International Law and EU Law: The Way Forward", in C. Baltag and A. Stanic (eds.), *The Future of Investment Treaty Arbitration in the EU: Intra-EU BITs, the Energy Charter Treaty, and the Multilateral Investment Court*, 2020, pp. 43-62.

a growing mistrust of elites and a desire to control them better; the feeling that the power of arbitrators is exercised opaquely and outside any control; the association of arbitration with globalisation and the accompanying challenge to the nation-State; and finally the idea that, in terms of investment protection, arbitration is an instrument in the hands of multinationals, designed to limit the exercise of legislative and regulatory powers by States and therefore inherently anti-democratic. In the face of this movement, arguments based on legality, efficiency and even fairness of the system carry little weight. The perfectly functional and rational nature of the international investment dispute settlement system has not prevented it from being abruptly swept away by a global wave of delegitimisation.

Arbitration, therefore, engages in a complex dialogue with the society surrounding it, in which not only its effectiveness and usefulness are at stake but also, and perhaps above all, political, philosophical or moral values that are external to it and which may lead to its legitimisation or delegitimisation. Generally speaking, it can be said that the values of political liberalism and economic openness have historically favoured arbitration, while the tendency towards sovereignty and the centralism of State power have tended to call it into question. Gary Born, for example, has highlighted how the Nazi regime, having only just come to power, adopted the *"Lignes Directrices du Reich concernant les Tribunaux Arbitraux"* (Guidelines of the Reich concerning arbitral tribunals), in which it was stated, contrary to the liberal tradition that had prevailed in Germany since the 1877 Code of Civil Procedure, that the continued development of arbitration was likely to undermine confidence in the State's jurisdiction and in the State itself[54].

However, the fact that the legitimacy of arbitration depends on values external to it, and over which it has no control, does not mean that the rules that arbitration sets for itself, and the discourse that the arbitration community develops about itself, cannot contribute to establishing the legitimacy of the institution. The *Alabama* arbitration provides a remarkable example of this, and authors have emphasised how this case, almost elevated to the rank of a founding myth, laid out the foundations for the legitimacy of arbitration in the settlement of inter-State disputes in the modern era[55]. More generally, the discourse that

54. 95 *Deutsche Justiz* 52, 821 (1933), in "The Right to Arbitrate: Historical and Contemporary Perspectives", *Asian Dispute Review*, 2015, 17, 56-60.

55. B. de Loynes de Fumichon and W. Park, "Retour sur l'affaire de l'*Alabama*: de l'utilité de l'histoire pour l'arbitrage international", *Revue de l'arbitrage*, Vol. 2019, No. 3, 2019, pp. 743-834.

arbitration develops about itself, and the way in which it communicates with society, are a powerful vector for the acceptance and development of the institution.

This brings us to another aspect of the dialectical process of legitimisation, namely the representations of arbitration. The legitimacy of arbitration presupposes not only favourable political, economic and social conditions but also the production, by those involved in arbitration themselves, of a set of discourses which, actively or reactively, are likely to produce or restore legitimacy. It is, therefore, to these representations (or self-representations) of arbitration as the basis of its legitimacy that we should now turn.

2. *Discourses and representations*

The debate on arbitration has been extraordinarily fertile – without a doubt a sign of the vitality of the discipline – proposing a number of possible representations of the institution, all of which claim to establish its legitimacy in a universal manner. Each of these representations offers a language of its own, capable of making sense of the acts, standards and discourse produced by the arbitration community as a whole and thus of responding to the criticisms levelled at it by society: the aim is for each of them to offer an overarching discourse capable of bringing coherence to a legal practice as old as it is polymorphous, in order to align it with the expectations of society at a particular moment in its history. This set of representations, whose value is as much analytical as propagandistic, forms a veritable ideology of arbitration, whose importance for the survival of the system cannot be underestimated: without the representations of arbitration, there is in fact no possible legitimacy, because arbitration remains unintelligible to society.

It will immediately be objected that many legal disciplines do not produce representations that intend to be coherent and universal. After all, nobody questions the legitimacy of maritime law or labour law. The legitimacy of this or that rule of maritime law or labour law can certainly be debated, but the discipline as a whole has no vocation to question its own legitimacy. Why should arbitration be any different? It would indeed be entirely conceivable to view arbitration as a simple set of legal standards and procedural techniques resulting from the combination of the practice and normative activity of States.

Arbitration occupies a special position, however, in that it is involved in the privatisation of one of the main sovereign functions on which the modern State was built: justice. Arbitration thus touches on two of the most central concerns of any government: the control exercised by the State over the development of the law, in other words, judicial policy, and the right of citizens to be judged according to standards that the State deems appropriate. Arbitration is a form of justice, which presupposes that its existence is acceptable to the State and legitimate in the eyes of society. However, the legitimacy of arbitration, in turn, presupposes that it is understood by society, which renders the ideological production that governs the construction of its representations necessary.

One must still define what is meant by "representation". It is not just a question of the legal nature of arbitration, which has given rise to numerous debates, particularly as to its jurisdictional or contractual nature, or its autonomy or territoriality, or the legal regime that applies to it. Such debates can certainly bring into play opposing legal conceptions and thereby influence the representations that each person may have of the institution, but they are not intended to offer a legitimisation discourse. The notion of representation must, therefore, refer to something else. A representation is, first and foremost, an arena of debate "where, in the competition between professionals who are involved, politically active and legitimate forms of perception and expression are created" [56], in other words, it is a language that acts and produces legitimacy. Emmanuel Gaillard thus refers to "concepts that provide a comprehensive account of the arbitral phenomenon, its sources, purposes and structures", adding that these representations should be "structuring" [57]. In other words, any representation of arbitration must give an account of its foundations, its coherence and its usefulness. A representation must indeed not only offer a comprehensive and structuring discourse, but also be militant in that its aim is to maintain belief in its legitimacy as an autonomous and private system of dispute resolution. But the arbitration discourse, beyond its structuring and militant dimension, must also be understood in its semiotic dimension. Any representation of arbitration, as we have said, is a language whose purpose is to transmit the values of legitimisation, to which we will return later, in which words have a performative as well as a descriptive value. As Gaillard said, no representation of

56. P. Bourdieu, *Language and Symbolic Power*, Seuil, 2001, p. 213. See also J. Habermas' idea of "discursive ethics" as an exercise of justification: *Morale et communication*, Cerf, 1986, p. 118.

57. E. Gaillard, *Aspects philosophiques du droit de l'arbitrage international*, Académie de droit international de La Haye, 2008, *op. cit*, No. 2, p. 34.

arbitration is true or false, as all are either fiction or belief; but every fiction or belief feeds on signs and codes, which, in turn, form, to use Hart's expression, the open texture of a law deeply shaped by words [58].

Gaillard identifies three possible representations of arbitration: the territorial conception, the Westphalian conception based on a plurality of State legal orders and the transnational conception of the arbitral legal order [59]. The first two, however, are essentially descriptive and, regardless of their underlying philosophical assumptions, pertain to legal analysis rather than forming a structuring discourse bearing a coherent and overarching vision. Moreover, the territorial and Westphalian representations, as described by the author, cannot account for the autonomy of arbitration, which is the only way in which it can make claims to legitimacy; to make arbitration an emanation of national legal orders is tantamount to denying its autonomy.

The third of these conceptions, which Gaillard proposes and supports, has however, by its transnational nature, not only a structuring value in that it offers a comprehensive explanation of the phenomenon of arbitration in its singularity, its unity and its universality, but also a justificatory value in that it proposes to lay the foundations of its legitimacy.

However, there are two other possible representations of arbitration, which Emmanuel Gaillard does not take into account: that which bases arbitration on natural law and that which focuses on the structures of the institution. Now, each of these last two representations, like the "Gaillardian" vision of the arbitral legal order, can claim to provide a comprehensive and structuring understanding of arbitration as an autonomous phenomenon.

We shall therefore posit, excluding territorialist conceptions, that the possible representations of arbitration as an autonomous legal phenomenon fall into three categories: jusnaturalist, transnational and structural. We will present each of them before attempting to propose a summary.

The first of these is that which postulates that the right to agree to arbitration is a matter of natural law. The decision of the Paris Court of Appeal dated 16 December 1809 (cited above) founded arbitration on the law of nations and, as Bruno Loynes de Fumichon noted [60], it was

58. Hart, *The Concept of Law*, Oxford, 1997, p. 135. On this point, see also the observations of S. Bollée in his lecture to the Academy on "The Inherent Powers of International Arbitrators", p. 155.

59. *Ibid.*

60. B. Loynes de Fumichon, *Cahiers de l'arbitrage*, 2019, 1, p. 50 *et seq.*

a continuation of the Grotius, Puffendorf and Vattel Rhine school of natural law:

> "For Grotius and the modern school of natural law, as for Gaïus, and for Aguesseau and the magistrates of the king's parliaments, the legal order is divided into three spheres: civil or national, international and universal. The classification of a body of rules in one category or another gives it its authority and force."

Rights acquired in the international sphere, of which the right to arbitration is one, are binding and enforceable everywhere, whereas rights acquired under natural law have a transcendent binding force independently of any foreign element. Recourse to the *ius gentium* thus forms the basis of an internationalist perspective on arbitration that is found in the French dualist tradition. But the spheres of *ius gentium* and of natural law may overlap. From such a perspective, the right of access to arbitration would be based on natural law and not only on *ius gentium*. It should not be forgotten that while the modern school of natural law distinguished natural law from *ius gentium*, the latter remained based on natural reason: Vitoria thus said, taking up the old definition of *Institutes*, "*Quod naturalis ratio inter omnes gentes constituit vocatur jus gentium*"; and as a commentator from the beginning of the last century, who was nevertheless sceptical about natural law, put it:

> "It is a commonly accepted principle of our old law that *ius gentium* derives at least in part from natural law and that the latter comprises the rules of conduct dictated by the consideration of man's reasonable and sociable nature." [61]

These rules include without a doubt, and have done so since the origins of Roman law, consensualism, good faith and keeping one's word [62].

---

61. A. Pillet, introduction to *Les fondateurs du droit international*, V. Giard et E. Brière, Paris, 1904, xiv.

62. "L'attenzione tutta particolare dedicata dai pretori – sia urbano, sia peregrino – alla protezione delle nuove realtà economiche della società schiavistico-mercantile mediterranea, che si veniva costruendo intorno alle vittorie militari romane, portò abbastanza rapidamente (fra II e I secolo a. C.), sempre all'interno della giurisdizione dei magistrati, al formarsi di una specie di diritto comune romano-mediterraneo, con contenuti soprattutto commerciali, che il pensiero giuridico e filosofico successivo definì *ius gentium* (diritto cioè idealmente condiviso non solo dai romani, ma da tutti i popoli mediterranei). Esso si articolava intorno a quattro contratti fondamentali (di compravendita, di locazione, di società, di mandato), e intorno a quattro principi guida, destinati a diventare altrettanti cardini di ogni successivo sviluppo giuridico: il consensualismo (il riconoscimento, cioè, dell'accordo tra le parti comunque manifestato, purché dimostrabile, indipendentemente dalla forma usata per la sua espressione); la buona fede (l'obbligo delle parti coinvolte in una

It could even be said that recourse to natural law is inseparable from arbitration's claim to autonomy: it is because arbitration seeks to be founded on natural reason that it must find its foundations elsewhere than in State legal orders, and it is because it asserts its autonomy that it requires this transfiguration through jusnaturalism [63]. Moreover, linking the foundations of arbitration's autonomy to natural law is far from being incongruous. Arbitration is in fact such an ancient and universally recognised institution that it is perfectly conceivable to give it the universal force that ancient law attached to natural law. Contrary to Carbonnier's suggestion [64], in fact, basing the right to arbitration on natural law is not necessarily incompatible with its historicity and, consequently, with the necessarily evolving nature of the discipline. In

---

transazione a un comportamento di cui l'inganno non fosse il fine determinante del loro agire); la reciprocità (secondo cui, alla prestazione economicamente onerosa, e già eseguita, di una delle parti impegnate in una transazione dovesse necessariamente corrispondere una prestazione simmetrica dell'altra, o un suo corrispettivo di pari entità economica...); l'equità (per cui nella valutazione processuale di ogni singolo caso l'applicazione letterale del *ius* poteva cedere il posto – ove essa avrebbe potuto dar luogo a risultati iniqui – a un criterio di misura più flessibile, e meglio aderente ai concreti interessi in gioco)". "The special attention devoted by the praetors – both urban and peregrine – to the protection of the new economic realities of the Mediterranean slave-trading society, which was taking shape around Roman military victories, led fairly quickly (between the 2nd and 1st centuries B.C.), always within the jurisdiction of the magistrates, to the formation of a sort of Roman-Mediterranean common law, with primarily commercial content, which subsequent legal and philosophical thought defined as ius gentium (that is, law ideally shared not only by the Romans but by all Mediterranean peoples). It was structured around four fundamental contracts (sale, lease, partnership, and mandate) and around four guiding principles, destined to become the cornerstones of all subsequent legal development: consensualism (that is, the recognition of an agreement between the parties, however expressed, provided it is demonstrable, regardless of the form used for its expression); good faith (the obligation of the parties involved in a transaction to act in a manner where deception was not the determining purpose of their conduct); reciprocity (according to which, an economically onerous performance, already executed, by one of the parties engaged in a transaction must necessarily be matched by a symmetrical performance from the other, or a consideration of equal economic value...); equity (whereby, in the judicial assessment of each individual case, the literal application of the ius could give way – where it might have led to unjust results – to a more flexible criterion of measurement, better aligned with the concrete interests at stake)",

A. Schiavone, *Diritto privato romano, un profilo storico*, Einaudi, 2003, pp. 44-45.

63. Here again, we dare to draw a perhaps audacious historical parallel by quoting Aldo Schiavone's analysis of the way in which Cicero, and the Roman jurists of the late-Republican period, sought to legitimise civil law: "Over the years, he sought to achieve his objective by essentially following two guidelines: the reaffirmation of law as an autonomous rational order in the face of political and economic power, and the representation in jusnaturalist terms of the Roman Legal experience". *Ius, l'invention du droit en Occident*, *op. cit.*, p. 396.

64. Flexible droit, *op. cit.*, pp. 10-11.

order to resolve this apparent contradiction, it is enough to conceive that the autonomy of the will is an intangible principle, with the consequence that a person who is able to dispose of his rights cannot be deprived of the possibility of agreeing to arbitration, while the norms governing the implementation of that right may be modified according to the circumstances. Evidence of such a view can be found in a judgment of the German Federal Court of Justice *(Bundesgerichtshof)*, which based the right to arbitration on the fundamental freedoms protected by the Constitution, such as the freedom of contract, freedom of association and other individual rights; according to this view, the denial of the right of citizens to arbitrate their disputes "is no less a threat to the rule of law and individual freedoms than the denial of freedoms of contract or association" [65].

Such a conception, which does not imply establishing arbitration as a legal order, therefore has certain merits. The fact that the right to arbitration is evolving and flexible in no way precludes it from being founded on higher values, which themselves are not. It must be said, however, that the recourse to natural law as a basis for the immanence of the right to arbitration has now become largely ineffective. As Leo Strauss has written, modern legal thought has downgraded natural law to the level of an ideal, or even of an ideology or a myth [66]; like

65. 3 April 2000, II ZR 373/98. This decision may be compared with the judgment handed down by the French Court of Cassation on 1 February 2005 in *NIOC* v. *Israel*, which characterised the impossibility for a party to access the arbitral tribunal as "a right falling within the scope of international public policy enshrined in the principles of international arbitration and Article 6.1 of the European Convention on Human Rights", and therefore as "a denial of justice that justifies the international jurisdiction of the President of the Tribunal de Grande Instance de Paris, in his role of assistance and cooperation with the State judge in the constitution of an arbitral tribunal insofar as there is a connection with France" (1-13.742 02-15.237). This is also the view defended by G. Born in his article "The Right to Arbitrate, Historical and Contemporary Perspectives", *op. cit.*

66. L. Strauss, *Droit naturel et histoire*, Flammarion, Paris, 1986, pp. 14-15. Strauss adds:

> "Nevertheless, the need for natural law is as clear today as it has been for centuries and even millennia. To reject natural law is to say that all law is positive, in other words that law is determined exclusively by the legislators and courts of different countries. Yet it is clear that it is perfectly sensible and sometimes even necessary to talk about unjust laws or decisions. By making such judgements, we imply that there is a standard of right and wrong that is independent of and superior to positive law: a standard by which we are able to judge positive law. Many people today consider that the standard in question is no more than the ideal adopted by our society or our 'civilisation', as it has taken shape in its ways of life or its institutions. But, according to this same opinion, every society has its own ideals, cannibal societies no less than civilized ones. If principles derive sufficient

him, we regret the setback that this represents for the law [67], but we can only observe that the undivided reign of positive law leaves little room for a representation of arbitration that would be based exclusively on natural reason. Arbitration thus no doubt loses the opportunity to anchor its universality and permanence on a standard that is superior to the rules that may limit its scope and effectiveness [68] to instead rely on more fragile assumptions. Pierre Mayer has accordingly grounded the arbitrator's power to exclude a legal rule that is deemed immoral on its own conscience [69]. One might think that such a point of view is not very far removed from the conceptions of natural law, since the arbitrator's decision to exclude an unjust rule must necessarily refer to a norm that is superior to it. As René David wrote more than sixty years ago, one might ask whether:

> "Under the guise of an alleged "interpretation" of positive law, and through the application of general formulations such as public policy, good faith and equity, our courts do not give effect to considerations that, rather than strict positive law, derive from the idea of natural law." [70]

However, in a perhaps more Kantian way, Pierre Mayer bases this power solely on the will of the arbitrator [71]. Yet, it is a very different

---

justification from the fact that they are accepted in a society, the principles of the cannibal are as defensible and as sound as those of the civilized man."

67. "There can be no natural law if human thought, despite its essential incompleteness, cannot resolve the problem of the principles of justice in an authentic and universally valid way. More generally, there can be no natural law if human thought is incapable of acquiring within a limited field of specific subjects, an authentic and universally valid form of knowledge", *op. cit.*, p. 34.

68. We will recall the words of A. Schiavone about natural law in Roman times:

> "It would... become be one of the founding elements of this universalist perspective which, during the Principate, jurisprudence would follow with even greater consistency, as a definitive legitimation of its choices and its practice";

A. Schiavone, *Ius, l'invention du droit en Occident*, Belin, 2008, p. 420.

69. P. Mayer, *La règle morale dans l'arbitrage international*, studies offered to P. Bellet, Paris, Litec, 1991.

70. R. David, "Droit naturel et arbitrage", *Natural Law and World Law*, Yuhikaku, Tokyo, 1954. R. David considered that arbitral justice was based, rather than on positive law, on the arbitrator's feelings of justice, morality and fairness, which he linked to a modern vision of natural law. Such a view is now clearly outdated in arbitration law and practice.

71. For a comparable approach, see M. Laazouzi, "L'arbitre international et les rapports entre ordres juridiques", in B. Bonnet (ed.), *Traité des rapports entre ordres juridiques*, LGDJ, 2016, p. 1043:

> "If [arbitrators] are free to adhere, or not, to a conception of their office guiding the intellectual process leading to the rendering of their award, it must be concluded

thing to ground the arbitrator's power on a legal order distinct from the one to which the excluded rule belongs, and to base it on the moral rule, the effectiveness of which ultimately results only from the absence of remedies on the merits and therefore from a freedom given to the arbitrator by the legal order itself. The latter conception, based entirely on the subjectivity of the arbitrator, does not, therefore, make it possible to structure a representation of arbitration in its entirety and autonomy [72]. It also presents certain political dangers, as the great discretion of arbitrators in applying the rule of law and the absence of review on the merits is one of the criticisms most often levelled against arbitration.

We may also find a trace of jusnaturalist conceptions in the elitist and moral vision, still widely held, according to which the value of arbitration lies in the personal merits of the individuals chosen by the parties to resolve their dispute, as illustrated by the adage, which goes back to Weber's vision of the charismatic judge, according to which "arbitration is only worth as much as the arbitrator" [73]; we also recall Duport's speech, which saw in the "trust" on which arbitration is based the means of strengthening "in the heart of man the primitive notions of morals and equity" [74]. But the reference to the actual or supposed moral values of arbitrators cannot in itself fulfil the role of a representation of arbitration. We can still detect the influence of jusnaturalist conceptions in Jan Paulsson, who, in his book *"The Idea of Arbitration"*, developed a vision of arbitration based entirely on the autonomy of the parties [75]. Since the parties can, by their own free will, create a legal space without any need for intervention by the State, each contract would form its own legal order, with all of them forming an autonomous normative

that they are fundamentally free and are not subject to the constraints imposed on the organs of State legal orders, on which the effectiveness of the arbitration will depend. The arbitrator's position, when confronted with relations between legal orders, is an illustration of this freedom."

72. See Gaillard, *Aspects philosophiques du droit de l'arbitrage international*, *op. cit.*, No. 2, p. 73.

73. It should be noted that the first attempt at a sociological description of modern arbitration bore the evocative title *Dealing in Virtue*, meaning that the value of arbitration lies entirely in the virtue of the arbitrator and, in the same vein, the title of the studies presented a few years ago to C. Brower, *Practicing Virtue*.

74. Note 30 above.

75. "Arbitration may be effective under arrangements that do not depend on national law or judges at all", J. Paulsson, *The Idea of Arbitration*, Oxford University Press, 2013, p. 30. See also, in the same vein, the aforementioned article by G. Born, "The Right to Arbitrate, Historical and Contemporary Perspectives".

system [76]; this vision is similar to that recently developed by Alain Pellet, who suggests that "there are as many legal orders as there are arbitral tribunals or treaties at the origin of their creation" [77]. It should be noted, however, that the notion of legal order is deprived of substance in such a vision; any legal relationship would, in fact, become its own legal order, whereas the notion only in our view takes on meaning, as conceived by Santi Romano, by reference to a social group which, because it is organised, is able to produce law. The vision proposed by Paulsson, on the other hand, has the merit of giving full effect to the creative power of the will; although this alone does not make it possible to grasp the complex set of relationships between arbitrators, parties, institutions, States and international organisations that characterise arbitration and the role it plays in contemporary society, it does lay the ontological foundations that allow arbitration to claim immanence.

Ultimately, natural law has fallen victim to the development of pluralist thought and legal sociology [78] as much as to the technification of the law, and the need for certainty in legal solutions has finally separated us from it. Having been suppressed by modern law, natural law remains however in a subliminal and degraded form, deeply rooted in the collective unconscious of arbitration [79]. As we shall see, the idea that the right to submit to arbitration is inherent in the freedom of each individual, and therefore has a superior value, is in fact indispensable to the construction of any discourse legitimising the institution. Natural

---

76. Paulsson, *op.cit.*, p. 30 *et seq*.

77. A. Pellet, "Le pluralisme juridique et les relations entre systèmes", *International Law in Motion, Some New Inshights, A Tribute to Late Professor François Rigaux*, PUL, 2020, p. 110. It is doubtful, however, contrary to what Pellet suggests, that Santi Romano thought of including contracts among the institutions likely to generate a legal order. For Santi Romano, a legal order emanates from an organised social body, which is not the case for the relationship between two contracting parties.

78. In the words of Strauss, it is a victim of Weber's idea that there is a plurality of principles of law that oppose each other with no means of proving the superiority of any one of them; Strauss, *op. cit.*, p. 45.

79. P. Franceskakis thus wrote that the multiplicity of historical conceptions of natural law did not allow to relate its operation to any one meaning of the term that may have prevailed at a particular time, as:

> "nothing indicates that this action is not also that of earlier ideas, that natural law has in sum not acted there with all its historical weight",

adding that this second explanation would be:

> "Somewhat better for those who believe that the action of ideas is not always that of isolated theses, but rather a matter of collective memory in its obscure corners",

Droit naturel et droit international privé, *Mélanges offerts à Jacques Maury*, tome 1, Paris, Dalloz, 1960, p. 116.

law remains the *logos* of any representation of arbitration as an autonomous institution. In this respect, it is noteworthy that the idea of the superior and universal nature of the right to agree to arbitration became positivized in the modern era by migrating from natural law to constitutional law. We can accordingly find traces of jusnaturalist conceptions in the tendencies towards the constitutionalization of arbitration observed in certain Latin American countries, a distant legacy of the French 16 August 1790 law that we have just mentioned [80].

A second possible representation of arbitration is that which postulates the existence of an arbitral legal order. The idea that arbitration constitutes its own legal order is inspired by modern theories of legal pluralism [81] which, faced with the questions posed by the coordination of State and non-State legal orders, drew on the efforts of legal thought in the Middle Ages to try to reconcile the universal concepts of Roman law and canon law, on which the Empire was based, and the political claims of the new free communes and guilds [82]. The post-glossators, first and foremost Bartole and Balde, had answered the question by recognising the existence of legal orders exercising their sovereignty in a particular field in the face of the *universalitas* of imperial rule and by adapting Roman law to organise the co-existence of these legal orders in their own domain and those of the Empire and Church [83]. The inquiry into the concept of legal order reappeared, in a completely different

---

80. Article 43 of the Constitution of Costa Rica provides that arbitration is a fundamental right. Article 116 of the Colombian Constitution, Article 109 of the Constitution of Ecuador, Article 23 of the Constitution of El Salvador, Article 17 of the Mexican Constitution and Article 138 of the Constitution of Peru also elevate the possibility of submitting a dispute to arbitration to the rank of constitutional value. The same is true of Article 209 of the Portuguese Constitution.

81. On the question as a whole, see *Le pluralisme*, Archives de philosophie du droit, tome 49, Dalloz, 2006.

82. "Nel secondo medioevo – medioevo sapientale – un'altra singolarissima convivenza ci segnalerà il marcato pluralismo di questa esperienza giuridica: nello stesso territorio avranno vigenza e applicazione – nei modi che si tenterà di precisare più innanzi – sia i cosiddetti *iura propria*, cioè le norme particolari consolidate in consuetudini o emanate localmente da monarchi e da città libere, sia lo *ius commune*, cioè il maestoso sistema giuridico universale elaborato sulla piattaforma romana e canonica". "In the second Middle Ages – the 'sapiental Middle Ages' – another highly distinctive coexistence will highlight the marked pluralism of this legal experience: within the same territory, both the so-called *iura propria*, that is, the specific rules established by custom or enacted locally by monarchs and free cities, and the *ius commune*, that is, the majestic universal legal system developed on the Roman and canonical foundation, will be in force and applied – in ways that we shall attempt to clarify further on",

P. Grossi, *L'ordine giuridico medievale*, Laterza, 2003, p. 54.

83. On the question as a whole, see F. Calasso, *Gli ordinamenti giuridici del rinascimento medievale*, Giuffré, Milan, 1965:

context, at the end of the nineteenth century, in the work of Anzilotti [84], then in Santi Romano's 1918 study [85]. Applied to arbitration, the notion of legal order has given rise to two representations of the institution, which share a common link to the transnational nature of arbitration but differ profoundly in their presuppositions.

The first of these representations is that which links the arbitral legal system to the *lex mercatoria*, an autonomous system of law created by and for the international trade community. The *lex mercatoria* is closely related to the law of nations. The first English text to analyse it, dating from 1622, states as follows:

> "I have entitled the book according to the ancient name of the *Lex Mercatoria* . . . because it is customary law approved by the authority of all kingdoms and commonwealths, and not by a law established by the sovereignty of any prince." [86]

The autonomy of the original *lex mercatoria* has been perfectly described in Berman's classic work:

> "The initial development of mercantile law was left largely, though not entirely, to the merchants themselves, who organized international fairs and markets, formed mercantile courts, and

"Il contrapposto tra la *singulae res* ed il *mundus* si risolve, sul terreno politico, in quello tra gli ordinamenti particolari e l'Impero universale; problema che abbiamo veduto sorgere da una realtà storica caratterizzata, per un verso, da una pluralità di ordinamenti particolari, per l'altro da un *dominatus mundi* che ha un solo titolare: l'imperatore" (pp. 236-237). "The contrast between the *singulae res* and the *mundus* resolves itself, in the political sphere, into that between particular legal systems and the universal Empire; a problem which we have seen arising from a historical reality characterised, on the one hand, by a plurality of particular legal systems, and on the other by a *dominatus mundi* which has but one holder: the emperor."

84. *Studi critici di diritto internazionale privato*, 1898, p. 148 *et seq.*

85. We have no doubt that S. Romano's thinking on the question of the plurality of legal orders was nourished by the reflections of medieval jurists. The Sicilian jurist writes as follows:

> "In the Middle Ages . . . by the very constitution of society, divided and fragmented into numerous and diverse communities, often independent or loosely linked to each other, the phenomenon of the plurality of legal orders imposed itself on the mind with such obviousness that it would have been impossible not to take it into account",

L'ordre juridique, Dalloz, 2002, p. 79.

86. G. Malynes, *Consuetudo vel Lex Mercatoria, or the Ancient Law Merchant*, quoted in Harold J. Berman, *Law and Revolution, the Formation of the Western Legal Tradition*, 1918, Harvard University Press, 1983, p. 342.

> established mercantile offices in the new urban communities that were springing up throughout western Europe."[87]

The emergence of this body of rules therefore raised the question of how to coordinate this new law of merchants with the restrictions imposed by ecclesiastical law on profit and interest, thus restating in another form the question of legal pluralism that the emergence of the new municipal powers had already raised at the political level. It is this reality which, perhaps at the risk of anachronism, was transposed by Berthold Goldman to the modern era and which subsequently founded a representation of arbitration as a legal order of the *lex mercatoria*. The question of the relationship between arbitration and the *lex mercatoria* has, however, generally been approached from a normative rather than an institutional perspective; Tom Carbonneau writes that the *lex mercatoria*

> "raises the issue of the substantive autonomy of arbitral determinations by allowing international arbitrators to apply the principles of an emerging law merchant regardless of whether the parties have designated an applicable national law"[88].

Arbitration would thus, in this view, be an expression of the legal order of the *lex mercatoria* rather than a legal order of its own. The disadvantage of such an analysis, however, is that it makes arbitration dependent on the *lex mercatoria* as an autonomous legal order. It has been argued that the modern *lex mercatoria* could not claim such status because of its uncertain or incomplete nature[89]. But it is entirely possible to postulate the existence of an autonomous legal order that does not have all the characteristics traditionally attributed to a State legal order, in particular that of completeness. It is, therefore, not decisive that the *lex mercatoria* does not provide a complete framework of rules. But other criticisms can more legitimately be directed against the idea that arbitration is the justice system of the *lex mercatoria*. First, as Emmanuel Gaillard[90] has observed, the debate as to the existence of the

---

87. Berman, *op. cit.*, p. 340.
88. Th. Carbonneau, *The Remaking of Arbitration, Design and Destiny*, Th. Carbonneau, *Lex Mercatoria and Arbitration*, Juris Publishing, 1998, p. 36.
89. P. Lagarde, "Approche critique de la *lex mercatoria*", *Le droit des relations économiques internationales, études offertes à B. Goldman*, Paris, 1982; E. Gaillard, "Transnational Law: A Legal System or a Method of Decision Making?", *Arbitration International*, Vol. 17, 2001, p. 66.
90. E. Gaillard, "Thirty Years of *Lex Mercatoria*: Towards the Selective Application of Transnational Rules", *ICSID Review*, Vol.10, Issue 2, 1995, p. 210.

lex mercatoria has thrived on a certain confusion as to the sources of the rules that would underpin the existence of such a legal order. Thus, in order to demonstrate the existence of such a body of autonomous rules, the advocates of the *lex mercatoria* place on the same level rules that have actually been developed by the international business community and that have acquired, in one form or another, the status of trade usages – many examples of which may be cited, ranging from Incoterms to the FIDIC rules, as well as the rules forming the *lex maritima*[91], the model contracts issued by associations such as the Association of International Petroleum Negotiators or the GAFTA rules – with general principles of law or transnational rules which, although they have sometimes been codified by scholarly institutions such as UNIDROIT, the Lando Commission or CENTRAL, are the result of a comparative approach rather than the generation of a spontaneous legal order. The *lex mercatoria* is thus assimilated to transnational law[92], whereas the latter is only partly the result of the spontaneous creation of legal rules by the international business community. Second, the equivalence between the *lex mercatoria* and the arbitral legal order is necessarily reductive, since the arbitration phenomenon goes far beyond the possible application of anational rules by international courts. It may even be argued that most of the activity of international arbitrators consists in applying rules of law of State origin, even if this is done from an internationalist perspective, rather than the customs of international trade or anational rules drawn up by the international business community.

In this respect, it is important to note that choice of law clauses inserted into international contracts refer, in the vast majority of cases, to a national law rather than to anational rules[93] and that, in such a case, arbitrators have a duty to respect the choice thus made without being able to set it aside in favour of non-national rules that are not part of international public policy[94]. It is, therefore, artificial to base the arbitral phenomenon on the *lex mercatoria*. Eric Loquin has attempted

91. On which, W. Tetley, "The *Lex Maritima*", in Th. Carbonneau, Lex Mercatoria *and Arbitration*, Juris Publishing, 1998, p. 43.

92. B. Goldman, "Nouvelles réflexions sur la *lex mercatoria*", in *Festschrift P. Lalive*, 1993, p. 245.

93. See ICC Dispute Resolution Statistics: 2020, p. 17, where it is stated that, for all cases handled in 2021, only "2 percent included a reference to rules or instruments other than national laws".

94. E. Gaillard, *Aspects philosophiques du droit de l'arbitrage international*, *op. cit.*, No. 2, p. 111.

to break this deadlock by describing arbitration as an instrument of coordination between legal orders [95], but this is tantamount to abandoning the idea of proposing a comprehensive and structuring representation.

A second possible representation of the arbitral legal order was proposed by Emmanuel Gaillard in his course at The Hague Academy of International Law [96]. This is close to the *lex mercatoria* thesis in that it links the autonomy of the arbitral phenomenon to the specific needs of international trade. The arbitral legal order thus corresponds

> "to the strong perception among international commercial arbitrators that they do not render justice on behalf of any State, but that they nonetheless exercise a jurisdictional function in the service of the international community" [97].

Nevertheless, for Gaillard, the arbitral legal order is not the expression of a legal infrastructure specific to the business world and distinct from national legal orders; rather, the transnational representation of arbitration is characterised by the fact that it "essentially consists in integrating the point of view of the arbitrators" [98]. The arbitral legal order would thus be essentially based on the idea that arbitration practitioners themselves have of their discipline, an idea that would be recognised by the normative practice of States. Gaillard thus firmly rejects the idea that arbitration is an expression of the *lex mercatoria* and of the international community of merchants, and he repudiates "the ideology of the existence of a community of merchants spontaneously generating a law of its own" [99]; he looks instead to sovereign States. In this self-centred perspective, the basis of the arbitrators' power to judge must be sought in the normative activity of all the State legal orders willing to recognise the validity of the award. In other words, it is the laws of the various States, assessed collectively, that form a "common law" of arbitration [100] that is "intended to address all the questions that may arise and to define its sources and its relationships with other legal orders" [101].

---

95. Lecture given at the E. Gaillard commemoration day organised by the French Arbitration Committee on 15 April 2022.
96. E. Gaillard, *Aspects philosophiques du droit de l'arbitrage international*, *op. cit.*, No. 2.
97. *Op. cit.*, p. 60.
98. *Op. cit.*, p. 61.
99. *Op. cit.*, p. 76.
100. P. 76.
101. P. 88.

However, the reference to the notion of legal order to offer such a representation of arbitration raises a number of difficulties. It is in fact difficult to postulate arbitration as an autonomous legal order [102] while at the same time maintaining that it is based on the normative activity of States, even if it is collective [103]. More fundamentally, a legal order cannot be understood independently of the social order that underpins it; to use a Marxist analysis, legal relationships cannot be understood in themselves but must be understood as the expression of social relationships [104]. For Santi Romano, the social dimension of the legal order is revealed by its institutional nature [105]; however, Gaillard's analysis does not at any point concern itself with the social reality and institutional structures of arbitration, limiting itself – in a rather Hegelian manner – to deriving from the arbitrators' own idea of their power the consequence that there is an arbitral legal order; such a hypostasised representation depends, however, on the assumption that there is an "arbitrators' point of view" with a sufficient degree of coherence. This remains largely unproven, even if, as we shall see, recent developments of the arbitration community are characterised by an increasing uniformity of behaviour and values.

Other commentators have endeavoured to explain the autonomy of the mechanisms of normative creation in arbitration without any recourse to the notion of legal order. Alec Stone Sweet and Florian Grisel have adopted an anthropological approach, describing arbitration as a triadic system that is the product of the spontaneous intervention of third parties responsible for resolving disputes within a human group [106]. These commentators, taking up an idea by Alexandre Kojève, thus explain the juridicity of the arbitral space by the mere interposition

102. P. 66: "without autonomy from the legal order of each sovereign State, one cannot speak of an arbitral legal order".

103. P. 77.

104. On the question as a whole, see M. Villey and N. Poulantzas (eds.), "Marx et le droit moderne", *Archives philosophie de droit*, 12, 1967, and to "Marx et le droit", *Droit et philosophie*, No. 10, Institut Villey, Paris, 2018.

105. "Law consists above all in the establishment and organisation of a social entity", S. Romano, *op. cit.*, p. 38.

106. "When two parties resolve a dispute themselves, they set themselves up as a dyadic legal system; when they ask a third party to help them resolve a dispute, they set themselves up as a triadic system";

A. Stone Sweet and F. Grisel, "L'arbitrage international: du contrat dyadique au système normatif", *Archives de philosophie du droit, L'arbitrage*, tome 52, Dalloz, Paris, 2009, p. 77.

of third parties in human interactions [107]. Such a representation of arbitration as a normative structure spontaneously created by an evolving, decentralised and non-hierarchical social practice certainly accounts for the autonomy of arbitration, but it reduces it to its infrastructural level by making the relationship between the parties and the arbitrator its sole vector of legitimisation [108].

What these different representations of arbitration have in common is that they largely ignore the social foundations of arbitration and its institutional reality. Yet, if we are to be faithful to Santo Romano's intuition, we must in our view base the legal order on an analysis of the institutions that structure this reality. This is where another possible representation of arbitration comes into play, which we will describe as structural.

Such a representation of arbitration was proposed by Stephan Schill at the 2014 ICCA Congress [109]. Schill describes arbitration as a heterarchical system, which refers to the idea of a network introduced in 1945 by Warren McCulloch in the field of cybernetics and developed twenty years ago in the field of legal institutions by François Ost and Michel van de Kerchove [110]. He then relies on various elements to conclude that this system has become a system of transnational governance: the institutionalisation of arbitration, the expansion of the field of arbitrability, the geographical diversification, the increasing use

---

107. According to Kojève,

> "For there to be a social structure, it is not enough for two people to interact with each other; it is necessary and sufficient for a third party to position himself in relation to their interaction",

op. cit., p. 78, citing A. Kojève, *Esquisse d'une phénoménologie du droit*, Gallimard, 1981, p. 73.

108. "By making social organisation the necessary and sufficient condition for legal existence, Santi Romano offers a theoretical framework whose lack of precision makes it particularly easy to criticise: any institution would be capable, in accordance with his theory, of generating legal norms. In relation to this explanatory framework, the theory of triadic normative creation offers greater precision by specifying this type of institution: the intervention of a neutral and impartial third party in the course of a dyadic dispute would be the basis of normative creation and the construction of a legal system", *op. cit.*, p. 84.

109. S. Schill, "Developing a Framework for the Legitimacy of International Arbitration", *ICCA Congress Series*, Vol. 18, pp. 789-827.

110. S. Schill, "Conceptions of Legitimation in International Arbitration", *Amsterdam Law School Legal Papers*, 2017-17, pp. 3-4:

> "International arbitration is a heterarchical system or network, in which different actors and institutions, including one-off arbitration tribunals, arbitration institutions, and reviewing courts exercise adjudicatory authority on the basis of norms that are grounded in a variety of legal systems."

of arbitration in transnational contracts and the global convergence in the practice of arbitration [111].

It is immediately clear that such an analysis embraces a very broad phenomenological spectrum, making it possible to give a much more accurate account of the reality of arbitration and its dialogue with society. However, it is striking that Schill never defines what he means by a system of governance. What does this system consist of, and what does it govern? The reference to an arbitration system is easy to understand, however: in Schill's view, arbitration has become a structured network that plays the role of a decentralised transnational jurisdiction [112]. It is a chiasmatic structure [113] within which arbitrators, who are born, evolve and grow within the same epistemic community [114], and who share the same values, contribute to the formation and interpretation of the rules of substantive and procedural law, on which those involved in international trade, in turn, base their expectations as to the conduct of arbitration proceedings and the substantive solutions to their disputes [115]. Ultimately, Schill supports the idea of a transnational justice system adapted to the needs of international trade. From this point of view, he could well have used the terms "justice system" rather than "governance system", without altering his conclusions. Such a perspective is both fruitful and dynamic, as the representation of arbitration as an autonomous system of justice is able to account for the most recent developments in arbitration: institutionalisation, heightened interaction within the arbitration community and increased transparency, making it possible to envisage the development of a consistent body of arbitral case law through the systematic publication of awards. However, in order to account for arbitration as a system of transnational governance, this representation still needs to integrate the social reality on which it is based, which is that of the international business community.

111. *Op. cit.*, pp. 796-797.

112. "Arbitration is not limited to a method for settling individual disputes, even though this remains its principal objective, but performs a host of other functions that are largely similar to those performed by permanent dispute settlement institutions, be they domestic or international courts", *op. cit.*, p. 797.

113. To borrow a phrase used by P. Bourdieu in *La noblesse d'Etat, grandes écoles et esprit de corps*, Editions de Minuit, 1989, p. 212.

114. As first described by Y. Dezalay and B. Garth in their book *Dealing in Virtue*, The University of Chicago Press, p. 16; cf. also G. Kaufmann-Kohler, "Arbitral Precedent: Dream, Necessity or Excuse?", *Arbitration International*, 2009, Vol. 25, No. 2, pp. 187-205.

115. *Op. cit.*, p. 798.

From this point of view, the reference to the *lex mercatoria* becomes more of a source of confusion than of clarity because, whether or not it survives today as a legal system, making it the basis of arbitration as an autonomous reality is necessarily reductive for the reasons we just set out. On the other hand, it is difficult to dispute that there is indeed a *societas mercatorum,* an international business community with its own players, values, structures and ideology, for which arbitration is its own system of justice. It is, therefore, to the social substratum that the international business community is rather than to the legal concept of *lex mercatoria* that reference should be made. Filali Osman has said, echoing Philippe Kahn's analysis:

> "the *Societas mercatorum (institution mercatique)*, despite the diversity of its components, such as professional associations, arbitration centres or individual merchants, is a single being, a social body endowed with coherence, permanence and stability" [116].

It is this international class of businessmen and women that find themselves at the heart of the movement towards the internationalisation of trade and the globalisation of the economy that has driven the development and expansion of transnational law. It is this community, united by a common awareness of its interests, sharing the same values – freedom of trade, free competition and protection of investments in particular – and defending its interests through multiple institutions – chambers of commerce, professional federations and employers' organisations – that arbitration is primarily designed to serve. Indisputably, arbitration cannot be reduced to international commercial arbitration; arbitration is an institution that existed centuries before the emergence of capitalism and even before medieval law developed a body of rules specific to commercial relations. And arbitration has been used for centuries to settle private non-commercial disputes as well as disputes between States. However, it is fair to say that without the tremendous impetus provided by the expansion of international

---

116. F. Osman, *Les principes généraux du droit de la* lex mercatoria. *Contribution à un ordre juridique anational*, LGDJ, Paris, 1992, p. 410. The author quotes Ph. Kahn, for whom

> "The mercantile order is formed and developed by a multiplicity of actors, such as the
> . . . companies that master international trade, those belonging to the industrial sector that control production units, the banks that direct monetary and financial flows."

trade since the end of the Second World War, arbitration law would not have undergone the extraordinary development that it has, and any idea of an arbitral legal order would have been preposterous. Similarly, it was the expansion in international trade and investment flows in the second half of the twentieth century that led to the development of this transnational law, made up of transnational practices, principles and rules, which arbitrators are called upon to apply. From this point of view, there is no need to postulate that this set of rules constitutes a legal order independent of the *lex mercatoria* in order to establish the autonomy of arbitration as a system of international justice. To do so, it is sufficient to note that the need to resolve international trade disputes neutrally and efficiently has given rise to the development of a specific international legal regime – the cornerstone of which is the New York Convention – distinct from private judicial law, then to the formation of a community of stakeholders, and finally to the structuring of a network of institutions. It is this reality that underpins the representation of arbitration as a system of justice for international trade. From this perspective, arbitration is less an autonomous legal order than an expression of the legal order of the *societas mercatorum* or, to use a concept borrowed from Marxism, the international capitalist class. In other words, the more globalised this class becomes, the greater the need for transnational dispute resolution, which need imposes itself on national legal systems, which explains why the success of arbitration is correlated with the development of cross-border trade and investment flows. The autonomy of arbitration, as expressed by the freedom granted to arbitrators by national legal systems to resolve international commercial disputes and in the minimum conditions laid down for the recognition and enforcement of awards, is thus the expression of a political and economic balance of power [117].

The criticism according to which the existence and effectiveness of arbitration depends on the support provided by States willing to promote it does not detract from the relevance of this representation. That State legal orders support an institution that expresses the needs of the *societas mercatorum* is no more contradictory than saying, as Marx did, that the State is an expression of the social domination of the

117. A view that makes it possible to incorporate the irreducible political element which, according to Gunther Teubner, is ignored by the ordoliberal conception of the economic constitution as an autonomous order and must not, however, be confused with State politics; *Fragments constitutionnels*, Garnier, 2016, p. 73 *et seq.*

bourgeoisie. Whatever residual validity such concepts may still have in today's world, it is certain that the institution of arbitration as we know it has developed into a global system for settling international trade disputes. Investment arbitration itself, which is admittedly a creature of public international law and is marked by a specificity that prevents its full inclusion within this representation, is not entirely immune to this observation, since the network of treaties that forms its framework has developed precisely to meet the needs of investors and has borrowed to a very large extent the rules and procedures that international commercial arbitration had developed long before it.

Ultimately, the structural representation of arbitration as a system of justice for international trade is certainly structuring and militant, but it is not all-encompassing if one intends to embrace the entire spectrum of arbitration, in that it does not allow for the full integration of investment arbitration and excludes arbitration in consumer and labour law matters. The structural representation would, therefore, not satisfy the requirement of completeness, althought we have already said that such completeness is not necessary for the production of a structuring discourse. Moreover, the completeness requirement must be assessed in light of what the discourse intends to represent, and positing the singularity of international commercial arbitration in relation to other areas where arbitration may be used calls for a vision of this reality that will necessarily be complete in its own field. Furthermore, the sectoral nature of the proposed representation is an advantage rather than a disadvantage. This representation makes it possible to integrate the three sociological, transnational and institutional dimensions of international commercial arbitration, the first reflecting its spontaneous nature and its link to the merchant society, the second its autonomy, and the third the structures that characterise its contemporary reality, while protecting it from political challenges. Recourse to arbitration in employment or consumer contracts, and more generally in legal relations involving a weaker party, has in fact given rise to legitimate criticism and legislative reactions which risk, through a spillover effect, destabilising international commercial arbitration [118]. Similarly, the use of procedural mechanisms applied to international commercial arbitration in the field of investment protection has provoked a backlash from certain States as well as in wide segments of public opinion.

118. Ch. Seraglini, "Les parties faibles face à l'arbitrage international : à la recherche de l'équilibre", *Cah. arb.*, IV, Pedone, 2008, p. 49; M. de Fontmichel and Th. Clay (eds.), *Le faible et l'arbitrage*, 2013, Economica.

The policy adopted by the European Union to create multilateral courts, the purpose of which is not to institutionalise the arbitration system in order to make it more predictable but simply to replace it, is a striking example. The representation of arbitration as a system of justice for international trade thus makes it possible to maintain its originality while defining its boundaries [119] in order to protect it from the spillover effects of legislative and political movements outside of the realm of international trade. It is still necessary to analyse how such a representation can contribute to the legitimisation of the institution.

3. Legitimacy, identification, recognition

Arbitration, seen as a complex network of structures constituting a decentralised system of justice, must be perceived both in its singularity – as the justice of international trade – and in the coherence of the social and institutional interactions between its various stakeholders. Understood as a whole constituted by, and for, the social function that it occupies, arbitration can thus be recognised as legitimate, i.e. produce what Bourdieu characterised, in taking up a Weberian idea, as a sociodicy through which a social group produces a theodicy of its own privilege [120]. This sociodicy of arbitration must account for the institutional, normative and ethical reality of arbitration, just as it must

119. On the idea of the "boundaries" of arbitration, see Ch. Jarrosson, "Les frontières de l'arbitrage", *Revue de l'Arbitrage*, Comité français de l'arbitrage, Vol. 2001, No. 1, pp. 5-42.

120. "Max Weber said that the dominant always need a 'theodicy of their privilege', or better still, a sociodicy, i.e. a theoretical justification for the fact that they are privileged", P. Bourdieu, *Contre-feux*, ed. Raisons d'agir, 1998, p. 48; P. Bourdieu illustrated the mechanisms of this production of legitimizing discourse in a study on the *grandes écoles*, in which he wrote:

> "No power can be content to exist as a power, that is, as a naked force, devoid of any justification, in a word, arbitrary; it must therefore justify its existence, and exist as it exists, or, at the very least, conceal the arbitrariness at its foundation and, by doing so, be recognised as legitimate. In practice, the question of legitimacy is inscribed in the very existence of a plurality of competing powers which, in and through their confrontation, and in the antithetical and often irreconcilable justifications they put forward, inevitably raise the question of their own justification. It follows that the strategies of reproduction by which the bearers of different kinds of capital work to preserve or increase their patrimony and, correlatively, to maintain or improve their position in the social space, inevitably involve symbolic strategies aimed at legitimising the social foundation of their domination, that is, the kind of capital on which their power rests and the mode of reproduction that is inseparable from it",

P. Bourdieu, *La noblesse d'Etat, grandes écoles et esprit de corps*, éditions de Minuit, 1989, p. 377.

define the conditions of its co-existence and discursive exchange with the State legal orders and societies in which it is embedded.

As we have said, arbitration is a decentralised network of tribunals and institutions of different kinds, some of which are administrative in nature, while others are educational, academic or propagandistic. The reticular nature of arbitration is characterised by the intensity of exchanges and interactions, both horizontal – within tribunals or directly at conferences or private meetings – and vertical – through institutions and their leaders – between arbitrators, administrative secretaries, parties and heads of institutions. The vitality of the arbitration community has been described by many commentators [121] and is undoubtedly a unique phenomenon that cannot be found in any other discipline or profession. This characteristic is combined with another, equally distinctive one, which is the entirely globalised nature of the exchanges between stakeholders of the system, whose relations with one another are unconstrained by geographical or linguistic borders. It can therefore be said that, although arbitral tribunals are set up for a given case, and are therefore not part of a hierarchical system or subject to the authority of an appeal body, they nevertheless operate to some extent as a network, with forums for exchange within the arbitral community providing a platform for comparing the procedural and substantive solutions adopted by each tribunal for each particular dispute.

The idea that jurisdictions or judicial authorities can operate as a network rather than in a hierarchical manner is now a classic one. The work of competition authorities within networks such as the *International Competition Network* is an interesting example [122]. The development of international co-operation between courts is another [123]. These phenomena are part of a significant tendency, which was studied by François Ost and Michel van de Kerchove in their now classic work [124]. However, the arbitration institutional network

121. Y. Dezalay and B. Garth, *Dealing in Virtue*, *op. cit.*, No. 106, p. 33; A. Mourre, "About Procedural Soft Law, the IBA Guidelines on Party Representation and the Future of Arbitration", in *The Powers and Duties of an Arbitrator, Liber Amicorum P. A. Karrer*, pp. 239-250.

122. M. Cardon, "Le réseau international de la concurrence (RIC/ICN) : une question de foi", in *Mondialisation et droit de la concurrence*, 2008, p. 187.

123. H. Muir Watt, "Governing Networks: A Global Challenge for Private International Law", *Maastricht Journal of European and Comparative Law*, Vol. 22, No. 3, 2015, p. 352.

124. "Network, regulation and governance form a new system which, while it would no doubt be excessive to say that it has replaced the classic triad of pyramid, regulation and government, certainly goes beyond it and sometimes subverts its modes of operation",

has specific heterogeneous characteristics that distinguish it from the interjurisdictional co-operation that was mentioned above. Within the network, organisations with different structures and objectives co-exist: there are institutions whose activity is to provide administrative services for the organisation of arbitration proceedings, others whose aim is to promote and develop the practice of arbitration and to develop standards of good practice and others still which set themselves particular objectives, such as that of promoting diversity or supporting the advancement of young practitioners. It is also important to consider the heterogeneity that characterises each of these categories, some of which are dependent on chambers of commerce, others not, some of which have a global or regional vocation, while others are local; governance structures and funding rules also vary considerably from one institution to another. It is nevertheless remarkable to note that the members and senior staff of all these institutions largely overlap, with the same individuals, counsel, arbitrators or experts specialising in international arbitration invariably being found in the same management bodies or teaching programmes. The homogeneity of the epistemic community thus counterbalances the heterogeneity of the institutional network and ultimately ensures its cohesion.

This cohesion, and sometimes even this *"entre-soi"*, enables the network to play its full role in the creation of a set of values, ideas, codes and standards which, despite the theoretical oppositions that persist within the community, form the basis of a veritable ideology of arbitration. It is this ideology which, whatever the representations adopted, underpins the legitimising discourse and forms the basis of an arbitral *habitus* in which the behaviour and interactions of its players are shaped. As Gabrielle Kaufmann-Kohler [125] noted, the members of the epistemic community are united by a strong sense of belonging, itself forged by the awareness of sharing foundational notions which, throught their unifying role, rise to the rank of quasi-existential values. These include the autonomy of arbitration and the idea that arbitration is governed by specific rules that differ from those applied in State courts [126]. This group dynamic is

---

F. Ost and M. van de Kerchove, *De la pyramide au réseau ? Pour une théorie dialectique du droit*, Presses de l'Université Saint-Louis, Brussels, 2002, p. 26.

125. G. Kauffman-Kohler, "Soft Law in International Arbitration: Codification and Normativity", 1 *J. Int'l Disp. Settlement* (2010), pp. 283-299, out of 295.

126. J. Carter writes that

> "Professor Karton announced the triumph of the international arbitration community, at least for the present, in what he agrees with Professors Dezalay and

powerfully fuelled by what Emmanuel Gaillard describes as the rituals of arbitration [127], which include not only the rules and symbolic codes observed at the hearing but also self-celebratory events such as award ceremonies and other grand masses at which the community gathers for several days, or even a whole week, to celebrate the correctness and legitimacy of its values [128]. There is thus an extraordinary proliferation of seminars, congresses, conferences, colloquia and other arbitration competitions, at which the same dominant messages are repeated by the same participants to the same audience in a multidimensional pattern of repetition that acts as a veritable echo chamber, messages further amplified by the arbitration press, which appeared at the beginning of this century and whose role has continued to grow ever since, acting as the glue that holds the arbitral clergy together and as the propagator of its sociodicy. It is this collective dimension, this common language, and the requirement imposed by the community to adhere to its rites, that enables these discourses to form the basis of a genuine arbitral ideology.

It is, therefore, remarkable to see that the expansion and diversification of the arbitration community over the last twenty years has not

---

> Garth has been a concerted effort to persuade domestic courts and legal elites of the necessary autonomy of an arbitral system of commercial justice. He said that the concept of party autonomy (meaning the right of the parties to opt out of all but minimal control by domestic courts by choosing international arbitration) has been enshrined 'within the treaties, national arbitration laws, rules of procedure, national court judgments, and international arbitration awards that collectively constitute the body of international arbitration law' precisely 'because arbitrators have dedicated themselves to expanding its scope'",

J. Carter, "The Culture of Arbitration and the Defense of Arbitral Legitimacy", in D. Caron, S. Schill, A. C. Smutny and E. Triantafilou (eds.), *Practising Virtue, Inside International Arbitration*, Oxford, 2015, p. 102. Carter quotes here from Joshua Karton, *The Culture of International Arbitration and the Evolution of Contract Law*, Oxford, 2013, 79.

127. "Rituals are characterized by a largely inflexible pattern of performance, adherence to form, symbology, and socially compulsory nature despite a lack of apparent benefit", E. Gaillard, *Sociology of International Arbitration, Practising Virtue, Inside International Arbitration*, *op. cit.*, p. 195.

128. Gaillard pertinently writes on this subject that:

> "These gatherings meet the characteristics of rituals as they feature a performance which is largely inflexible, with participants acting consistently with prescribed expectations. The symbolic value of these events is real, not only for the speakers who reinforce their symbolic capital in demonstrating their cognitive legitimacy, but also for all participants whose presence demonstrates adherence to the values of the community. Arbitration players who regularly attend these mass gatherings experience in the flesh that rituals operate as gatekeepers by excluding non-believers unprepared to engage in costly actions incommensurate with their benefits. In other words, costly ritual behaviours represent signs of commitment to a group, discouraging insincere members from joining", *op. cit.*, p. 199.

been at the expense of its homogeneity. It is even possible to think that the ideological and theoretical oppositions within the arbitration community were stronger at a time when it was made up of a small number of practitioners. This seemingly paradoxical observation is easily explained: while the number of arbitrators has increased over the last two decades and there has been genuine regional and generational diversification, the professional profiles of its members also became more homogenous; thirty or forty years ago, arbitration was the domain of men and women whose main activity was not arbitration, but rather substantive law (civil, commercial or comparative law), and who came to arbitration from different horizons and with different cultural backgrounds, whereas today's generation of arbitrators is essentially made up of specialists in arbitral procedure who have been educated and developed in and through the values of arbitration. It is thus knowledge of arbitral procedure, rather than expertise in areas of substantive law, that has become the gateway into the group of these new clerics of the arbitration religion, who have obtained the long-awaited pass to the community by adopting its dominant values and language; and it is this knowledge that gives the community its integrative and organicist character. Lastly, the cohesion of the arbitration community has been strengthened by a need for legitimacy that is all the more pressing now that arbitration is facing growing opposition within civil society.

Of course, it should not be overlooked that the members of the community still sometimes hold different theoretical views on arbitration. However, we must not exaggerate the significance that the opposition between one or another representation, whether territorial, Westphalian, delocalised, jusnaturalistic or otherwise, may have on the cohesion of the community. Despite these debates, the essential point remains the prevalence of the arbitral *habitus* and collective adherence to an ideology that acts as cement for the community by grounding a powerful discourse on legitimisation. Far from being polarised [129], the arbitration community today is in fact characterised by a great uniformity of language and practice and by a certain ability to exclude those who deny or question the *doxa* and legitimacy of the system [130]. The cohesive, structuring and expansive effect of the arbitration discourse has enabled

129. As E. Gaillard said, *op. cit.*, p. 199.

130. For example, the authors of a pamphlet such as *Profiting from Injustice*, far from expressing a divergent point of view within the arbitration community, stand outside it by denying its foundational values.

the arbitration community, through the establishment of treaties such as the New York Convention and the development of case law in the main arbitration hubs that is highly favourable to the principles it upholds, to convince States and courts around the world of the usefulness of the values it advances, thereby paving the way for the undisputed triumph of arbitration in the resolution of international commercial disputes. This power of conviction has been accompanied by the community's great confidence in the system's ability to adapt and self-regulate. As one commentator has noted [131], the legitimising discourse produced by this collective dynamic, because it is geared towards maintaining the system and the privileges it generates, also feeds a conservative and largely self-referential culture that rejects any proposal that might be perceived as an attack on the system [132].

The question that then arises is whether and to what extent this discourse remains sufficient to establish the legitimacy of arbitration as a system of international justice in contemporary society. As we have said, this analysis must be confined to international trade. In modern times, arbitration is no longer an accepted means of resolving disputes in all fields, as it was in the thirteenth and fourteenth centuries; the hegemony it has acquired has been accompanied by a process of specialisation that renders its legitimacy ineffective in the many fields that do not involve professional or business relations; arbitration is also weakened in relationships characterised by an imbalance of power between the parties or involving a vulnerable party, such as employment or consumer contracts, as shown by a recent decision of the Supreme Court of Canada [133]. The contemporary reality of arbitration, as a social phenomenon, and therefore its very legitimacy, is rooted today in the *societas mercatorum* and the settlement of international commercial disputes. And if we accept that it is as a global system of justice for

131. J. Carter, *op. cit.*

132. A reflex that Carter describes as "Burkian" and which is perfectly illustrated by the following comments on investment arbitration, made by three eminent scholars:

> "Any proposal that would alter any of the fundamental elements of international arbitration constitutes an unacceptable assault on the very institution of international arbitration. Conversely, any proposal that does not attack those fundamental elements, but instead is designed to enhance them, should be considered carefully and may be found to be an improvement of it."

Ch. Brower, M. Pulos and Ch. Rosenberg, "So Is There Anything Really Wrong with International Arbitration as We Know It?", in *Contemporary Issues in International Arbitration and Mediation, The Fordham Papers*, 2013, p. 3.

133. *Uber Technologies Inc* v. *Heller*, 2020 SCC 16, Supreme Court of Canada, 26 June 2020.

international commerce that arbitration can establish its legitimacy, we must also accept that the durability of the system in the area of investment protection rests on necessarily more fragile foundations, and that arbitration cannot claim in this area the privileges it enjoys in its own field [134]. Unlike recourse to arbitration between States, which is based on a long historical tradition, and of which the *Alabama* arbitration is a particularly significant example, recourse to arbitration in the context of the modern law of investment protection, where States find themselves directly opposed to private parties elevated to the status of subjects of international law, raises questions of legitimacy for States that are difficult to confront at a time when globalisation is being seriously questioned and public opinion is stirred by strong sovereignist sentiments and dangerous nationalist impulses; in such a context, the political cost of maintaining the system inherited from the proliferation of investment protection treaties containing a unilateral offer to arbitrate may have been perceived by the European Union and by certain States as disproportionate to its supposed benefits, particularly at a time when the Union was embarking on a very ambitious trade policy, which led to the decisions that we all know. While investment arbitration, which is characterised by the importation of the rules of international commercial arbitration into the field of international law, will certainly continue to exist alongside other forms of dispute resolution where States agree to maintain it, its legitimacy will remain largely subject to political uncertainties over which the arbitration community has no control and over which the discourses on legitimisation that it has developed to promote arbitration in the commercial field will have little impact. It may further be added that importing the procedural mechanisms applied in international commercial arbitration into the field of public international law runs the risk of contaminating the former, as the criticisms levelled at investment arbitration regarding its lack of transparency, the absence of a proper code of ethics and the

---

134. It should be noted that, only recently, the Advocate General of the Court of Justice of the European Communities, in his observations on the case of *Poland* v. *PL Holdings* (C-109/20) drew a clear distinction between "private" commercial arbitration in which the European legal system accepts the limited scope of review of awards, and investor-State arbitration:

> "The judgment in Achmea distinguishes commercial arbitration between private parties, which is permissible in accordance with that case-law, from the impermissible arbitration between a private party and a Member State on the basis of investment treaties, in that the former originate in the freely expressed wishes of the parties, whereas the latter derive from a treaty between the Member States" (para. 47).

existence of new types of conflicts of interest – relationships with third-party funders, with experts, double-hatting, issue conflicts, etc. – being passed to the very different context of commercial arbitration.

However, in order to answer the question of the relevance to contemporary society of the legitimising discourse produced by the arbitration community, it is necessary to go beyond these sociological and political observations to consider the concept of system of justice, as we have applied it to arbitration. The question raised here is that of the conditions under which all institutions, social and professional interactions, values, principles and rules produced by arbitration can be perceived by civil society as an organised and legitimate system. In other words, it is a question of defining the conditions under which a legal system acquires what François Ost and Michel van de Kerchove have called an *identity* [135]. According to these legal theorists, the identity of the legal system rests first of all on a principle of unity, which may be static or dynamic, formal or material, linear or circular; it is this principle of unity that links together the different components of the system. The system must also achieve a certain degree of autonomy, which may be social, organic or organisational. The system, so defined, enters into relations with other legal systems in a manner that they describe, drawing from Santi Romano, as one of relevance or irrelevance [136]. If we apply the intellectual framework proposed by Ost and van de Kerchove to arbitration, we are led to question the extent to which it has reached a degree of unity and autonomy such that it can be *identified* as a global justice system or, to use the concept put forward by Stephan Schill, as a system of transnational governance. We still need to define what is meant by these terms of unity and autonomy. In the case of a justice system such as arbitration, it refers to the set of characteristics, or rather of signs, since what is at stake is the construction of a language, which enables society to recognise – implying both identification and acceptance – a body of rules and institutions as a coherent, useful, and enduring system that responds to a social need. These characteristics of unity and autonomy are, therefore, closely linked, as the coherence of the rules is necessary for the formation of a system capable of claiming autonomy in relation to State legal orders and of producing a representation of itself that is structured, comprehensive and assertive.

135. *De la pyramide au réseau*, *op. cit.*, p. 184 *et seq.*
136. Neologisms derived from the Italian words *rilevanza* and *irrilevanza*.

As Eduardo Silva Romero said, the autonomy of arbitration is both a legal fiction [137] and a sociological and political reality. The autonomy of the arbitration agreement from the contract containing it, a utilitarian solution designed to ensure the effectiveness of arbitration, has given rise in French case law to substantive rules designed to separate it entirely, not only from the law applicable to the contract but also from any State law, while also proclaiming the complete delocalisation of the award, which can survive even its annulment in its country of origin. These solutions have, in turn, fuelled a delocalising ideology whose ambition is to assert the existence of an arbitral legal order distinct from State legal orders, an ideology which, in turn, operates – despite the differences of opinion that persist within it – as a powerful factor of cohesion for the social group that constitutes the arbitral community. However, the foundations of this representation of the autonomy of arbitration remain fragile, and it is undoubtedly insufficient to assert that it is a fiction or a belief in order to dispose of the issue. First of all, it is based on a case law that may evolve, as we have seen with the developments concerning the degree of control exercised over the award on the basis of public policy [138]. Secondly, one may doubt the coherence of the theoretical assumptions underlying the delocalising representation of arbitration maintained by French case law; for example, the principle according to which a foreign decision to set aside an award would not, in principle, be capable of recognition has never truly been explained, other than by a fiction according to which an award is not rooted in any legal system, a fiction that is itself weakened by the fact that the French legal system recognises the right to set aside awards made on its territory [139]. Above all, however, the delocalising solutions promoted by French law are far from constituting the majority position in comparative law. As regards the autonomy of the arbitration agreement and the degree of control exercised over the award, profound differences persist between countries as prominent and as

137. On the legal fictitiousness of delocalizing conceptions, see E. Silva Romero's lecture at The Hague Academy of International Law, August 2019.

138. After establishing the principle of a review limited to "obvious" illegality that "leaps to the eye", the case law, under the impetus of an influential doctrine, affirmed an expanded review of public policy, leading to the reintroduction of review on the merits; on this question, see A. Mourre, "Plaidoyer pour un retour à un minimalisme mesuré", in *The System of International Arbitration – Liber Amicorum Emmanuel Gaillard.*

139. A. Mourre, "A propos des articles V et VII de la Convention de New York et de la reconnaissance des sentences annulées dans leur pays d'origine : où va-t-on après les arrêts *Putrabali* et *Termo Rio ?*", *Revue de l'arbitrage*, 2008/2, pp. 263-298.

proximate as France, Switzerland and the United Kingdom [140]. As for the delocalisation of the award, France stands alone, as the countries that have accepted the enforcement of an award set aside in its country of origin have done so on intellectual grounds that are fundamentally distinct from the premises adopted by French doctrine [141].

The idea of delocalisation, which is fruitful in law and useful in practice, is therefore insufficient as a basis for representing arbitration as an autonomous legal order, as a global system of justice, and as a social fact. But to posit the autonomy of arbitration does not require that it be constituted as a legal order; arbitration can exist perfectly well as a global system of justice without presenting the characteristics of an autonomous legal order. Indeed, in order to lay the foundations for its legitimacy as a global system of justice, it is sufficient for three conditions to be satisfied: on the ontological level, that the right to submit to arbitration be a matter of individual autonomy, so that freedom is the rule and prohibition the exception; on the axiological level, that the institutional and regulatory structures of arbitration provide a framework for the exercise of this freedom in conditions compatible with the values of society at a given moment in its development; and on a sociological level, that arbitration is based on a social and economic substratum that is of such significance for the community that the latter accepts its claims. This is a process that is both discursive and reflexive: it is the combination of these three ontological, sociological and axiological conditions that underpins, on the one hand, the awareness that arbitration acquires of its own legitimacy through the discourse it develops about itself and, on the other hand, the society's acceptance of the discourse of legitimisation that arbitration presents to it.

The first of these three conditions refers to natural law, which has already been discussed. Any discourse that legitimises arbitration as a permanent and autonomous institution is rooted in the immanence of its connection to the primacy of the creative power of individual autonomy as a superior and intangible principle: natural law, even if not sufficient

140. On the autonomy of the arbitration agreement, see the French and English decisions in *Kabab-Ji SAL Company* v. *Kout Food Group Company Food*: Cour d'appel de Paris, 23 June 2020, No. 17/22943; Supreme Court of the United Kingdom, UKSC 48, 27 October 2021. On the degree of control, the French and English decisions in *Alstom* v. *ABL*: Cour de cassation, 29 September 2021, No. 19-19769; High Court of Justice of England and Wales, EWHC 1584, 18 June 2020.

141. Or the refusal to recognise the decision on annulment, see A. Mourre, "A propos des articles V et VII de la Convention de New York et de la reconnaissance des sentences annulées dans leur pays d'origine : où va-t-on après les arrêts *Putrabali* et *Termo Rio*?", *op. cit.*, No. 131.

to fully account for the phenomenon of arbitration, is the *pathos* of arbitration, without which it is reduced to a more or less useful and accepted technique. But the invocation of the immanence of individual autonomy cannot be confined to raising a moral and philosophical question on which, ultimately, legal science does not have the last word; rather, what is at stake is the establishment, in practical terms, of the superior value of the right to resort to arbitration. To do this, we must go beyond the impracticable and precarious postulate [142] that would deduce, from a principle of individual freedom existing in the state of nature, that the right to arbitration has an absolute and universal nature, in favour of accepting natural law as a method for asserting, in given historical conditions, the pre-eminence of certain rights. Michel Villey has shown how Ockham's nominalist philosophy contributed, in an anti-Aristotelian and personalist perspective, to transforming the traditional conception of objective natural rights into a modern theory of individual subjective rights during the legal debates that arose at the beginning of the fourteenth century from the dispute over Franciscan poverty [143]. Villey concludes that with the *via moderna* inaugurated by Ockham, "there can no longer be a legal order that does not derive from the individual will" [144]. A contradiction then immediately arises: if law is entirely occupied by subjective rights, what place is left for natural law, and how can arbitration legitimise its claim to universality and permanence? One historian has shown, however, that Ockham's individualist thinking was part of a rich legal tradition that did not oppose personalism and natural law but accepted that the legitimate exercise of subjective rights may itself fall under natural law [145]; from this perspective, natural law ceases to be fixed and immutable to become capable of evolution, making it possible to effectively ground the legitimacy of the institution of arbitration on free will through

142. M. Villey, *Le droit et les droits de l'homme*, PUF, Paris, 1983, p. 145.

143. Ockham, a Benedictine friar, undertook to defend, against John XXII, the claim of the Franciscan communities to use their goods while having renounced all rights over them, while the Pope intended to force them to recognise such property rights. Ockham objected, distinguishing between the right of property and the *de facto* use, stating that while the former is a power deriving from positive human law, the latter is a matter of the state of nature. On this question: M. Villey, "La genèse du droit subjectif chez Guillaume d'Ockham", *Archives de philosophie du droit*, 9, 1964, pp. 97-102; *La formation de la pensée juridique moderne*, PUF, Paris, 2003, p. 220 *et seq* and p. 250 *et seq*; M. Villey, *Le droit et les droits de l'homme*, *op. cit.*, p. 118 *et seq*.

144. M. Villey, *La formation de la pensée juridique moderne*, PUF, p. 261.

145. B. Tierney, *The Idea of Natural Rights. Studies on Natural Rights, Natural Rights and Church Law, 1150-1625*, Scholars Press for Emory University, Atlanta, 1997, and in Italian published by Il Mulino, Milan, 2002, p. 58 *et seq*.

the exercise of individual rights[146]. This subjectification of natural law permits one to posit that arbitration, insofar as it is a matter of personal autonomy, is in principle only lawful within the limits that are strictly necessary for the protection of the general interest. Restrictions on the exercise of this right – whether relating to inarbitrability or to the conduct of the proceedings and the review of the award – must, therefore, remain exceptional. Ockham already said that the law consists in the exercise of a lawful power[147], a statement that applies perfectly to arbitration. The extent to which the exercise of the power to resort to arbitration will be considered lawful by society will, however, depend on two other legitimising factors, sociological and axiological, which do not fall under natural law.

We will not dwell at length on the sociological factor of legitimisation, which we have already addressed. As we have said, international commercial arbitration may, from a systemic perspective, be defined as the autonomous justice system of the *societas mercatorum*, i.e. of all those involved in international trade, including States and sovereign entities when they act *de iure gestionis*. In this respect, it is a mechanism for regulating international trade, the importance of which, in a globalised society, is obvious to all. Without access to arbitration as a neutral forum for resolving international disputes, contractual risks, and the premiums paid in this respect by international investors and contractors, increase. This naturally results in higher investment costs and a weakening of international trade, which is the lifeblood of global growth. The legitimacy of arbitration is, therefore, based on the existence of an international class of merchants, industrialists and bankers, united by a community of interests and sharing common values – in other words, what Marx called a class for itself – which forms a legal order in the sense that Santi Romano gave to this term. The legitimacy of arbitration as a global system of justice thus derives directly from this social substratum and from the role played by this social class in an open society founded on the free flow of capital, goods and people. This does not mean, of course, as we have said, that arbitration is not a method of dispute resolution commonly used in the settlement of disputes other

---

146. J. Habermas:

> "only the autonomy of isolated and equal individuals and their recognition of the rational coherence of the norms of natural law can constitute the prerequisite for positive natural law".

Théorie et Pratique, Payot, Paris, 2006, p. 112.

147. *Ius utendi est potestas licita utendi et intrinseca*, Tierney, *op. cit.*, p. 52.

than those between stakeholders of international trade: arbitration between States, which has existed for centuries, arbitration in matters of investment protection or arbitration in matters of employment law or consumer contracts are all areas, outside international trade, where arbitration has developed considerably. But if we reason in terms of legitimacy rather than legality, the terms of the question change entirely depending on whether we are referring to international trade or not. While arbitration may claim to impose its rules and its discourse of legitimacy in international commercial relations, the same claims become much weaker outside this field.[148] The way in which French[149] and Canadian[150] case law has either made arbitration in consumer matters subject to the consumer's consent once the dispute has arisen, or has allowed the consumer to repudiate the clause – which results in the same outcome – demonstrates this. Another example is the crisis in investment arbitration, a detailed analysis of which is beyond the scope of this lecture.

Society's assessment of the legitimacy of arbitration provides, in counterpoint, the extent to which the State may legitimately restrict its use. For example, when the European Union decides to ban arbitration from its investment protection treaties, it is difficult to describe this decision as illegitimate. One may consider, or not, that this decision constitutes poor policymaking, based on a flawed analysis of the advantages and disadvantages of arbitration, or a misplaced hostility towards this method of dispute resolution, but that does not make it a decision contrary to the fundamental values of society, which could be perceived as infringing an inalienable right. On the contrary, it is a political decision whereby the State refuses to submit the merits of sovereign decisions to private adjudicators, which may resonate with public opinion at a time when questions of sovereignty are becoming particularly acute everywhere. In the same vein, the rule that an arbitration agreement cannot be enforced against an employee is certainly considered entirely legitimate in view of the need to protect

---

148. This is the case in investment arbitration insofar as it involves the exercise of sovereign prerogatives of the State or obligations of treatment subject to public international law.

149. See Cass. Civ. 1re, 21 May 1997, *Jaguar* case, *Rev. arb.* 1997, p. 538, note E. Gaillard; Cass. Civ. 1re, 30 March 2004, *Dame Rado* v. *sté Painvewebber* et al., Bull. Civ., I, No. 97, *Rev. arb.* 2005.115, note X. Boucobza.

150. *Kanitz* v. *Rogers Cable Inc.* (2002) 58 O.R. (3d) 299; *Dell Computer* v. *Union des Consommateurs*, 2007 SCC 34; *Rogers Wireless inc.* v. *Muroff*, 2007 SCC 35; *Seidel* v. *Telus Communications Inc*, 2011 SCC 15.

the weaker party, to which society undoubtedly attaches greater importance than the principle of freedom of contract. On the other hand, if a State, in repudiation of its international commitments, were to ban arbitration in international commercial relations, such a decision would undoubtedly be perceived by the community as an unjustifiable attack on individual autonomy and contractual freedom, which would immediately result in a migration of proceedings to other seats. There is, of course, a whole range of possible situations and possible restrictions on the recourse to international commercial arbitration, ranging from the introduction of more or less expansive conceptions of public policy to more or less intrusive practices for reviewing the validity of awards. However, while arbitration may be viewed with suspicion in matters involving State sovereignty or vulnerable parties, its legitimacy is in principle established in the field of international commercial relations, and this is explained by the sociological condition to legitimacy that we have just described.

The third factor legitimising arbitration is axiological. The aim here is to find the values with which international commercial arbitration must align in order to be recognised as a system of justice for international trade. Such an inquiry depends on a society's conception of the fundamental principles that any system of justice must respect at a given moment in its history, which is necessarily evolving; it also requires a reflection on the conditions allowing for the intelligibility of arbitration by society, i.e. the content of the messages that arbitration must communicate if it is to be identified by society not only as a legal institution but also as a system that forms part of the general organisation of society.

This raises the question of the relationships between legal orders: under what conditions can the arbitral legal system be recognised and accepted as such by State legal orders? The global and transnational nature of the arbitral legal system obviously makes it impossible for States to validate arbitration in a hierarchical, Kelsenian way, and a retreat to the idea of a community of States recognising the values of arbitration [151] does not advance the discussion either, since it fails to address the issue of how such values of recognition are chosen and projected by State legal orders onto the arbitral system. To borrow an image employed by François Rigaux:

---

151. E. Gaillard, *Aspects philosophiques du droit de l'arbitrage international*, *op. cit.*, p. 35.

> "Legal systems can be listed on a stock exchange, in which each is valued according to the value attributed to it by all the others." [152]

The recognition of legitimacy, in this perspective, arises from a process of evaluation and valorisation [153]. On the one hand, for evaluation to take place, a dialogue must be established between the systems involved, enabling society to identify arbitration as a system of justice or, in other words, making it functionally intelligible. Secondly, for the valorization process to operate, it is necessary to define the values that society expects arbitration to respect. We therefore speak of values on identification and values on recognition. This dialectic, in turn, places the arbitration system under pressure; the growing demand for transparency in all areas of society, whether politics, economic governance or justice, brings the private and contractual nature of arbitration into conflict with its public role as a system of justice.

Society's identification of arbitration as a system of justice includes both structural and functional considerations. There is primarily a need for coherence in terms of the rules, structures and governance. First, the rules: international commercial arbitration, as we know it today, developed on the foundations of a process of harmonisation and transnationalisation of procedural rules. Indeed, it was the need for a common procedural language between parties from different traditions and cultures, as well as the need to establish a neutral forum for the resolution of international commercial disputes, that forged the epistemic community that forms the basis of the global justice system that arbitration has become; this movement has led to the emergence of a transnational procedural law that, until recently, was rarely contested and which remains a powerful factor in the identification of arbitration by society. Indeed, it is because arbitration is capable of generating its own procedural rules that it can claim both the coherence and the autonomy of any legal system: coherence, since what forms the basis of arbitration practice does not vary according to national traditions and the cultural origins of the parties; autonomy, because these written rules constitute *soft law* spontaneously generated by the system

152. F. Rigaux, "Le droit au singulier et au pluriel", *RIEJ*, No. 9, 1982, p. 1 *et seq*. Quoted by F. Ost and M. van de Kerchove, *De la pyramide au réseau*, *op. cit*., p. 202, who speak of "reticular structuring of normativity".

153. For Niklas Luhmann, the concept of legitimacy has moved from the sphere of positive law "to the level of the concept of recognition or acceptance", *La légitimation par la procédure*, PUL/CERF, 2001, p. 24.

without the intervention of State legal orders [154]. The isonomic value of the emergence of this body of transnational rules has been largely underestimated. The transition from an unwritten body of arbitration law, entrusted to the memory of a small circle of practitioners, to a written body of rules, accessible to all and internationally recognised, is in fact an essential step in the process of arbitration's maturation as a system of justice for international trade [155]. However, this global convergence in arbitration rules and practice now seems to be taking a step backwards, as illustrated by the debate on the respective merits of the IBA Rules and the Prague Rules on the taking of evidence in international arbitration [156]. A number of commentators have spoken out against the risks of a supposed standardisation of the arbitration practice, proposing a return to local traditions or practices in force before the courts [157]. Apart from the area of evidence, which is still largely covered by the IBA Rules, the arbitration community has not yet shown itself capable of reaching a consensus on uniform rules in several other areas. The rules governing the disclosure of conflicts of interest are still the subject of divergent approaches, with the co-existence of the objective standard proposed by the Model Law, the UNCITRAL Rules and several national laws on the one hand, and the subjective standard adopted by the IBA Guidelines and several arbitral institutions, such as the ICC, on the other [158]. It should also be noted that the arbitration community has, so far, been unable to reach a consensus on issues as important as the ethical rules applicable to counsel and

---

154. On this issue, see A. Mourre, "Soft Law as a Condition for the Development of Trust in International Arbitration", *Revista Brasileira de Arbitragem*, CBAr & IOB, Kluwer Law International 2016, Vol. XIII, Issue 51, pp. 82-98; G. Kaufmann-Kohler, "Soft Law in International Arbitration: Codification and Normativity", *Journal of International Dispute Settlement*, Vol. 1, No. 2, 2010, p. 284.

155. A parallel can be drawn with the democratic irruption of written law in archaic Rome, with the legislation of the Twelve Tables and the break it represented with the patrician tradition and the orality of the pontiffs, cf. Aldo Schiavone, *Ius, l'invention du droit en Occident*, Belin, 2008, pp. 136-140.

156. G. Kaufmann-Kohler, "Soft Law in International Arbitration: Codification and Normativity", in Thomas Schultz (ed.), *Journal of International Dispute Settlement*, Oxford University Press, 2010, Vol. 1, No. 2, pp. 283-299; M. Kocur, "Why Civil Law Lawyers Do Not Need the Prague Rules", Kluwer Arbitration Blog, 19 August 2018.

157. M. Schneider, "ASA President's Messages (2010-2013)", in B. Ehle and D. Baizeau (eds.), *Stories from the Hearing Room: Experience from Arbitral Practice (Essays in Honour of Michael E. Schneider)*, 2015, p. 270; S. Perloff, "The Ties That Bind: The Limits of Automony and Uniformity in International Commercial Arbitration Comment", *University of Pennsylvania Journal of International Business Law*, 1993.

158. A. Mourre, "Conflicts Disclosures: The IBA Guidelines and beyond", *Austrian Yearbook on International Arbitration*, 2015, pp. 291-300.

representatives of the parties [159] or legal privilege [160]. This normative disorder poses an existential threat to arbitration; the absence of a coherent and autonomous body of procedural rules can only constitute an obstacle to its legitimacy as a system of justice.

Second, we turn to the coherence of institutional structures and their governance. It has already been said that the structuring of arbitration as a global justice system has largely involved a process of institutionalisation. Arbitral institutions have become the backbone of the arbitral system: as administrators of the proceedings, they have naturally become the guardians of the system's integrity, in particular through the control they exercise over arbitrators' remuneration and their power to dismiss arbitrators who have a conflict of interest or who fail to comply with the rules of ethics; as guardians of the integrity of the arbitration system, they have become its natural legislators [161]. The idea that there is a global and autonomous system of arbitral justice is now largely based on the existence of a network of arbitral institutions able to avail themselves of their experience, the stability of their rules of governance and the transparency of their practices to gain the confidence of both international commercial actors and States. However, the global network of arbitral institutions is far from uniform, with reputable and well-established institutions rubbing shoulders with others that lack experience or were even created for suspicious or fraudulent purposes, as was recently observed in Egypt [162]. Institutional arbitration is also characterised by a significant lack of homogeneity, with some institutions being public and others private, some being the offshoot of chambers of commerce and others independent, and some having a global reach while others are regional or local. Finally, there are no common rules of governance for the institutions, despite an attempt in this direction by the *Club Espanol de Arbitraje* [163]. This issue naturally

159. A. Mourre and E. Zuleta, "The IBA Guidelines on Party Representation in International Arbitration", in Nassib G. Ziadé (ed.), *Festschrift Ahmed Sadek El-Kosheri*, pp. 109-120. For a contrary view, see F. Dasser, *Soft Law in International Commercial Arbitration*, Hague Academy of International Law, Offprint from *Collected Courses*, Vol. 402, 2019, p. 552.

160. T. Stouten, *Legal Privilege Issues: At the Mercy of the Arbitral Tribunal*, International Bar Association (2021).

161. On the whole issue, see A. Mourre, "Arbitral Institutions and Professional Organizations as Lawmakers", *ICCA Congress Series*, Vol. 20, pp. 86-111.

162. A. Mourre, *On Arbitral Institutional Cooperation*, Hendrix Lecture, Atlanta, 6 March 2018.

163. Código de Buenas Prácticas Arbitrales del Club Español del Arbitraje, CEA, 2019. On the question, as a whole, see A. Mourre, *On Arbitral Institutional Cooperation*, *op. cit.*

raises the question of regulation. Can we accept over the long term that an arbitral institution may be created without any oversight, that its governing bodies may be selected without any transparency and that these institutions, which play such a fundamental role in the administration of arbitral justice, may carry out their activities without being subject to any supervision? This question immediately raises another: if the regulation of institutional arbitration is necessary, who should take the initiative? Should it be governments, as some have attempted to do, notably by introducing licences [164]? However, given the international nature of the activities of many institutions, it is difficult to imagine that such attempts could produce positive results, and they are, moreover, hardly compatible with the autonomy of arbitration as a global justice system; recent examples of State regulation of institutional arbitration show that, in the few countries where such attempts have been implemented, they often pursued the disguised objective of protecting or favouring local interests to the detriment of the freedom and integrity of arbitration [165]. It is equally inconceivable that institutional arbitration could be regulated by an international treaty. It must, therefore, be concluded that rules on the governance of arbitral institutions could only be introduced by the arbitration institutions themselves, by way of *soft law*. Yet reflection on this subject is still in its infancy, and the aforementioned initiative of the *Club Espanol de Arbitraje* remains isolated. Admittedly, there have been mergers between institutions, such as in Spain [166] and Switzerland [167], leading to the adoption of more effective arbitration rules and more efficient systems of governance; there is also an institution whose specific purpose is to lay the foundations for inter-institutional cooperation [168], but it has never truly sought to establish rules of

164. As we have seen recently in Russia, where the 2016 law introduced a licensing requirement for the operation of arbitral institutions, and more recently in Ukraine; see in this regard O. Sendetska, "Draft Bills on Registration Requirements for Arbitral Institutions: Is Ukraine Joining the Regional Trend?", Kluwer Arbitration Blog, 2022; E. Burova, "New Rules of the Game for Arbitral Institutions in Russia: Two Recent Governmental Authorizations", Kluwer Arbitration Blog, 2017. China, of course, has also long exercised such control.

165. A. Mourre, *On Arbitral Institutional Cooperation, op. cit.*, No. 154.

166. J. Caínzos, "The Madrid International Arbitration Centre Takes off Powered by the Unification of Spain's Largest Arbitral Institutions", Kluwer Arbitration Blog, 2019.

167. S. Nessi, "A Swiss '(R)Evolution': SCAI Becomes the Swiss Arbitration Centre and Enacts New Arbitration Rules", Kluwer Arbitration Blog, 2021.

168. P. Davidson, "The International Federation of Commercial Arbitration Institutions", *Journal of International Arbitration*, 1988, pp. 131-138.

governance common to the main institutions. The task is, of course, made all the more difficult by the fact that arbitral institutions operate in a highly competitive market, which forces them to differentiate their services and discourages them from co-ordinating their activities. But the question arises as to whether arbitration will be able to develop sustainably as a system of justice without a common framework that will enable the main institutions to be subject to minimum standards of transparency, ethics and good governance. In this respect, we could perhaps imagine that an institution such as the ICCA, after being reformed to give it unquestionable legitimacy to regulate the system, could play a role in developing such standards and in monitoring their application.

The identification of the arbitration system by society is also subject to considerations of a functional nature. The very nature of any system of justice is to participate, through the production of standards, in the creation and development of the law. In other words, the question is whether, and to what extent, arbitral awards can contribute to the creation of law. The answer to this question, in turn, determines whether arbitration may claim to operate as a system of justice and be legitimised as such. Here, we will not address the question of the *res judicata* effect of awards, nor the absence, in the arbitral system, of an appeallate mechanism enabling a higher court to resolve conflicting decisions and produce decisions with general authority. As we have had occasion to write elsewhere [169], rather than *res judicata*, what is needed in arbitration is to create the conditions for the emergence of a form of *jurisprudence constante*, enabling consolidated decision-making trends to acquire normative value, either by way of persuasion or as an expression of commercial practice. However, this type of normative production presupposes that awards be made public, not in part or in excepts, as is currently most often the case, but systematically and in full. Yet, such a development encounters considerable resistance, as shown by the criticism levelled against the ICC's policy on transparency, and in particular its policy on publishing awards [170]. This issue is made particularly acute by the fact that, in many industrial sectors, virtually all international disputes are now submitted to arbitration,

169. A. Mourre, "The Case for the Publication of Arbitration Awards, The Rise of Transparency in International Arbitration", *Juris*, 2013, p. 53.

170. P. Cavalieros, "La publication intégrale des sentences: (r)évolution ou régression de la justice arbitrale ?", *Revue de l'Arbitrage*, Comité français de l'arbitrage 2020, Vol. 2020, No. 3, pp. 727-758.

with the result that the principle of non-publication of awards may be perceived as a barrier to the creation and evolution of the law; it is this concern that was expressed by Lord Thomas in 2016 [171], in a fierce critique of the confidentiality of arbitration [172]. This culture of secrecy, in which arbitration is immersed today, can thus function as a powerful delegitimising factor.

We turn now to the values for which arbitration is recognised – that is, those that enable it to claim legitimacy – which pertain to its legality and effectiveness, as well as its ethical and political objectives.

We will not dwell on questions of the legality of arbitration. As we said at the beginning of this lecture, the notions of legality and legitimacy must be distinguished; however, the legality of arbitration contributes to its legitimacy, since a system that refuses to comply with the law cannot claim to be accepted by society. One of the particular features of the dialogue between society and arbitration is that the arbitration agreement touches upon one of the most fundamental sovereign functions, namely that of administering justice. The advance waiver of the right to access State justice must, therefore, necessarily be accompanied by guarantees – sanctioned under procedural public policy – ensuring compliance with the fundamental principles of due process, which are, by the way, scrupulously observed in arbitration. From a substantive point of view, the review exercised by the courts of the seat over arbitral awards ensures that arbitration is not used to introduce into the legal order decisions that are contrary to its public

---

171. Lord Thomas considers that the systematic submission of disputes to arbitration in certain sectors "reduces the potential for the courts to develop and explain the law" and that "this consequence provides fertile ground for transforming the common law from a living instrument into 'an ossuary'"; The Right Hon. Lord Thomas of Cwmgiedd, Lord Justice of England and Wales, "Developing Commercial Law Through the Courts: Rebalancing the Relationship between the Courts and Arbitration", The Bailii Lecture 2016, 9 March 2016, p. 10.

172. "There are . . . issues which arise from the resolution of disputes firmly behind closed doors – retarding public understanding of the law, and public debate over its application. A series of decisions in the courts may expose issues that call for Parliamentary scrutiny and legislative revision. A series of similar decisions in arbitral proceedings will not do so, and those issues may then carry on being taken account in future arbitrations. As had been put: 'Arbitration confidentiality perpetuates public ignorance of continuing hazards, systemic problems, or public needs . . .'. Such lack of openness equally denudes the ability of individuals, and lawyers apart from the few who are instructed in arbitrations, to access the law, to understand how it has been interpreted, and applied. It reduces the degree of certainty in the law that comes through the provision of authoritative decisions of the court. As such it reduces individual's ability to fully understand their rights and obligations", *op. cit.*, p. 10.

policy, whether involving fraud, corruption, money laundering or competition law.

Furthermore, the legitimacy of arbitration as a system of justice depends on its effectiveness. It goes without saying that an ineffective system, which generates unnecessary costs, cannot be supported by society for long; this calls for a cost-benefit analysis that falls outside the scope of this study. We will limit ourselves to noting that the need to control the often excessive duration and cost of arbitration proceedings has led certain institutions to act in a prescriptive manner, thus limiting the space reserved for the contractual freedom of parties who have submitted to their rules. By way of example, the ICC International Court of Arbitration adopted a system of expedited arbitration, which is compulsory unless all the parties agree otherwise, where the amounts in dispute are below a certain threshold, and which allows it to disregard the provisions of the arbitration agreement as to the number of arbitrators. The question that arises, once again, is that of the tension between the principle of contractual autonomy on which arbitration is based and the restrictions arising from the development of an institutional framework intended to respond to societal demand: to what extent may arbitration develop as a system of justice without reneging on the promise of freedom on which it is based?

Finally, the legitimacy of arbitration depends on a certain number of behavioural objectives assigned to it by society.

First and foremost, there is an increased ethical expectation, which raises issues of a different nature for counsel and arbitrators. With regard to the ethics of counsel, the question raised is essentially whether a system of justice that administers a very significant proportion of international commercial disputes may continue to do so without uniform rules on the representation of parties before arbitral tribunals. Arbitration today does not have a uniform professional code governing issues as important as the conditions under which arbitrators may refuse to accept the introduction of new counsel during the proceedings when this creates a conflict of interest with one or more of the arbitrators, the extent and conditions under which arbitrators may maintain unilateral contacts with the parties for the purpose of their appointment or the selection of the third arbitrator; the duty of the parties not to mislead the tribunal by making false statements in their submissions or in witness statements; the duty of counsel to inform the parties of their obligation to disclose documents that the tribunal orders them to produce or not to destroy documents that are potentially relevant to the resolution of the dispute and the conditions under which counsel may prepare witnesses and experts for cross-examination. Despite several attempts in this direction, first by the IBA and then the LCIA, these issues still give rise to deep fragmentations within the arbitration community, as shown by the successive positions adopted on the matter by the Swiss Arbitration Association [173]. This lack of consensus on such fundamental issues affects the coherence and autonomy of the arbitration system, and the fact that these issues are left to national laws and to professional bar rules, with all the conflicts of standards that this entails, can only undermine its legitimacy.

The question of the ethics of arbitration also arises for the arbitrators themselves, essentially regarding the extent of their disclosure obligations. Two observations are in order. First, as has been said on this issue of prime importance, the co-existence of an objective standard and a subjective standard applicable to disclosures gives rise to a normative disorder that is difficult to reconcile with the idea that arbitration is a global and autonomous system of justice. However, we can observe the emergence of a consensus among institutions in favour of the subjective standard, which is certainly more likely to ensure greater transparency in the practice of conflict disclosures. Yet this development remains fragile: in this respect, it is interesting to note that, after initially adopting the subjective standard "in the eyes of the parties", the draft code of ethics prepared in the field of investment protection by UNCITRAL and ICSID appears, regrettably, to have backtracked from that position in its fourth version [174]. This hesitation only highlights the gap that persists between the subjective standard applied by a large number of arbitral institutions and the objective standard of the UNCITRAL Rules and the Model Law. Secondly, the question arises as to whether the IBA Guidelines on Conflicts of Interest in International Arbitration remain adequate in light of the desire for greater transparency expressed by civil society. To a certain extent, when these guidelines were adopted in 2003, they represented a compromise between the need to establish a common framework enabling arbitrators to fulfill their disclosure obligations on a uniform and transparent basis and what was then perceived as a need to protect

173. E. Geisinger, "President's Message: Counsel Ethics in International Arbitration – Could One Take Things a Step Further?", *ASA Bull*, 2014, 453.

174. ICSID-UNCITRAL, Code of Conduct for Adjudicators in International Investment Disputes, Third and Fourth versions, Article 10.1.

arbitrators and arbitration proceedings against a tendency, originating in the United States, to demand excessive disclosures, which were perceived to be counterproductive given the incidents and challenges that would ensue. However, since 2003, the arbitration paradigm in relation to conflicts of interest has changed significantly, without the IBA having however introduced any substantial changes in the new version of its guidelines adopted in 2014. The question today is, in fact, no longer to limit arbitrators' disclosure obligations, but rather to extend them [175]. Given the multiplicity of connections that may exist between arbitrators, counsel, parties, experts and other stakeholders in arbitration, only a principle of full transparency, resulting in comprehensive disclosures, is likely to maintain confidence in arbitration. Here again, the lack of consensus on this issue acts as a regressive factor. It should be added, as shown by the recent emergence of rules requiring parties to disclose their relationships with third-party funders, that the duty of disclosure should not be imposed only on arbitrators, but also on the parties, counsel and the institutions themselves. In addition to the question of arbitrators' disclosure obligations, there also arises the issue of whether arbitration will be able to maintain the system of unilateral nominations whereby each party may choose "its" arbitrator; this system presents two disadvantages: first, it creates a relationship between the arbitrator and the party that appointed him or her, which may constitute a conflict of interest depending on the number of other appointments received by that arbitrator and all the other circumstances of the case. Second, it casts doubt on the complete impartiality of an arbitrator who owes his or her appointment to one of the parties [176]. Once again, it should be noted that the parties and the arbitration community are strongly attached to this system, for reasons that are not all illegitimate [177]. Banning unilateral appointments may also raise the concern of a "politicization" of the community of arbitrators, by transforming competing private practitioners in institution insiders. Moreover, any reform of this system, even if it were desirable, could

175. On this question, see A. Mourre, "Conflicts Disclosures: The IBA Guidelines and beyond, The Evolution and Future of International Arbitration", *op. cit.*, No. 148.

176. On this debate, see J. Paulsson, "Ethics, Elitism, Eligibility", *Journal of International Arbitration*, 1997, pp. 13-22.

177. A. Mourre, "Are Unilateral Appointments Defensible? On Jan Paulsson's Moral Hazard in International Arbitration", in S. M. Kröll and L. A. Mistelis *et al.* (eds.), *International Arbitration and International Commercial Law: Synergy, Convergence and Evolution*, pp. 381-386; A. Mourre, "Is the Free-Market of Adjudication Dysfunctional?", in A. Jan van den Berg (ed.), *International Arbitration: The Coming of a New Age?*, ICCA Congress Series, Vol. 17, pp. 67-73.

only be initiated by the arbitration community itself and its institutions; legislative intervention or intervention by way of an international treaty would be neither desirable nor realistic. But here again, what is as stake is the balance between regulation and contractual freedom. In any case, given the public's sensitivity to the issue of conflicts of interest, it is certain that the existing system of unilateral appointments can only be sustained if two conditions are met: the first, as we have said, is that there must be complete transparency in arbitrators' disclosures of potential conflicts; the second is that arbitral institutions must stand firm in their control, which is their responsibility, over nominations made by the parties, which shows that the legitimacy of the arbitration institution remains, in any event, directly linked to the strengthening of the regulatory and disciplinary role of arbitral institutions.

We have mentioned the issue of transparency in relation to the publication of awards, as a condition for society's recognition of the arbitral justice system, as well as the issue of arbitrators' disclosure obligations. Yet the question of transparency arises in a much broader manner, with regard to the underlying trends that run through all sectors of society, in relation to which the culture of secrecy and confidentiality that still characterises arbitration today appears profoundly out of step. John Rawls said almost thirty years ago, in *Justice et Démocratie*:

> "Publicity ensures that, insofar as the practicable form of institutions permits, free and equal individuals are able to know and to accept the influences of the social context that shape their conception of themselves as persons as well as their character and their conception of good. Being in such a situation is a precondition to freedom; it means that nothing is hidden, nor needs be hidden . . . In public matters, the methods of reasoning used and the rules for establishing the evidence that make it possible to reach generally true beliefs on the basis of which one may determine whether an institution is just should be such that everyone can recognise them." [178]

This requirement of full publicity, which is at the heart of any legitimisation process, also applies to arbitration, for several reasons. First, secrecy naturally fuels public suspicion – made all the stronger as public opinion becomes increasingly hostile to capitalism and finance

178. J. Rawls, *Justice et démocratie*, Seuil, Paris, 1993, pp. 106-107.

– towards a special form of justice that derogates from ordinary judicial law and is accessible only to those with sufficient means; as the *Tapie* case has shown, this is as true for commercial arbitration as it is for investment arbitration. Second, transparency implies that certain administrative decisions, such as decisions issued by arbitral institutions on challenges of arbitrators or refusals to initiate arbitration, must be reasoned, which is a safeguard against arbitrariness. Third, transparency in the constitution and composition of the governing bodies of arbitral institutions serves to ensure their legitimacy and avoids conflicts of interest. Fourth, transparency in the composition of arbitral tribunals that is, the publication of the names of the arbitrators serving on them, as well as the manner in which they were appointed – assists in combatting conflicts of interest, sometimes more effectively than through disclosures of conflict left to the arbitrators themselves. Finally, in addition to strengthening the normative role of arbitration, as mentioned above, publicising awards ensures that parties wishing to appoint an arbitrator are better informed and that decisions are of a higher quality. Transparency should, therefore, apply to all aspects of arbitration: the governance and decision-making practices of the institutions, the disclosure obligations of arbitrators and parties, the openness of hearings and proceedings in both public and commercial matters and the publication of awards in a non-anonymised manner. Arbitration and arbitral institutions, in other words, should be a house of glass to the society. However, this requirement comes up against the autonomy of the parties, who remain strongly attached to the confidentiality of arbitration, illustrating once again the tension between institutionalisation and freedom that characterises the assertion of arbitration as a system of justice. When it comes to transparency, however, these reservations remain difficult to explain, other than by certain attitudes of comfort encouraged by a culture of secrecy that still permeates the arbitration community in all its components.

The last, although certainly not the least, of the values of recognition that should be mentioned at the end of this lecture is diversity. Arbitration cannot remain indifferent to the growing aspiration to overcome the male and white domination that has characterised our societies for millennia. In this respect, immense progress has been made over the last decade, in particular under the impetus of the institutions, but much remains to be done: to take only the example of the most prominent of international arbitral institutions, the ICC, nearly 70 per cent of all arbitrators appointed or confirmed under its rules are European or North American, and nearly 80 per cent of them are men.

We shall conclude by saying that arbitration is a living body, in constant search of legitimacy, which evolves and transforms through an ongoing dialogue with the society surrounding it. It is, to use a term borrowed from neuroscience [179], an autopoietic system organised as a network, having functional autonomy in relation to State legal orders, capable of continual self-regeneration, and whose social substratum enables it to function as a global system of justice for international commerce, a function that is the source of its legitimacy. However, this functional legitimacy remains subject to the system's ability to be identified by society and to respond to the values of recognition that enable society, at a given moment in its development, to adopt it. The extent to which arbitration can produce a discourse that enables it to align itself with these values will be the measure of the legitimacy to which it may aspire.

179. Applied to legal scholarship by G. Teubner: *Law as an Autopoietic System*, Oxford, Blackwell, 1993.

BIOGRAPHICAL NOTE

Alexis Mourre, born on 25 March 1963 in Suresnes.

Awarded a master's degree in law from the University of Paris-X and a postgraduate degree in international trade law from the University of Paris-I. Member of the Paris Bar since January 1988.

As a founding partner of Mourre, Gutierrez, Chessa Arbitration since October 2021, he has acted as counsel to parties, sole arbitrator, co-arbitrator, chairman of the tribunal and expert in more than 300 international arbitration proceedings, both *ad hoc* and under the aegis of most arbitral institutions.

He set up his own firm in May 2015, having founded *Castaldi Mourre et Associés* in 1996. He was a member of the ICC International Court of Arbitration for twelve years, first as Vice-Chairman (2009-2015) and then as Chairman (1 July 2015-30 June 2021). He was also Vice-President of the ICC Institute of World Business Law from 2011 to 2015, Co-Chairman of the Arbitration Committee of the International Bar Association (2012-2013), a member of the LCIA Court (2012-2015) and of the Council of the Milan Chamber of Arbitration (2006-2014).

He was a member of the ICC France Board (2010-2015) and Chairman of the ICC France Competition Commission (2003-2009). He has authored numerous works on international business law, private international law and arbitration law. Founder and former editor-in-chief *of Les Cahiers de l'Arbitrage – The Paris Journal of International Arbitration*, one of the world's leading arbitration journals.

He is also a member of a large number of scholarly and professional institutions dedicated to private international law and arbitration. Founder and former chairman of the association *Paris Place d'Arbitrage/Paris the Home of International Arbitration*.

Alexis Mourre is a lecturer at the University of Paris II and the *Institut d'études politiques*.

He is fluent in French, English, Italian and Spanish and has a working knowledge of Portuguese.

PRINCIPAL PUBLICATIONS

Articles

"L'avocat face aux marchés de capitaux", *Bulletin des thèses*, No. 19, 1988. "Les contrats spéculatifs sur les taux", *Bulletin des thèses*, No. 21, 1988.

"Le délit d'initié en droit français", *Gazette du Palais (GP)*, 1989, 253-255.

"La loi du 2 août 1989 et la répression des infractions boursières", *GP*, 15 May 1990.

"Les arrêts Rothmans et Arizona Tobacco du Conseil d'Etat: la séparation des pouvoirs en question ?", *GP*, 1992, 297-298.

"A propos de la compétence internationale du juge des référés", *GP*, 1992, 218-219.

"La compétence juridictionnelle dans les litiges relatifs à la rupture d'un contrat de concession exclusive", *GP*, 1992, 341-343.

"Aspects procéduraux de l'affaire Parretti : nouveaux développements du droit de l'exequatur", *GP*, 1993, 251-252.

"Bruxelles attend sa nuit du 4 août", *Libération*, 2 June 1993.

"Prophylaxie sociale et tentation répressive", *Le Journal du sida*, No. 61, April 1994. "Doubles fonds judiciaires", *Libération*, 11 May 1994.

"A propos de l'application de l'article 5-1° de la Convention de Bruxelles aux litiges nés de la rupture d'un contrat de représentation", *GP*, 8 July 1994.

"La Convention de Bruxelles et les pouvoirs du juge des référés", *GP*, 1993, 290-292.

"Pour la présomption d'innocence, pour Omar Raddad", *Globe Hebdo*, February 1994. "Réflexions sur le serment décisoire", *GP*, 1994, 163-165.

"Trente ans après la Convention de Bruxelles, bilan et perspectives de la jurisprudence concernant la détermination de la juridiction compétente en matière contractuelle", *International Business Law Journal*, 1999, No. 4.

"L'arrêt van Uden de la Cour de Justice des Communautés européennes : les jours du référé-provision en matière européenne sont-ils comptés ?", *GP*, 1999, 150-152.

The French Approach to the Application of the Brussels and Lugano Conventions, Transnational Publishers, 1999.

"Les rapports de l'arbitrage et du droit communautaire après l'arrêt Eco Swiss de la Cour de Justice des Communautés Européennes", *Les Cahiers de l'Arbitrage, Recueil*, ed. Gaz. Pal., Vol. 1, 2002, p. 77.

"Le droit français de l'arbitrage international face à la Convention européenne des droits de l'homme", *Les Cahiers de l'Arbitrage, Recueil*, ed. Gaz. Pal., Vol. 1, 2002, p. 22.

"Recent Trends in French Arbitration Case Law", *LCIA News*, Vol. 5, Issue 4, 2000.

"L'intervention des tiers à l'instance arbitrale", *Les Cahiers de l'Arbitrage, Recueil*, ed. Gaz. Pal., Vol. 1, 2002, p. 100.

"Survey of International Private Law Applied to Business", *Tilburg Foreign Law Review*, 2001, Vol. 9, No. 1, pp. 89-118.

"Réflexions sur quelques aspects du droit à un procès équitable en matière d'arbitrage après les arrêts des 6 novembre 1998 et 20 février 2001 de la Cour de cassation", in *L'arbitrage et la Convention européenne des droits de l'homme*, Droit et Justice, 31 Bruylant, Brussels, October 2001, p. 23.

"La médiation en droit français : quelques points de repères législatifs et jurisprudentiels récents", *ICC Court of International Arbitration Bulletin*, Special Issue, ADR, International Applications, November 2001.

"The Absorption of Judicial Co-operation in Civil Matters by Community Law, *International Business Law Journal*, 2001/6, Paris.

"Réflexions critiques sur la suppression du contrôle de motivations des sentences arbitrales en droit français", *ASA Bulletin*, 2001/4, p. 634.

"Diritto di accesso alla giustizia ed ordine pubblico internazionale: spunti di riflessione sul forum necessitatis in materia arbitrale", *Rivista dell'Arbitrato*, 2002/1, p. 25.

"L'impact de la réforme de la clause compromissoire sur les litiges relatifs aux sociétés", *Cahiers de l'arbitrage, Recueil*, ed. Gaz. Pal., Vol. 2, 2004, p. 125.
"Enforcement of Provisional Orders in Arbitration: Is French Law in a Deadlock?" *IBA Committee D News*, February 2003.
"Référé pré-arbitral de la CCI : to be or not to be a judge?", *Cahiers de l'arbitrage, Recueil*, ed. Gaz. Pal., Vol. 2, 2004, p. 77.
"Les distorsions de concurrence peuvent entraver le libre accès aux marchés, Interview", *Echanges Internationaux*, No. 66/2003.
"The Nature of the ICC Pre-Arbitral Referee Proceedings", *IBA Committee D News*, September 2003.
"L'inadmissabilité est-elle la sanction appropriée en cas de violation d'une clause de conciliation obligatoire ?", *Cahiers de l'arbitrage, Recueil*, ed. Gaz. Pal., Vol. 2, 2004, p. 197.
"Arbitrage, conflits de juridictions et ADR dans la résolution des litiges entre actionnaires", *Revue de droit des affaires internationales*, 2004/3, p. 287.
"La réforme du droit communautaire des concentrations", *International Exchanges*, No. 69/2004.
"Chronique de droit international privé des affaires (2004) – La Construction de l'espace judiciaire européen : L'exécution des créances incontestées et l'interdiction des anti-suit Injunctions", *Revue de droit des affaires internationales*, 2004/4, p. 538.
"La réception des principes d'UNIDROIT dans les contrats modèles de la Chambre de commerce internationale (avec E. Jolivet)", *Uniform Law Review*, 2004/2, p. 275.
"L'administration de la preuve dans l'arbitrage international : état actuel de la pratique et perspectives d'évolution", in *Les Arbitres internationaux*, Paris, *Société de législation comparée*, December 2005, p. 153.
"La résolution des litiges dans les contrats spatiaux", in *Le droit des activités spatiales à l'aube du XXIe siècle*, LexisNexis Litec, 2005, p. 197.
"Arbitration in Space Contracts", *Arbitration International*, 2005/1, p. 37.
"La aportación de la prueba oral en el arbitraje internacional: el estado actual de la práctica y las perspectivas de evolución", *Revista Internacional de arbitraje*, 2005/3, p. 76.
"Faut-t-il un statut communautaire de l'arbitrage ?", *RAE*, 2005/2 and *ASA Bulletin*, 2005/3.
"Private Arbitration and Regulatory Adjudication in the Telecommunications Industry: New Trends", *Journal of International Arbitration*, 2005/3, p. 207.
"Arbitration and Criminal Law: Reflections on the Duties of the Arbitrator", *Arbitration International*, 2006/1, p. 595.
"L'application par l'arbitre de la Convention de Vienne sur la vente internationale de marchandises", *Bulletin of the ICC International Court of Arbitration*, 2006/1.
"La aplicación por el árbitro de la Convención de Viena sobre la venta internacional de mercaderías de 11 de abril de 1980", *Revista Internacional de arbitraje*, Colombia, 2006, p. 173.
"Towards Finality of Arbitration Awards: Two Steps Forward and One Step Back", with L. Radicati di Brozolo, *Journal of International Arbitration*, 2006/2, p. 171.
"Arbitraje y derecho de la competencia: un panorama desde la perspectiva europea, *Revista Brasileira de arbitraje*, 2006, p. 63.
"Canada Dry Arbitrations ?", *International Construction Law Journal*, 2006, p. 422.
"Plaidoyer pour une meilleure efficacité du droit français de la concurrence dans l'économie mondiale", *Concurrences*, December 2006, p. 10.
"Perspectives of International Arbitration in Latin America", *The American Review of International Arbitration*, 2006, 597.
"Arbitraje y Derecho Concursal: Reflexiones sobre el Papel del Juez y del Árbitro", *Revista de la Corte Española de Arbitraje*, 2007, p. 227.
"Arbitrage et droit de la faillite : Réflexions sur l'office du juge et de l'arbitre", in *Faillite internationale et conflit de juridiction*, Bruylant, 2007, p. 153.

"*Apropos* the Draft Best Practice Note on the European Commission acting as *Amicus Curiae* in International Arbitration, Dissenting Opinion on a Dangerous Project, European Business Law Review", 2008, 19-1, 210, French version in *Revue Lamy Concurrences*, June/September 2007.
"Arbitrators' Impartiality and Provisional Measures", *LCIA News*, 2007/2.
"Los méritos de la constitucionalización del procedimiento civil y del derecho de arbitraje", in *Constitucionalización del derecho privado*, Universidad Externado de Colombia/Universidad del Rosario, 2007, p. 281.
"La ejecución forzada de laudos internacionales", *Revista Peruana de Arbitraje*, 2007/5, p. 153.
"Can the Statutory Grounds for Review of Arbitral Awards Be Changed by the Parties? A French Law Perspective", *The American Review of International Arbitration*, 2007, p. 279.
"La paradoja de la compensación en el arbitraje internacional", *Spain Arbitration Review*, 2008/1, p. 97.
"La responsabilidad internacional del Estado por incumplimiento de su obligación de ejecutar un laudo extranjero", in *El Arbitraje en el Perú y el Mundo*, Lima, 2008, p. 573.
"La protección del inversionista frente a la denegación de justicia", *Revista de Arbitragem e Mediaçao*, 2008, p. 333.
"May or Must? Las causales de no reconocimiento de laudos previstas en el articulo V de la Convención de Nueva-York ¿son ellas facultativas?", in G. Tawil and E. Zuleta, *El Arbitraje Comercial Internacional, Estudio de la Convención de Nueva York con Motivo de su 50º aniversario*, Abeledo Perrot, Bogotá, 2008, p. 361.
"Judicial Penalties and Specific Performance in International Arbitration", in *ICC Institute Dossiers V*, ICC Publishing 2008.
"A propos des articles V et VII de la Convention de New-York et de la reconnaissance des sentences annulées dans leur pays d'origine : où va-t-on après les arrêts Putrabali et Termo Rio ?", *Revue de l'arbitrage*, 2008/2, p. 263.
"Sul controllo dei lodi e delle norme di applicazione inmediata", in *I rapporti economici internazionali e l'evoluzione del loro regime giuridico*, Soggetti, valori e strumenti XII Convegno Milano, 8-9 giugno 2007, Editoriale Scientifica, Napoli, 2008.
"The Set-Off Paradox in International Arbitration", *Arbitration International*, 2008, p. 387.
"Competencia, Arbitrabilidad y Derechos del Tribunal Arbitral", *Revista Internacional de Arbitraje*, 2008, p. 11.
"Problemas del control de los laudos bajo el orden publico, en particular en materia de derecho de competencia", in *Convención de Nueva York de 1958, Reconocimiento y Ejecución de Sentencias Arbitrales Extranjeras*, Instituto Peruano de Arbitraje, 2009, p. 505.
"Precedent and Confidentiality in International Commercial Arbitration: The Case for the Publication of Arbitral Awards", in *Precedent in International Arbitration*, Yas Banifatemi (ed.), Juris Publishing, 2008, p. 39.
"Gentili tra Rinascimento e Controriforma", in *La Crisi del Disarmo nel Diritto Internazionale, Nel Quarto Centenario della Morte di Alberico Gentili, Editoriale Scientifica*, Rome, 2009, p. 47.
"The Arbitration Exclusion in Regulation 44/2001 after West Tankers (with A. Vagenheim)", *International Arbitration Law Review*, 2009/5, p. 75.
"A propos de la portée de l'exclusion de l'arbitrage dans le Règlement No. 44/2001, notamment après l'arrêt West Tankers de la CJCE (with A. Vagenheim)", *Cahiers de l'arbitrage*, 2009/2, p. 20.
"The Regulation of International Arbitration by European Law: What Does the Future Hold?", *Kluwer Arbitration Blog*, 4 May 2009.
"Extension" of the Arbitration Agreement, Joinders, Review of Awards Declining Jurisdiction and Public Policy: News from Paris and Lausanne", *Kluwer Arbitration Blog*, 12 May 2009.

"Conflicts of Interest: Towards Greater Transparency and Uniform Standards of Disclosure", *Kluwer Arbitration Blog*, 19 May 2009.
"Arbitral Jurisprudence in International Commercial Arbitration: The Case for a Systematic Publication of Arbitral Awards in 10 Questions", *Kluwer Arbitration Blog*, 28 May 2009.
"Arbitrabilidad del Derecho antimonopolio desde la perspectiva europea y estadounidense", Arbitraje: *Revista de Arbitraje Comercial y de Inversiones*, Centro Internacional de Arbitraje, Mediación y Negociación (CIAMEN), IproLex 2009, Vol. 2, Issue 1, pp. 81-138.
"Arbitration and Criminal Law: Jurisdiction, Arbitrability and Duties of the Arbitral Tribunal", in A. Loukas, A. Mistelis and S. Brekoulakis (eds.), *Arbitrability: International and Comparative Perspectives*, International Arbitration Law Library, Vol. 19, Kluwer Law International, 2009, pp. 207-240.
"El Reconocimiento de los laudos", in *Arbitraje Internacional & Medios Alternativos de Solución de Litigios: Retos y Realidades*, Asociación Andrès Bello, 2010, p. 97.
"L'Arbitrabilité du droit de la concurrence et le contrôle judiciaire des sentences après le Règlement (CE) n° 1/2003", in *L'arbitrage et le droit de la concurrence*, Bruylant, 2010, p. 67.
"Courts in France and Belgium Confirm Limited Review of Awards under European Competition Law", *Kluwer Arbitration Blog*, 7 February 2010.
"Circulez, il n'y a rien à voir!", A Response to Professor Hess, *Kluwer Arbitration Blog*, 3 March 2010.
"French Courts Firmly Reject Anti-Arbitration Injunctions", *Kluwer Arbitration Blog*, 6 May 2010.
"The INSERM Decision of the Tribunal des Conflits: A Storm in a Teacup?", *Kluwer Arbitration Blog*, 7 June 2010.
"Can Discovery Costs Be Treated as Arbitration Costs?", *Kluwer Arbitration Blog*, 13 July 2010.
"Good Faith and Ethics in International Arbitration: An Important Initiative by the IBA Arbitration Committee", *Kluwer Arbitration Blog*, 31 August 2010.
"Challenges: Do Institutional Rules Matter? The Situation after Tecnimont II", *Kluwer Arbitration Blog*, 5 November 2010.
"Algunos Comentarios sobre la denegación de justicia en el derecho internacional pùblico y privado después de Loewen y Saipem", *Revista Internacional de Arbitraje*, No. 13, 2010/2, Colombia.
"Arbitrability of Antitrust Law from the European and US Perspectives", in *EU and US Antitrust Arbitration*, Vol. 2, Wolters Kluwer, 2011, p. 3.
"La competencia del juez de apoyo francés, en particular en caso de denegación de justicia: el nuevo art. 1505 del Código Procesal Civil", with B. Amezaga, *Spain Arbitration Review*, No. 11/2011, p. 95.
"The New French Arbitration Law: Innovation and Consolidation" (with V. Chessa), *Dispute Resolution Journal,* May-July 2011.
"Is There a Life after the Award?", *ASA Annual Series*, 2011.
"Differenze e convergenze tra *common law* e *civil law* nell'amministrazione della prova: spunti di riflessione sulle IBA Rules on the Taking of Evidence", *Quaderni dell'Arbitrato*, Edizioni Lapis, 2011, p. 82.
"*Sed quis custodiet ipsos custodes?* On Jurisdiction upon Arbitrators", *ICC Institute of International Business Law Dossiers*, Vol. VIII, 2011, p. 13.
"Multas coercitivas y ejecución en especie en arbitraje internacional", *Spain Arbitration Review, Revista del Club Español del Arbitraje*, Wolters Kluwer España 2011, Vol. 2011, Issue 10, pp. 17-36.
"Panorama de Jurisprudencia Francesa, Panorama of French Case Law", with F. Mantilla-Serrano *et al.*, *Spain Arbitration Review, Revista del Club Español del Arbitraje*, Wolters Kluwer España 2012, Vol. 2012, Issue 15, pp. 133-133.
"Reflexiones sobre el arbitraje y el Derecho Europeo de la Competencia, Arbitrabilidad y control de los laudos respecto del orden público europeo", *Arbitraje Comercial*

Internacional en Europa, aspecto actuales y regímenes jurídicos, ed. Palestra, February 2013.
"Arbitrage Tapie, de quoi parle-t-on vraiment?", *Le Figaro*, 7 June 2013.
"Is the Current System of Free Adjudication Dysfunctional?", *ICCA Congress Series*, No. 17, Wolters Kluwer, October 2013, p. 67.
"The IBA Guidelines on Party Representation in International Arbitration", *Dispute Resolution International*, Vol. 7, Issue 2, November 2013.
"Le règlement Bruxelles I 'refondu' évite le risque d'une régionalisation de l'arbitrage", with M. Nioche, *Les Cahiers de l'Arbitrage, Journal of International Arbitration* 2013/3, Paris, p. 567.
"The Case for the Publication of Arbitral Awards", in A. Malatesta and R. Sali (eds.), *The Rise of Transparency in International Arbitration*, Juris Publishing, 2013, p. 53.
"The IBA Guidelines on Party Representation in International Arbitration (with E. Zuleta Jaramillo), *Revista Brasileira de Arbitragem*, Comitê Brasileiro de Arbitragem, Vol. X, Issue 39, pp. 105-114.
"ICC France au cœur du mouvement de l'arbitrage international", *ICC France*, editorial No. 18, 1st quarter 2014.
"Panorama de jurisprudencia francesa (with B. Amezaga)", *Spain Arbitration Review, Revista del Club Español del Arbitraje*, Wolters Kluwer España 2014, Vol. 2014, Issue 19, pp. 117-117.
"Conflicts Disclosures: The IBA Guidelines and beyond", in C. Klausegger, P. Klein *et al.* (eds.), *Austrian Yearbook on International Arbitration 2015*, Vol. 2015, Manz'sche Verlags- und Universitätsbuchhandlung 2015, pp. 291-300.
"Los méritos de la constitucionalizacion del procedimiento civil y del derecho de arbitraje", *Ediçoes especiáis Revista dos Tribunais, Doutrinas essenciais, Arbitragem e Mediaçao*, 2014, Vol. 1, p. 613, Sao Paulo, Brasil.
"The IBA Guidelines on Party Representation in International Arbitration", in N. G. Ziadé (ed.), *Festschrift Ahmed Sadek El-Kosheri*, Kluwer Law International 2015, pp. 109-120.
"Soft Law as a Condition for the Development of Trust in International Arbitration", *Conferencia Hugo Grocio*, CEU Ediciones, 2018; and *Revista Brasileira de Arbitragem*, No. 51, 2016, p. 82.
"Gas Price Reopeners: Is Arbitration Still the Answer?", *Dispute Resolution International*, Vol 9, No. 2, October 2015, pp. 139-147.
"The Proper Use of Med-Arb in the Resolution of International Disputes", *Asian Dispute Review*, Hong Kong International Arbitration Centre (HKIAC) 2016, Vol. 18, Issue 2, pp. 94-99.
"La convenzione arbitrale" (with V. Chessa), in *Commentario breve al diritto dell'arbitrato nazionale ed internazionale*, Giuffré, Milan, 2017, p. 663.
"Arbitral Institutions and Professional Organizations as Law Makers", *ICCA Congress Series*, No. 20, 2020, p. 86.
"ICC Rules and Arbitration in India" (with A. Bhushan), *Indian Journal of Arbitration Law*, Centre for Advanced Research and Training in Arbitration Law, National Law University, Jodhpur 2018, Vol. VII, Issue 1, pp. 1-8.

Articles on investment arbitration

"*The Virtuous Arbitrator*, The MENA Arbitrators' Handbook", Juris, to be published.
"Are *Amici Curiae* the Proper Response to the Concern on Transparency in Investment Arbitration?", *The Law and Practice of International Tribunals*, 2006, p. 257 in Spanish in *Revista Brasileira de Arbitragem*, No. 12, p. 60.
"Some Comments on Denial of Justice in Private and Public International Law after Loewen and Saipem", *Liber Amicorum Bernardo Cremades*, ed. La Ley, Madrid, 2010, p. 843 (with A. Vagenheim).
"Expropriation by Courts: Is It Expropriation or Denial of Justice?", *Contemporary Issues in International Arbitration and Mediation*, 2011 Fordham University Conference, ed. A. W. Rovine, New York, 2012, p. 60.
"Le Chapitre X de l'accord économique et commercial global Canada-Union

Européenne: une solution équilibrée au débat sur le recours à l'arbitrage dans le règlement des différends entre investisseurs et Etats?", in *Mélanges en l'honneur du Professeur Pierre Mayer*, p. 571, LGDJ Lextens, 2015.

"Chapter 23: Provisional Measures in Investment Arbitration: Recent Problems", in C. Leben (ed.), *Droit international des investissements et de l'arbitrage transnational*, ed. A. Pedone, 2015, pp. 861-882.

Books

L'instance arbitrale, Juris-Classeur, Fasc. 586-8-1, 2012 (with A. Vagenheim).

Les mesures provisoires et conservatoires dans l'arbitrage international, Juris-Classeur, fasc. 780, 2020 (with B. Amezaga).

Droit judiciaire privé européen des affaires, Bruylant, 2003, Brussels.

Consolidation et intervention des tiers, litispendance et sursis à statuer, Jurisclasseur, forthcoming (with B. Amezaga).

Les règles de compétence, de reconnaissance et d'exécution des décisions en matière civile et commerciale dans l'Union européenne et dans les Etats parties aux Conventions de Bruxelles et de Lugano, Encyclopédie Lamy Contrats internationaux, December 2002, updated in 2010 (with M. Nioche) and 2014 (with A. Pinna).

Written Evidence and Discovery in International Arbitration, ICC Institute Dossiers VI, ICC Publications, 2009 (ed.).

Players' Interaction in International Arbitration, CCI Institute Dossiers IX, CCI Publications, 2012 (ed.).

Le nouveau droit communautaire de la concurrence, Bruylant, Brussels, December 2004 (ed.).

Mondialisation, politique industrielle et droit communautaire de la concurrence, Bruylant, Brussels, September 2006 (ed.).

Liber Amicorum

"Alberico Gentili (1552-1608) aux sources du droit international", *Liber Amicorum Guy Horsmans*, Brussels, Bruylant, 2004.

"L'aveuglement de Zaleucus, ou variations sur l'arbitrage et l'ordre public", *Mélanges François Knoepfler*, Helbing & Lichtenhahn, December 2005.

"A propos de trois arrêts récents et du contrôle de la compétence de l'arbitre, notamment dans l'arbitrage institutionnel", *Liber Amicorum Christian Larroumet*, Economica, 2009.

"Some Comments on Denial of Justice in Private and Public International Law after Loewen and Saipem", *Liber Amicorum Bernardo Cremades*, ed. La Ley, Madrid, 2010.

"Are Unilateral Appointments Defensible? On Jan Paulsson's Moral Hazard in International Arbitration", *Liber Amicorum Eric Bergsten*, Wolters Kluwer.

"Serge Lazareff, une vision de l'arbitre à travers 10 ans d'éditoriaux des Cahiers de l'Arbitrage", *Liber Amicorum in Honour of Serge Lazareff*, Pedone éditeurs, 2011.

"Institutional Arbitration Rules: Do They Deserve More Deference from the Judiciary? – Comments on Tecnimont and Other Cases", *Essays in Honour of Hans Van Houtte*, p. 149, P. Wautelet, T. Kruger and G. Coppens (eds.), Hart Publishing, 2012.

"La paradoja de la compensación en el arbitraje internacional", *Homenaje a Yves Derains y Bernardo Cremades*, Lima, Perú, 2013.

"¿Quien tiene Competencia sobre los árbitros? Reflexiones sobre el contrato de árbitro?", *Liber Amicorum Luiz Olavo Baptista*, ed. Latin Quarter do Brasil, 2013.

"L'espropriazione giudiziale: Espropriazione o diniego di giustizia?", in *Persona e Attività Economica tra Libertà e Regola. Studi dedicati a Diego Corapi* (B. De Donno, F. Pernazza, R. Torino, G. Scarchillo, D. Benincasa (eds.)), Editoriale Scientifica Napoli, 2016.

"A Comparative Approach to the Standard of Review of Arbitral Awards under Substantive Public Policy", *The Challenges and the Future of Commercial and Investment Arbitration, Liber Amicorum Professor Jerzy Rajski*, Lewiatan, 2015 (with V. Chessa).

"Le Chapitre X de l'accord économique et commercial global Canada-Union européenne: une solution équilibrée au débat sur le recours à l'arbitrage dans le règlement des différends entre investisseurs et Etats?", *Mélanges en l'honneur du Professeur Pierre Mayer*, LGDJ, Lextenso editions, 2015 (with J. Fouret).

"About Procedural Soft Law, the IBA Guidelines on Party Representation and the Future of Arbitration", *Liber Amicorum Pierre A. Karrer*, Wolters Kluwer, 2017.

"Should Post-Final Award Challenges against Arbitrators Be Admitted?", *Liber Amicorum pour Yves Derains*, Pedone, Paris, 2021.

"Aplicação da Convenção Internacional de Compra e Venda de Mercadorias na arbitragem", *A evolução do Direito no século XXI, Homenagem ao Professor Arnoldo Wald*, Editora IASP, 2022, p. 237 (with Bingen Amezaga).

"Plaidoyer pour un retour à un minimalisme mesuré", *The System of International Arbitration, Liber Amicorum Emmanuel Gaillard*, 2022, forthcoming.

"Les contre-procès internationaux dans l'histoire judiciaire contemporaine", *Arbitration beyond Borders: Essays in Memory of Guillermo Aguilar Alvarez*, Kluwer, forthcoming.

Case notes

Note on Cass. Com. 2 June 2004, *Alstom Power*, *Journal du droit international* (Clunet), 2005/1, p. 1.

Note on Paris, 18 November 2004, *Thalès* v. *Euromissile*, *Journal du droit international* (Clunet), 2005/2, p. 357.

Note on Paris, 7 October 2004, *Otor* v. *Carlyle*, *Journal du droit international* (with P. Pedone), (Clunet), 2005/2, p. 341.

Note on Paris, 29 September 2005, *United Arab Emirates* v. *Bechtel*, *Stockholm International Arbitration Review* (with Ph. Pinsolle), 2005/3, p. 151.

Note on Cass. Civ. 1re, 7 June 2006, *ABS* v. *Jules Verne*, *Journal du droit international* (Clunet) 2006/4, p. 1384.

Note on European Court of Justice, 26 October 2006, *Mostaza Claro* v. *Centro Movil Milenium SL*, *Journal du droit international* (Clunet) 2007/2, p. 581.

Note on Trib. Brussels, *SNF* v. *Cytec*, *Revue de l'arbitrage*, 2007, p. 303, with L. Radicati di Brozolo.

Note on Cour d'appel de Bruxelles, *Cytec* v. *SNF*, *Revue de l'arbitrage*, 2009, p. 574.

Note on Cass. Civ. 1re, 4 June 2008, *SAS SNF* v. *Sté Cytec Industries BV*, *Journal du droit international* (Clunet), 2008/4, p. 1107.

Note on Cass. Com. 29 June 2011, *Société Smeg NV* v. *Société La Poupardine, Confirmation du caractère limité du contrôle des sentences au regard de l'ordre public de fond, et en particulier du droit communautaire*, *Les Cahiers de l'Arbitrage/Paris Journal of International Arbitration*, 2012/2, p. 393.

Note on Cass. Civ. 1re, 28 March 2013, *Z* v. *Elf Neftegaz, Une inutile et dangereuse porte ouverte à l'interférence du juge dans l'arbitrage*, *Les Cahiers de l'Arbitrage/Paris Journal of International Arbitration* 2013/4, p. 1049 (with P. Pinsolle).

Note on Paris, 17 December 2013, *Jnah* v. *Marriott*, *Les Cahiers de l'Arbitrage/Paris Journal of International Arbitration* 2014/3, p. 579 (with P. Pedone).

PUBLICATIONS OF THE
HAGUE ACADEMY OF INTERNATIONAL
LAW

PUBLICATIONS DE L'ACADÉMIE
DE DROIT INTERNATIONAL
DE LA HAYE

COLLECTED COURSES

Since 1923 the top names in international law have taught at The Hague Academy of International Law. All the volumes of the *Collected Courses* which have been published since 1923 are available, as, since the very first volume, they are reprinted regularly in their original format.

Since 2008, certain courses have been the subject of a pocketbook edition.

In addition, the total collection now exists in electronic form. All works already published have been put "on line" and can be consulted under one of the proposed subscription methods, which offer a range of tariffs and possibilities.

INDEXES

Up till now seven General Indexes have been published. They cover the following volumes:

1 to 101	(1923-1960)	379 pages	ISBN 978-90-218-9948-0
102 to 125	(1961-1968)	204 pages	ISBN 978-90-286-0643-2
126 to 151	(1969-1976)	280 pages	ISBN 978-90-286-0630-2
152 to 178	(1976-1982)	416 pages	ISBN 978-0-7923-2955-8
179 to 200	(1983-1986)	260 pages	ISBN 978-90-411-0110-5
201 to 250	(1987-1994)	448 pages	ISBN 978-90-04-13700-4
251 to 300	(1995-2002)	580 pages	ISBN 978-90-04-15387-7

From Volume 210 onwards it has been decided to publish a full index covering, each time, ten volumes of the *Collected Courses*. The latest Index published covers the following volumes:

311 to 320 (2004-2006) 392 pages Volume 320A ISBN 978-90-04-19695-7

WORKSHOPS

The Academy publishes the discussions from the Workshops which it organises. The latest titles of the Workshops already published are as follows: *The Peaceful Settlement of International Disputes in Europe: Future Prospects* (1990) ; *The Development of the Role of the Security Council* (1992); *The Convention on the Prohibition and Elimination of Chemical Weapons: A Breakthrough in Multilateral Disarmament* (1994); *Topicality of the 1907 Hague Conference, the Second Peace Conference* (2007).

CENTRE FOR STUDIES AND RESEARCH

The scientific works of the Centre for Studies and Research in International Law and International Relations of The Hague Academy of International Law, the subjects of which are chosen by the Curatorium of the Academy, have been published, since the Centre's 1985 session, in a publication in which the Directors of Studies reported on the state of research of the Centre under their direction. This series has been discontinued and the title of the latest booklet published is as follows: *Rules and Institutions of International Humanitarian Law Put to the Test of Recent Armed Conflicts.* Nevertheless, when the work of the Centre has been of particular interest and originality, the reports of the Directors of Studies together with the articles by the researchers form the subject of a collection published by the Academy.

RECUEIL DES COURS

Depuis 1923, les plus grands noms du droit international ont professé à l'Académie de droit international de La Haye. Tous les tomes du *Recueil* qui ont été publiés depuis cette date sont disponibles, chaque tome étant, depuis les tout premiers, régulièrement réimprimé sous sa forme originale.

Depuis 2008, certains cours font l'objet d'une édition en livres de poche.

En outre, toute la collection existe en version électronique. Tous les ouvrages parus à ce jour ont été mis en ligne et peuvent être consultés moyennant un des abonnements proposés, qui offrent un éventail de tarifs et de possibilités.

INDEX

A ce jour, il a paru sept index généraux. Ils couvrent les tomes suivants:

1 à 101	(1923-1960)	379 pages	ISBN 978-90-218-9948-0
102 à 125	(1961-1968)	204 pages	ISBN 978-90-286-0643-2
126 à 151	(1969-1976)	280 pages	ISBN 978-90-286-0630-2
152 à 178	(1976-1982)	416 pages	ISBN 978-0-7923-2955-8
179 à 200	(1983-1986)	260 pages	ISBN 978-90-411-0110-5
201 à 250	(1987-1994)	448 pages	ISBN 978-90-04-13700-4
251 à 300	(1995-2002)	580 pages	ISBN 978-90-04-15387-7

A partir du tome 210 il a été décidé de publier un index complet qui couvrira chaque fois dix tomes du *Recueil des cours*. Le dernier index paru couvre les tomes suivants:

311 à 320 (2004-2006) 392 pages Tome 320A ISBN 978-90-04-19695-7

COLLOQUES

L'Académie organise également des colloques dont les débats sont publiés. Les derniers volumes parus de ces colloques portent les titres suivants: *Le règlement pacifique des différends internationaux en Europe: perspectives d'avenir* (1990); *Le développement du rôle du Conseil de sécurité* (1992); *La Convention sur l'interdiction et l'élimination des armes chimiques: une percée dans l'entreprise multilatérale du désarmement* (1994); *Actualité de la Conférence de La Haye de 1907, Deuxième Conférence de la Paix* (2007).

CENTRE D'ÉTUDE ET DE RECHERCHE

Les travaux scientifiques du Centre d'étude et de recherche de droit international et de relations internationales de l'Académie de droit international de La Haye, dont les sujets sont choisis par le Curatorium de l'Académie, faisaient l'objet, depuis la session de 1985, d'une publication dans laquelle les directeurs d'études dressaient le bilan des recherches du Centre qu'ils avaient dirigé. Cette série a été arrêtée et la dernière brochure parue porte le titre suivant: *Les règles et les institutions du droit international humanitaire à l'épreuve des conflits armés récents*. Néanmoins, lorsque les travaux du Centre se révèlent particulièrement intéressants et originaux, les rapports des directeurs et les articles rédigés par les chercheurs font l'objet d'un ouvrage collectif.

Les demandes de renseignements ou de catalogues et les commandes doivent être adressées à

MARTINUS NIJHOFF PUBLISHERS

B.P. 9000, 2300 PA Leyde Pays-Bas **http://www.brill.nl**

INDEX BY VOLUME OF THE COURSES PUBLISHED THESE LAST YEARS

TABLE PAR TOME DES COURS PUBLIÉS CES DERNIÈRES ANNÉES

Tome/Volume 248 (1994)

Capotorti, F.: Cours général de droit international public, 9-344.
Frowein, J. A.: Reactions by Not Directly Affected States to Breaches of Public International Law, 345-438.

(ISBN 978-90-411-0164-8)

Tome/Volume 249 (1994)

Pfund, P. H.: Contributing to Progressive Development of Private International Law: The International Process and the United States Approach, 9-144.
Borrás, A.: Les ordres plurilégislatifs dans le droit international privé actuel, 145-368.
Fadlallah, I.: L'ordre public dans les sentences arbitrales, 369-430.

(ISBN 978-90-411-0260-7)

Tome/Volume 250 (1994)

Juillard, P.: L'évolution des sources du droit des investissements, 9-216.
Simma, B.: From Bilateralism to Community Interest in International Law, 217-384.

(ISBN 978-90-411-0419-9)

Tome/Volume 251 (1995)

Jayme, E.: Identité culturelle et intégration: le droit privé postmoderne. Cours général de droit international privé, 9-268.
Nygh, P. E.: The Reasonable Expectations of the Parties as a Guide to the Choice of Law in Contract and in Tort, 269-400.

(ISBN 978-90-411-0261-4)

Tome/Volume 252 (1995)

Brilmayer, L.: The Role of Substantive and Choice of Law Policies in the Formation and Application of Choice of Law Rules, 9-112.
Waters, D. W. M.: The Institution of the Trust in Civil and Common Law, 113-454.

(ISBN 978-90-411-0168-6)

Tome/Volume 253 (1995)

Fallon, M.: Les conflits de lois et de juridictions dans un espace économique intégré. L'expérience de la Communauté européenne, 9-282.
Murase, S.: Perspectives from International Economic Law on Transnational Environmental Issues, 283-432.

(ISBN 978-90-411-0279-9)

Tome/Volume 254 (1995)

Morin, J.-Y.: L'Etat de droit: émergence d'un principe du droit international, 9-464.

(ISBN 978-90-411-0354-3)

Tome/Volume 255 (1995)

Brownlie, I.: International Law at the Fiftieth Anniversary of the United Nations. General Course on Public International Law, 9-228.

Hage-Chahine, F.: La prescription extinctive en droit international privé, 229-338.

Quéneudec, J.-P.: La notion d'Etat intéressé en droit international, 339-462.

(ISBN 978-90-411-0318-5)

Tome/Volume 256 (1995)

Goldblat, J.: The Nuclear Non-Proliferation Régime: Assessment and Prospects, 9-192.

Torres-Bernárdez, S.: L'intervention dans la procédure de la Cour internationale de Justice, 193-458.

(ISBN 978-90-411-0420-5)

Tome/Volume 257 (1996)

Bedjaoui, M.: Le cinquantième anniversaire de la Cour internationale de Justice (communication), 9-34.

Carrillo-Salcedo, J.-A.: Droit international et souveraineté des Etats. Cours général de droit international public, 35-222.

De Boer, Th. M.: Facultative Choice of Law: The Procedural Status of Choice-of-Law Rules and Foreign Law, 223-428.

(ISBN 978-90-411-0440-3)

Tome/Volume 258 (1996)

Reisman, W. M.: The Supervisory Jurisdiction of the International Court of Justice: International Arbitration and International Adjudication, 9-394.

(ISBN 978-90-411-0441-0)

Tome/Volume 259 (1996)

Kreuzer, K.: La propriété mobilière en droit international privé, 9-318.

Voulgaris, I.: Le crédit-bail (leasing) et les institutions analogues en droit international privé, 319-412.

(ISBN 978-90-411-0529-5)

Tome/Volume 260 (1996)

McClean, J. D.: A Common Inheritance? An Examination of the Private International Law of the Commonwealth, 9-98.

McRae, D. M.: The Contribution of International Trade Law to the Development of International Law, 99-238.

Francioni, F.: La conservation et la gestion des ressources de l'Antarctique, 239-404.

(ISBN 978-90-411-0517-2)

Tome/Volume 261 (1996)

Koh, H. H.: International Business Transactions in United States Courts, 9-242.

Pérez Vera, E.: Citoyenneté de l'Union européenne, nationalité et condition des étrangers, 243-426.

(ISBN 978-90-411-1054-1)

Tome/Volume 262 (1996)

Stern, B.: La succession d'Etats, 9-438.

(ISBN 978-90-411-1393-1)

Tome/Volume 263 (1997)

Bermann, G. A.: Regulatory Federalism: European Union and United States, 9-148.

Sánchez Rodríguez: L'*uti possidetis* et les effectivités dans les contentieux territoriaux et frontaliers, 149-382.

(ISBN 978-90-411-0539-4)

Tome/Volume 264 (1997)

Basedow, J.: Souveraineté territoriale et globalisation des marchés: le domaine d'application des lois contre les restrictions de la concurrence, 9-178.

Kerameus, K. D.: Enforcement in the International Context, 179-410.

(ISBN 978-90-411-1016-9)

Tome/Volume 265 (1997)

Rideau, J.: Le rôle de l'Union européenne en matière de protection des droits de l'homme, 9-480.

(ISBN 978-90-411-1178-4)

Tome/Volume 266 (1997)

Zemanek, K.: The Legal Foundations of the International System. General Course on Public International Law, 9-336.

Hartley, T. C.: Mandatory Rules in International Contracts: the Common Law Approach, 337-426.

(ISBN 978-90-411-0590-5)

Tome/Volume 267 (1997)

Plender, R.: Procedure in the European Courts: Comparisons and Proposals, 9-344.

Oreja Aguirre, M.: La révision institutionnelle de l'Union européenne, 345-386.

(ISBN 978-90-411-1006-0)

Tome/Volume 268 (1997)

Moulay Rchid, A.: Les droits de l'enfant dans les conventions internationales et les solutions retenues dans les pays arabo-musulmans, 9-290.

Von Bar, C.: Environmental Damage in Private International Law, 291-412.

(ISBN 978-90-411-1292-7)

Tome/Volume 269 (1997)

Damrosch, L. F.: Enforcing International Law through Non-forcible Measures, 9-250.
Sacerdoti, G.: Bilateral Treaties and Multilateral Instruments on Investment Protection, 251-460.

(ISBN 978-90-411-1111-1)

Tome/Volume 270 (1997)

Ranjeva, R.: Les organisations non gouvernementales et la mise en œuvre du droit international, 9-106.
Xu, D.: Le droit international privé en Chine: une perspective comparative, 107-236.
Matscher, F.: Quarante ans d'activités de la Cour européenne des droits de l'homme, 237-398.

(ISBN 978-90-411-1331-3)

Tome/Volume 271 (1998)

Struycken, A. V. M.: La contribution de l'Académie au développement de la science et de la pratique du droit international privé (Conférence prononcée à l'occasion du soixante-quinzième anniversaire de l'Académie), 11-56.
Skubiszewski, K.: The Contribution of the Academy to the Development of the Science and Practice of Public International Law (Address Delivered on the Occasion of the 75th Anniversary of the Academy), 57-100.
Charney, J. I.: Is International Law Threatened by Multiple International Tribunals?, 101-382.

(ISBN 978-90-411-1210-1)

Tome/Volume 272 (1998)

Wolfrum, R.: Means of Ensuring Compliance with and Enforcement of International Environmental Law, 9-154.
Mendelson, M. H.: The Formation of Customary International Law, 155-410.

(ISBN 978-90-411-1237-8)

Tome/Volume 273 (1998)

Sur, S.: Vérification en matière de désarmement, 9-102.
Caminos, H.: The Role of the Organization of American States in the Promotion and Protection of Democratic Governance, 103-238.
Ginsburg, J. C.: The Private International Law of Copyright in an Era of Technological Change, 239-406.

(ISBN 978-90-411-1251-4)

Tome/Volume 274 (1998)

Pastor Ridruejo, J. A.: Le droit international à la veille du vingt et unième siècle: normes, faits et valeurs. Cours général de droit international public, 9-308.
Carreau, D.: Le système monétaire international privé (UEM et euromarchés), 309-392.

(ISBN 978-90-411-1300-9)

Tome/Volume 275 (1998)

Elwan, O.: La loi applicable à la garantie bancaire à première demande, 9-218.
Mestral, A. de: The North American Free Trade Agreement: A Comparative Analysis, 219-416. (ISBN 978-90-411-1486-0)

Tome/Volume 276 (1999)

Picone, P.: Les méthodes de coordination entre ordres juridiques en droit international privé. Cours général de droit international privé, 9-296.
Baxi, U.: Mass Torts, Multinational Enterprises Liability and Private International Law, 297-428. (ISBN 978-90-411-1394-8)

Tome/Volume 277 (1999)

Verwilghen, M.: Conflits de nationalités. Plurinationalité et apatridie, 9-484.
(ISBN 978-90-411-1395-5)

Tome/Volume 278 (1999)

Barboza, J.: International Criminal Law, 9-200.
Maupain, F.: L'OIT, la justice sociale et la mondialisation, 201-396.
(ISBN 978-90-411-1396-2)

Tome/Volume 279 (1999)

Jonkman, H.: The Role of the Permanent Court of Arbitration in International Dispute Resolution (Addresses), 9-50.
Hascher, D.: Principes et pratique de procédure dans l'arbitrage commercial international, 51-194.
Degan, V.-D.: Création et disparition de l'Etat (à la lumière du démembrement de trois fédérations multiethniques en Europe), 195-376.
(ISBN 978-90-411-1397-9)

Tome/Volume 280 (1999)

Droz, G. A. L.: L'activité notariale internationale, 9-134.
Abellán Honrubia, V.: La responsabilité internationale de l'individu, 135-428.
(ISBN 978-90-411-1487-7)

Tome/Volume 281 (1999)

Tomuschat, C.: International Law: Ensuring the Survival of Mankind on the Eve of a New Century. General Course on Public International Law, 9-438.
(ISBN 978-90-411-1488-4)

Tome/Volume 282 (2000)

Jayme, E.: Le droit international privé du nouveau millénaire: la protection de la personne humaine face à la globalisation (conférence), 9-40.
McClean, D.: De Conflictu Legum. Perspectives on Private International Law at the Turn of the Century. General Course on Private International Law, 41-228.
Smith, B. L.: The Third Industrial Revolution: Law and Policy for the Internet, 229-464. (ISBN 978-90-411-1489-1)

Tome/Volume 283 (2000)

Bucher, A.: La famille en droit international privé, 9-186.
Dolinger, J.: Evolution of Principles for Resolving Conflicts in the Field of Contracts and Torts, 187-512.

(ISBN 978-90-411-1490-7)

Tome/Volume 284 (2000)

Schlosser, P.: Jurisdiction and International Judicial and Administrative Co-operation, 9-428.

(ISBN 978-90-411-1605-5)

Tome/Volume 285 (2000)

Slaughter, A.-M.: International Law and International Relations, 9-250.
Lucchini, L.: L'Etat insulaire, 251-392.

(ISBN 978-90-411-1606-2)

Tome/Volume 286 (2000)

Boutros-Ghali, B. : Le droit international à la recherche de ses valeurs : paix, développement, démocratisation (conférence inaugurale), 9-38.
Scovazzi, T. : The Evolution of International Law of the Sea : New Issues, New Challenges, 39-244.
Kronke, H. : Capital Markets and Conflict of Laws, 245-386.

(ISBN 978-90-411-1607-9)

Tome/Volume 287 (2000)

González Campos, J. D. : Diversification, spécialisation, flexibilisation et matérialisation des règles de droit international privé. Cours général, 9-426.

(ISBN 978-90-411-1608-6)

Tome/Volume 288 (2001)

Kowalski, W. W. : Restitution of Works of Art pursuant to Private and Public International Law, 9-244.
Caflisch, L. : Cent ans de règlement pacifique des différends interétatiques, 245-468.

(ISBN 978-90-411-1609-3)

Tome/Volume 289 (2001)

Grigera Naón, H. A. : Choice-of-Law Problems in International Commercial Arbitration, 9-396.

(ISBN 978-90-411-1610-9)

Tome/Volume 290 (2001)

Fernández Rozas, J. C. : Le rôle des juridictions étatiques devant l'arbitrage commercial international, 9-224.
Villani, U. : Les rapports entre l'ONU et les organisations régionales dans le domaine du maintien de la paix, 225-436.

(ISBN 978-90-411-1611-6)

Tome/Volume 291 (2001)

Rosenne, Sh. : The Perplexities of Modern International Law. General Course on Public International Law, 9-472.

(ISBN 978-90-411-1746-5)

Tome/Volume 292 (2001)

Momtaz, D. : Le droit international humanitaire applicable aux conflits armés non internationaux, 9-146.

Jacquet, J.-M. : La fonction supranationale de la règle de conflit de loi, 147-248.

Mengozzi, P. : Private International Law and the WTO Law, 249-386.

(ISBN 978-90-411-1854-7)

Tome/Volume 293 (2001)

Fitzmaurice, M. A. : International Protection of the Environment, 9-488.

(ISBN 978-90-411-1855-4)

Tome/Volume 294 (2002)

Camdessus, M. : Organisations internationales et mondialisation (conférence), 9-38.

Zoller, E. : Aspects internationaux du droit constitutionnel. Contribution à la théorie de la fédération d'Etats, 39-166.

McWhinney, E. : Self-determination of Peoples and Plural-ethnic States (Secession and State Succession and the Alternative, Federal Option), 167-264.

Thirlway, H. : Concepts, Principles, Rules and Analogies : International and Municipal Legal Reasoning, 265-406.

(ISBN 978-90-411-1856-1)

Tome/Volume 295 (2002)

Von Mehren, A. : Theory and Practice of Adjudicatory Authority in Private International Law : A Comparative Study of the Doctrine, Policies and Practices of Common- and Civil-Law Systems. General Course on Private International Law (1966), 9-432.

(ISBN 978-90-411-1857-8)

Tome/Volume 296 (2002)

Van der Stoel, M. : The Role of the OSCE High Commissioner on National Minorities in the Field of Conflict Prevention (Address), 9-24.

Hanotiau, B. : L'arbitrabilité, 25-254.

Heiskanen, V. : The United Nations Compensation Commission, 255-398.

(ISBN 978-90-411-1858-5)

Tome/Volume 297 (2002)

Dupuy, P.-M. : L'unité de l'ordre juridique international. Cours général de droit international public (2000), 9-496.

(ISBN 978-90-411-1859-2)

Tome/Volume 298 (2002)

Symeonides, S. C. : The American Choice-of-Law Revolution in the Courts : Today and Tomorrow, 9-448.

(ISBN 978-90-411-1860-8)

Tome/Volume 299 (2002)

Roucounas, E. : Facteurs privés et droit international public, 9-420.
(ISBN 978-90-411-1861-5)

Tome/Volume 300 (2002)

Bennouna, M. : Les sanctions économiques des Nations Unies, 9-78.
Kessedjian, C. : Codification du droit commercial international et droit international privé. De la gouvernance normative pour les relations économiques transnationales, 79-308.
Smits, R. : Law of the Economic and Monetary Union, 309-422.
(ISBN 978-90-411-1862-2)

Tome/Volume 301 (2003)

Meron, T. : International Law in the Age of Human Rights, 9-490.
(ISBN 978-90-04-14020-2)

Tome/Volume 302 (2003)

Black, V. : Foreign Currency Obligations in Private International Law, 9-196.
Leben, Ch. : La théorie du contrat d'Etat et l'évolution du droit international des investissements, 197-386. (ISBN 978-90-04-14021-9)

Tome/Volume 303 (2003)

Daudet, Y. : Actualités de la codification du droit international, 9-118.
Mezghani, A. : Méthodes de droit international privé et contrat illicite, 119-430.
(ISBN 978-90-04-14022-6)

Tome/Volume 304 (2003)

Mosk, R. M. : The Role of Facts in International Dispute Revolution, 9-180.
Jänterä-Jareborg, M. : Foreign Law in National Courts : A Comparative Perspective, 181-386.
(ISBN 978-90-04-14023-3)

Tome/Volume 305 (2003)

Audit, B. : Le droit international privé en quête d'universalité. Cours général (2001), 9-488.
(ISBN 978-90-04-14307-4)

Tome/Volume 306 (2003)

Casanovas, O. : La protection internationale des réfugiés et des personnes déplacées dans les conflits armés, 9-176.
Reed, L. : Mixed Private and Public Law Solutions to International Crises, 177-410.
(ISBN 978-90-04-14545-0)

Tome/Volume 307 (2004)

Jorda, M. C. : Du Tribunal pénal international pour l'ex-Yougoslavie à la Cour pénale internationale : De quelques observations et enseignements (conférence), 9-24.
Muir Watt, H. : Aspects économiques du droit international privé (Réflexions sur l'impact de la globalisations économique sur les fondements des conflits de lois et de juridictions), 25-384.
(ISBN 978-90-04-456-7)

Tome/Volume 308 (2004)

Rigo Sureda, A. : The Law Applicable to the Activities of International Development Banks, 9-252.
González Lapeyre, E. : Transport maritime et régime portuaire, 253-378.

(ISBN 978-90-04-14547-4)

Tome/Volume 309 (2004)

Karaquillo, J.-P. : Droit international du sport, 9-124.
Maresceau, M. : Bilateral Agreements Concluded by the European Community, 9-452.

(ISBN 978-90-04-14548-1)

Tome/Volume 310 (2004)

Kamto, M. : La volonté de l'Etat en droit international, 9-428.

(ISBN 978-90-04-14552-8)

Tome/Volume 311 (2004)

Struycken, A. V. M. : Co-ordination and Co-operation in Respectful Disagreement. General Course on Private International Law, 5-552.

(ISBN 978-90-04-14553-5)

Tome/Volume 312 (2005)

Gaudemet-Tallon, H. : Le pluralisme en droit international privé : richesses et faiblesses (Le funambule et l'arc-en-ciel). Cours général, 9-488.

(ISBN 978-90-04-14554-2)

Tome/Volume 313 (2005)

Mani, V. S. : "Humanitarian" Intervention Today, 9-324.
David, E. : La Cour pénale internationale, 325-454.

(ISBN 978-90-04-14555-9)

Tome/Volume 314 (2005)

Draetta, U. : Internet et commerce électronique en droit international des affaires, 9-232.
Daillier, P. : Les opérations multinationales consécutives à des conflits armés en vue du rétablissement de la paix, 233-432.

(ISBN 978-90-04-14557-3)

Tome/Volume 315 (2005)

Dogauchi, M. : Four-Step Analysis of Private International Law, 9-140.
Mohamed Salah, M. M. : Loi d'autonomie et méthodes de protection de la partie faible en droit international privé, 141-264.
Radicati di Brozolo, L. G. : Arbitrage commercial international et lois de police. Considérations sur les conflits de juridictions dans le commerce international, 265-502.

(ISBN 978-90-04-14558-0)

Tome/Volume 316 (2005)

Cançado Trindade, A. A. : International Law for Humankind : Towards a New *Jus Gentium* (I). General Course on Public International Law, 9-440.

(ISBN 978-90-04-15375-2)

Tome/Volume 317 (2005)

Cançado Trindade, A. A. : International Law for Humankind : Towards a New *Jus Gentium* (II). General Course on Public International Law, 9-312.
Borrás, A. : Le droit international privé communautaire : réalités, problèmes et perspectives d'avenir, 313-536. (ISBN 978-90-04-15376-9)

Tome/Volume 318 (2005)

Kinsch, P. : Droits de l'homme, droits fondamentaux et droit international privé, 9-332.
Bothe, M. : Environment, Development, Resources, 323-516.
(ISBN 978-90-04-15377-6)

Tome/Volume 319 (2006)

Hartley, T. C. : The Modern Approach to Private International Law. International Litigation and Transactions from a Common-Law Perspective. General Course on Private International Law, 9-324.
Crawford, J. : Multilateral Rights and Obligations in International Law, 325-482.
(ISBN 978-90-04-15378-3)

Tome/Volume 320 (2006)

Goldstein, G. : La cohabitation hors mariage en droit international privé, 9-390.
(ISBN 978-90-04-15379-0)

Tome/Volume 321 (2006)

Shaker, M. I. : The Evolving International Regime of Nuclear Non-Proliferation, 9-202.
Klein, P. : Le droit international à l'épreuve du terrorisme, 203-484.
(ISBN 978-90-04-16100-0)

Tome/Volume 322 (2006)

Loquin, E. : Les règles matérielles internationales, 9-242.
Dinstein, Y. : The Interaction between Customary International Law and Treaties, 243-428.
(ISBN 978-90-04-16101-6)

Tome/Volume 323 (2006)

Fernández Arroyo, D. P. : Compétence exclusive et compétence exorbitante dans les relations privées internationales, 9-260.
Silberman, L. J.. : Co-operative Efforts in Private International Law on Behalf of Children : The Hague Children's Conventions, 261-478.
(ISBN 978-90-04-16102-3)

Tome/Volume 324 (2006)

Bedjaoui, M. : L'humanité en quête de paix et de développement (I). Cours général de droit international public, 9-530.
(ISBN 978-90-04-16103-0)

Tome/Volume 325 (2006)

Bedjaoui, M. : L'humanité en quête de paix et de développement (II). Cours général de droit international public, 9-542. (ISBN 978-90-04-16104-7)

Tome/Volume 326 (2007)

Collins, L. : Revolution and Restitution : Foreign States in National Courts (Opening Lecture, Private International Law Session, 2007), 9-72.
Gotanda, J. Y. : Damages in Private International Law, 73-408.

(ISBN 978-90-04-16616-5)

Tome/Volume 327 (2007)

Mayer, P. : Le phénomène de la coordination des ordres juridiques étatiques en droit privé. Cours général de droit international privé (2003), 9-378.

(ISBN 978-90-04-16617-2)

Tome/Volume 328 (2007)

Garcimartín Alférez, F. J., Cross-border Listed Companies, 9-174.
Vrellis, S., Conflit ou coordination de valeurs en droit international privé. A la recherche de la justice, 175-486.

(ISBN 978-90-04-16618-9)

Tome/Volume 329 (2007)

Pellet, A. : L'adaptation du droit international aux besoins changeants de la société internationale (conférence inaugurale, session de droit international public, 2007), 9-48.
Gaillard, E. : Aspects philosophiques du droit de l'arbitrage international, 49-216.
Schrijver, N. : The Evolution of Sustainable Development in International Law : Inception, Meaning and Status, 217-412.

(ISBN 978-90-04-16619-6)

Tome/Volume 330 (2007)

Pamboukis, Ch. P. : Droit international privé holistique : droit uniforme et droit international privé, 9-474.

(ISBN 978-90-04-16620-2)

Tome/Volume 331 (2007)

Pinto, M. : L'emploi de la force dans la jurisprudence des tribunaux internationaux, 9-160
Brown Weiss, E. : The Evolution of International Water Law, 161-404.

(ISBN 978-90-04-17288-3)

Tome/Volume 332 (2007)

Carlier, J.-Y. : Droit d'asile et des réfugiés. De la protection aux droits, 9-354.
Fatouros, A. A. : An International Legal Framework for Energy, 355-446.

(ISBN 978-90-04-17198-5)

Tome/Volume 333 (2008)

Müllerson, R. : Democracy Promotion : Institutions, International Law and Politics, 9-174.
Pisillo Mazzeschi, R. : Responsabilité de l'Etat pour violation des obligations positives relatives aux droits de l'homme, 174-506.

(ISBN 978-90-04-17284-5)

Tome/Volume 334 (2008)

Verhoeven, J. : Considérations sur ce qui est commun. Cours général de droit international public (2002), 9-434. (ISBN 978-90-04-17289-0)

Tome/Volume 335 (2008)

Beaumont, P. R.: The Jurisprudence of the European Court of Human Rights and the European Court of Justice on the Hague Convention on International Child Abduction, 9-104.

Moura Vicente, D.: La propriété intellectuelle en droit international privé, 105-504. (ISBN 978-90-04-17290-6)

Tome/Volume 336 (2008)

Decaux, E.: Les formes contemporaines de l'esclavage, 9-198.

McLachlan, C.: *Lis Pendens* in International Litigation, 199-554. (ISBN 978-90-04-17291-3)

Tome/Volume 337 (2008)

Mahiou, A.: Le droit international ou la dialectique de la rigueur et de la flexibilité. Cours général de droit international public, 9-516. (ISBN 978-90-04-17292-0)

Tome/Volume 338 (2008)

Thürer, D.: International Humanitariam Law : Theory, Practice, Context, 9-370. (ISBN 978-90-04-17293-7)

Tome/Volume 339 (2008)

Sicilianos, L.-A.: Entre multilatéralisme et unilatéralisme : l'autorisation par le Conseil de sécurité de recourir à la force, 9-436. (ISBN 978-90-04-17294-4)

Tome/Volume 340 (2009)

Beaumont, P. R.: Reflections on the Relevance of Public International Law to Private International Law Treaty Making (Opening Lecture, Private International Law Session, 2009), 9-62.

Carbone, S. M.: Conflits de lois en droit maritime, 63-270.

Boele-Woelki, K.: Unifying and Harmonizing Substantive Law and the Role of Conflict of Laws, 271-462. (ISBN 978-90-04-17295-1)

Tome/Volume 341 (2009)

Bucher, A.: La dimension sociale du droit international privé. Cours général, 9-526. (ISBN 978-90-04-18509-8)

Tome/Volume 342 (2009)

Musin, V.: The Influence of the International Sale of Goods Convention on Domestic Law Including Conflict of Laws (with Specific Reference to Russian Law), 9-76.

Onuma, Y.: A Transcivilizational Perspective on International Law. Questioning Prevalent Cognitive Frameworks in the Emerging Multi-Polar and Multi-Civilizational World of the Twenty-First Century, 77-418. (ISBN 978-90-04-18510-4)

Tome/Volume 343 (2009)

Abou-el-Wafa, A.: Les différends internationaux concernant les frontières terrestres dans la jurisprudence de la Cour internationale de Justice, 9-570.

(ISBN 978-90-04-18513-5)

Tome/Volume 344 (2009)

Villiger, M. E.: The 1969 Vienna Convention on the Law of Treaties – 40 Years After, 4-192.

Alvarez, J. E.: The Public International Law Regime Governing International Investment, 193-452.

(ISBN 978-90-04-18512-8)

Tome/Volume 345 (2009)

Meziou, K.: Migrations et relations familiales, 9-386.

Lauterpacht, Sir Elihu: Principles of Procedure in International Litigation, 387-530.

(ISBN 978-90-04-18514-2)

Tome/Volume 346 (2009)

Kawano, M.: The Role of Judicial Procedures in the Process of the Pacific Settlement of International Disputes, 9-474.

(ISBN 978-90-04-18515-9)

Tome/Volume 347 (2010)

Salmon, J.: Quelle place pour l'Etat dans le droit international d'aujourd'hui? 9-78.

Boisson de Chazournes, L.: Les relations entre organisations régionales et organisations universelles, 79-406.

(ISBN 978-90-04-18516-6)

Tome/Volume 348 (2010)

Bogdan, M.: Private International Law as Component of the Law of the Forum. General Course, 9-252.

Baratta, R.: La reconnaissance internationale des situations juridiques personnelles et familiales, 253-500. (ISBN 978-90-04-18517-3)

Tome/Volume 349 (2010)

Malenovský, J.: L'indépendance des juges internationaux, 9-276.

Wang, G.: Radiating Impact of WTO on Its Members' Legal System: The Chinese Perspective, 277-536. (ISBN 978-90-04-18518-0)

Tome/Volume 350 (2010)

Van Gerven, W.: Plaidoirie pour une nouvelle branche du droit: le « droit des conflits d'ordres juridiques » dans le prolongement du « droit des conflits de règles » (conférence inaugurale), 9-70.

Bonomi, A.: Successions internationales: conflits de lois et de juridictions, 71-418.

Oxman, B. H.: Idealism and the Study of International Law (Inaugural Lecture), 419-440.

(ISBN 978-90-04-18519-7)

Tome/Volume 351 (2010)

Reisman, W. M.: The Quest for World Order and Human Dignity in the Twenty-first Century: Constitutive Process and Individual Commitment. General Course on Public International Law, 9-382. (ISBN 978-90-04-22725-5)

Tome/Volume 352 (2010)

Daví, A.: Le renvoi en droit international privé contemporain, 9-522. (ISBN 978-90-04-22726-2)

Tome/Volume 353 (2011)

Meeusen, J.: Le droit international privé et le principe de non-discrimination, 9-184.

Gowlland-Debbas, V.: The Security Council and Issues of Responsibility under International Law, 185-444.

(ISBN 978-90-04-22727-9)

Tome/Volume 354 (2011)

Lamm, C. B.: Internationalization of the Practice of Law and Important Emerging Issues for Investor-State Arbitration (Opening Lecture), 9-64.

Briggs, A.: The Principle of Comity in Private International Law, 65-182.

Davey, W. J.: Non-discrimination in the World Trade Organization: The Rules and Exceptions, 183-440.

(ISBN 978-90-04-22728-6)

Tome/Volume 355 (2011)

Chemillier-Gendreau, M.: A quelles conditions l'universalité du droit international est-elle possible? (conférence inaugurale), 9-40.

Xue Hanqin: Chinese Contemporary Perspectives on International Law – History, Culture and International Law, 41-234.

Arrighi, J. M.: L'Organisation des Etats américains et le droit international, 235-438. (ISBN 978-90-04-22729-3)

Tome/Volume 356 (2011)

Talpis, J.: Succession Substitutes, 9-238.

Lagrange, E.: L'efficacité des normes internationales concernant la situation des personnes privées dans les ordres juridiques internes, 239-552.

(ISBN 978-90-04-22730-9)

Tome/Volume 357 (2011)

Dugard, J.: The Secession of States and Their Recognition in the Wake of Kosovo, 9-222.

Gannagé, L.: Les méthodes du droit international privé à l'épreuve des conflits de cultures, 223-490.

(ISBN 978-90-04-22731-6)

Tome/Volume 358 (2011)

Brand, R. A.: Transaction Planning Using Rules on Jurisdiction and the Recognition and Enforcement of Judgments, 9-262.

Hafner, G.: The Emancipation of the Individual from the State under International Law, 263-454.

(ISBN 978-90-04-22732-3)

Tome/Volume 359 (2012)

Opertti Badán, D.: Conflit de lois et droit uniforme dans le droit international privé contemporain: dilemme ou convergence? (conférence inaugurale), 9-86.

Chen Weizuo: La nouvelle codification du droit international privé chinois, 87-234.

Kohler, Ch.: L'autonomie de la volonté en droit international privé: un principe universel entre libéralisme et étatisme, 285-478.

(ISBN 978-90-04-25541-8)

Tome/Volume 360 (2012)

Basedow, J.: The Law of Open Societies — Private Ordering and Public Regulation of International Relations. General Course on Private International Law, 9-516.

(ISBN 978-90-04-25550-0)

Tome/Volume 361 (2012)

Pinto, M. C. W.: The Common Heritage of Mankind: Then and Now, 9-130.

Kreindler, R.: Competence-Competence in the Face of Illegality in Contracts and Arbitration Agreements, 131-482.

(ISBN 978-90-04-25552-4)

Tome/Volume 362 (2012)

Arsanjani, M. H.: The United Nations and International Law-Making (Opening Lecture), 9-40.

Alland, D.: L'interprétation du droit international public, 41-394.

(ISBN 978-90-04-25554-8)

Tome/Volume 363 (2012)

Sur, S.: La créativité du droit international. Cours général de droit international public, 9-332.

Turp, D.: La contribution du droit international au maintien de la diversité culturelle, 333-454.

(ISBN 978-90-04-25556-2)

Tome/Volume 364 (2012)

Gaja, G.: The Protection of General Interests in the International Community. General Course on Public International Law (2011), 9-186.

Glenn, H. P.: La conciliation des lois. Cours général de droit international privé (2011), 187-470.

(ISBN 978-90-04-25557-9)

Tome/Volume 365 (2013)

Crawford, J.: Chance, Order, Change: The Course of International Law. General Course on Public International Law, 9-390.

(ISBN 978-90-04-25560-9)

Tome/Volume 366 (2013)

Hayton, D.: "Trusts" in Private International Law, 9-98.

Hobér, K.: Res Judicata and Lis Pendens in International Arbitration, 99-406.

(ISBN 978-90-04-26395-6)

Tome/Volume 367 (2013)

Kolb, R. : L'article 103 de la Charte des Nations Unies, 9-252.
Nascimbene, B. : Le droit de la nationalité et le droit des organisations d'intégration régionales. Vers de nouveaux statuts de résidents ?, 253-454.
(ISBN 978-90-04-26793-0)

Tome/Volume 368 (2013)

Caflisch, L : Frontières nationales, limites et délimitations. – Quelle importance aujourd'hui ? (conférence inaugurale), 9-46.
Benvenisti, E. : The International Law of Global Governance, 47-280.
Park, K. G. : La protection des personnes en cas de catastrophes, 281-456.
(ISBN 978-90-04-26795-4)

Tome/Volume 369 (2013)

Kronke, H. : Transnational Commercial Law and Conflict of Laws : Institutional Co-operation and Substantive Complementarity (Opening Lecture), 9-42.
Ortiz Ahlf, L. : The Human Rights of Undocumented Migrants, 43-160.
Kono, T. : Efficiency in Private International Law, 161-360.
Yusuf, A. A. : Pan-Africanism and International Law, 361-512.
(ISBN 978-90-04-26797-8)

Tome/Volume 370 (2013)

Dominicé, Ch. : La société internationale à la recherche de son équilibre. Cours général de droit international public, 9-392. (ISBN 978-90-04-26799-2)

Tome/Volume 371 (2014)

Lagarde, P. : La méthode de la reconnaissance est-elle l'avenir du droit international privé ?, 9-42.
Charlesworth, H. : Democracy and International Law, 43-152.
de Vareilles-Sommières, P. : L'exception d'ordre public et la régularité substantielle internationale de la loi étrangère, 153-272.
Yanagihara, M. : Significance of the History of the Law of Nations in Europe and East Asia, 273-435.
(ISBN 978-90-04-28936-9)

Tome/Volume 372 (2014)

Bucher, A. : La compétence universelle civile, 9-128.
Cordero-Moss, G. : Limitations on Party Autonomy in International Commercial Arbitration, 129-326.
Sinjela, M. : Intellectual Property : Cross-Border Recognition of Rights and National Development, 327-394.
Dolzer, R. : International Co-operation in Energy Affairs, 395-504.
(ISBN 978-90-04-28937-6)

Tome/Volume 373 (2014)

Cachard, O. : Le transport international aérien de passagers, 9-216.
Audit, M. : Bioéthique et droit international privé, 217-447.
(ISBN 978-90-04-28938-3)

Tome/Volume 374 (2014)

Struycken, A. V. M.: Arbitration and State Contract, 9-52.
Corten, O., La rébellion et le droit international : le principe de neutralité en tension, 53-312.
Parra, A.: The Convention and Centre for Settlement of Investment Disputes, 313-410.

(ISBN 978-90-04-29764-7)

Tome/Volume 375 (2014)

Jayme, E.: Narrative Norms in Private International Law – The Example of Art Law, 9-52.
De Boer, Th. M.: Choice of Law in Arbitration Proceedings, 53-88.
Frigo, M.: Circulation des biens culturels, détermination de la loi applicable et méthodes de règlement des litiges, 89-474.

(ISBN 978-90-04-29766-1)

Tome/Volume 376 (2014)

Cançado Trindade, A. A.: The Contribution of Latin American Legal Doctrine to the Progressive Development of International Law, 9-92.
Gray, C.: The Limits of Force, 93-198.
Najurieta, M. S.: L'adoption internationale des mineurs et les droits de l'enfant, 199-494.

(ISBN 978-90-04-29768-5)

Tome/Volume 377 (2015)

Kassir, W. J.: Le renvoi en droit international privé – technique de dialogue entre les cultures juridiques, 9-120.
Noodt Taquela, M. B.: Applying the Most Favourable Treaty or Domestic Rules to Facilitate Private International Law Co-operation, 121-318.
Tuzmukhamedov, B.: Legal Dimensions of Arms Control Agreements, An Introductory Overview, 319-468.

(ISBN 978-90-04-29770-8)

Tome/Volume 378 (2015)

Iwasawa, Y.: Domestic Application of International Law, 9-262.
Carrascosa Gonzalez, J.: The Internet – Privacy and Rights relating to Personality, 263-486.

(ISBN 978-90-04-32125-0)

Tome/Volume 379 (2015)

Lowe, V.: The Limits of the Law.
Boele-Woelki, K.: Party Autonomy in Litigation and Arbitration in View of The Hague Principles on Choice of Law in International Commercial Contracts.
Fresnedo de Aguirre, C.: Public Policy: Common Principles in the American States.
Ben Achour, R.: Changements anticonstitutionnels de gouvernement et droit international.

(ISBN 978-90-04-32127-4)

Tome/Volume 380 (2015)

Van Loon, J. H. A.: The Global Horizon of Private International Law.
Pougoué, P.-G.: L'arbitrage dans l'espace OHADA.
Kruger, T.: The Quest for Legal Certainty in International Civil Cases.
(ISBN 978-90-04-32131-1)

Tome/Volume 381 (2015)

Jayme, E.: Les langues et le droit international privé, 11-39.
Bermann, G.: Arbitrage and Private International Law. General Course on Private International Law (2015), 41-484.
(ISBN 978-90-04-33828-9)

Tome/Volume 382 (2015)

Cooper, D., and C. Kuner: Data Protection Law and International Dispute Resolution, 9-174.
Jia, B. B.: International Case Law in the Development of International Law, 175-397.
(ISBN 978-90-04-33830-2)

Tome/Volume 383 (2016)

Bennouna, M.: Le droit international entre la lettre et l'esprit, 9-231.
Iovane, M.: L'influence de la multiplication des juridictions internationales sur l'application du droit international, 233-446.
(ISBN 978-90-04-34648-2)

Tome/Volume 384 (2016)

Symeonides, S. C.: Private International Law Idealism, Pragmatism, Eclecticism, 9-385.
(ISBN 978-90-04-35131-8)

Tome/Volume 385 (2016)

Berman, Sir F.: Why Do we Need a Law of Treaties?, 9-31.
Marrella, F.: Protection internationale des droits de l'homme et activités des sociétés transnationales, 33-435.
(ISBN 978-90-04-35132-5)

Tome/Volume 386 (2016)

Murphy, S. D.: International Law relating to Islands, 9-266.
Cataldi, G.: La mise en œuvre des décisions des tribunaux internationaux dans l'ordre interne, 267-428.
(ISBN 978-90-04-35133-2)

Tome/Volume 387 (2016)

Lequette, Y.: Les mutations du droit international privé: vers un changement de paradigme?, 9-644.
(ISBN 978-90-04-36118-8)

Tome/Volume 388 (2016)

Bonell, M. J.: The Law Governing International Commercial Contracts: Hard Law versus Soft Law, 9-48.

Hess, B.: The Private-Public Divide in International Dispute Resolution, 49-266.

(ISBN 978-90-04-36120-1)

Tome/Volume 389 (2017)

Muir Watt, H.: Discours sur les méthodes du droit international privé (des formes juridiques de l'inter-altérité). Cours général de droit international privé, 9-410.

(ISBN 978-90-04-36122-5)

Tome/Volume 390 (2017)

Rau, A. S.: The Allocation of Power between Arbitral Tribunals and State Courts, 9-396.

(ISBN 978-90-04-36475-2)

Tome/Volume 391 (2017)

Cançado Trindade, A. A.: Les tribunaux internationaux et leur mission commune de réalisation de la justice : développements, état actuel et perspectives, Conférence spéciale (2017), 9-101.

Mariño Menéndez, F. M. : The Prohibition of Torture in Public International Law, 103-185.

Swinarski, C.: Effets pour l'individu des régimes de protection de droit international, 187-369.

Cot, J.-P.: L'éthique du procès international (leçon inaugurale), 371-384.

(ISBN 978-90-04-37781-3)

Tome/Volume 392 (2017)

Novak, F.: The System of Reparations in the Jurisprudence of the Inter-American Court of Human Rights, 9-203.

Nolte, G.: Treaties and their Practice – Symptoms of their Rise or Decline, 205-397.

(ISBN 978-90-04-39273-1)

Tome/Volume 393 (2017)

Tiburcio, C.: The Current Practice of International Co-Operation in Civil Matters, 9-310.

Ruiz De Santiago, J.: Aspects juridiques des mouvements forcés de personnes, 311-468.

(ISBN 978-90-04-39274-8)

Tome/Volume 394 (2017)

Kostin, A. A.: International Commercial Arbitration, with Special Focus on Russia, 9-86.

Cuniberti, G.: Le fondement de l'effet des jugements étrangers, 87-283.

(ISBN 978-90-04-39275-5)

Tome/Volume 395 (2018)

Salerno, F.: The Identity and Continuity of Personal Status in Contemporary Private International Law, 9-198.
Chinkin, C. M.: United Nations Accountability for Violations of International Human Rights Law, 199-320.

(ISBN 978-90-04-40710-7)

Tome/Volume 396 (2018)

Jacquet, J.-M.: Droit international privé et arbitrage commercial international, 9-36.
Brown Weiss, E.: Establishing Norms in a Kaleidoscopic World. General Course on Public International Law, 37-415.

(ISBN 978-90-04-41002-2)

Tome/Volume 397 (2018)

D'Avout, L.: L'entreprise et les conflits internationaux de lois, 9-612.

(ISBN 978-90-04-41221-7)

Tome/Volume 398 (2018)

Treves, T.: The Expansion of International Law, General Course on Public International Law (2015), 9-398.

(ISBN 978-90-04-41224-8)

Tome/Volume 399 (2018)

Kanehara, A.: Reassessment of the Acts of the State in the Law of State Responsibility, 9-266.
Buxbaum, H. L.: Public Regulation and Private Enforcement in a Global Economy: Strategies for Managing Conflict, 267-442.

(ISBN 978-90-04-41670-3)

Tome/Volume 400 (2018)

Chedly, L.: L'efficacité de l'arbitrage commercial international, 9-624.

(ISBN 978-90-04-42388-6)

Tome/Volume 401 (2019)

Wood, P.: Extraterritorial Enforcement of Regulatory Laws, 9-126.
Nishitani, Yuko: Identité culturelle en droit international privé de la famille, 127-450.

(ISBN 978-90-04-42389-3)

Tome/Volume 402 (2019)

Kinsch, P.: Le rôle du politique en droit international privé. Cours général de droit international privé, 9-384.
Dasser, F.: "Soft Law" in International Commercial Arbitration, 385-596.

(ISBN 978-90-04-42392-3)

Tome/Volume 403 (2019)

Daudet, Y.: 1919-2019, le flux du multilatéralisme, 9-48.
Kessedjian, C.: Le tiers impartial et indépendant en droit international, juge, arbitre, médiateur, conciliateur, 49-643.

(ISBN 978-90-04-42468-5)

Tome/Volume 404 (2019)

Rajamani, L.: Innovation and Experimentation in the International Climate Change Regime, 9-234.
Sorel, J.-M.: Quelle normativité pour le droit des relations monétaires et financières internationales ?, 235-403.

(ISBN 978-90-04-43142-3)

Tome/Volume 405 (2019)

Paulsson, J.: Issues arising from Findings of Denial of Justice, 9-74.
Brunée, J.: Procedure and Substance in International Environmental Law, 75-240.

(ISBN 978-90-04-43300-7)

Tome/Volume 406 (2019)

Bundy, R.: The Practice of International Law, Inaugural Lecture, 9-26.
Gama, L.: Les principes d'UNIDROIT et la loi régissant les contrats de commerce, 27-343.

(ISBN 978-90-04-43611-4)

Tome/Volume 407 (2020)

Wouters, J.: Le statut juridique des standards publics et privés dans les relations économiques internationales, 9-122.
Maljean-Dubois, S.: Le droit international de la biodiversité, 123-538.

(ISBN 978-90-04-43643-5)

Tome/Volume 408 (2020)

Cançado Trindade, A. A.: Reflections on the Realization of Justice in the Era of Contemporary International Tribunals, 9-88.
González, C.: Party Autonomy in International Family Law, 89-361.

(ISBN 978-90-04-44504-8)

Tome/Volume 409 (2020)

Shany, Y: The Extraterritorial Application of International Human Rights Law, 9-152.
Besson, S.: La *due diligence* en droit international, 153-398.

(ISBN 978-90-04-44505-5)

Tome/Volume 410 (2020)

Koh, H. H.: American Schools of International Law, 9-93.
Peters, A.: Animals in International Law, 95-544.

(ISBN 978-90-04-44897-1)

Tome/Volume 411 (2020)

Cahin, G: Reconstrution et construction de l'Etat en droit international, 9-573.
(ISBN 978-90-04-44898-8)

Tome/Volume 412 (2020)

Momtaz, D: La hiérarchisation de l'ordre juridique international, cours général de droit international public, 9-252.
Grammaticaki-Alexiou, A.: Best Interests of the Child in Private International Law, 253-434.
(ISBN 978-90-04-44899-5)

Tome/Volume 413 (2021)

Ferrari, F.: Forum Shopping Despite Unification of Law, 9-290.
(ISBN 978-90-04-46100-0)

Tome/Volume 414 (2021)

Pellet, A.: Le droit international à la lumière de la pratique: l'introuvable théorie de la réalité. Cours général de droit international public, 9-547.
(ISBN 978-90-04-46547-3)

Tome/Volume 415 (2021)

Trooboff, P. D.: Globalization, Personal Jurisdiction and the Internet. Responding to the Challenge of adapting settled Principles and Precedents. General Course of Private International Law, 9-321. (ISBN 978-90-04-46730-9)

Tome/Volume 416 (2021)

Wolfrum, R: Solidarity and Community Interests: Driving Forces for the Interpretation and Development of International Law. General Course on Public International Law, 9-479. (ISBN 978-90-04-46827-6)

Tome/Volume 417 (2021)

d'Argent, P.: Les obligations internationales, 9-210.
Schabas, W. A.: Relationships Between International Criminal Law and Other Branches of International Law, 211-392. (ISBN 978-90-04-47239-6)

Tome/Volume 418 (2021)

Bollée, S.: Les pouvoirs inhérents des arbitres internationaux, 9-224.
Tladi, D.: The Extraterritorial Use of Force against Non-State Actors, 225-360.
(ISBN 978-90-04-50380-9)

Tome/Volume 419 (2021)

Kolb, R.: Le droit international comme corps de «droit privé» et de «droit public». Cours général de droit international public, 9-668.
(ISBN 978-90-04-50381-6)

Tome/Volume 420 (2021)

Perrakis, S.: La protection internationale au profit des personnes vulnérables en droit international des droits de l'homme, 9-497.
(ISBN 978-90-04-50382-3)

Tome/Volume 421 (2021)

Estrella Faria, J. A.: La protection des biens culturels d'intérêt religieux en droit international public et en droit international privé, 9-333.

(ISBN 978-90-04-50829-3)

Tome/Volume 422 (2021)

Karayanni, M.: The Private International Law of Class Actions: A Functional approach, 9-248.

Mahmoudi, S.: Self-Defence and "Unwilling or Unable" States, 249-399.

(ISBN 978-90-04-50830-9)

Tome/Volume 423 (2022)

Kinnear, M.: The Growth, Challenges and Future Prospects for Investment Dispute Settlement, 9-36.

Weller, M.: "Mutual Trust": A Suitable Foundation for Private International Law in Regional Integration Communities and Beyond?, 37-378.

(ISBN 978-90-04-51411-9)

Tome/Volume 424 (2022)

Asada, M.: International Law of Nuclear Non-proliferation and Disarmament, 9-726.

(ISBN 978-90-04-51769-1)

Tome/Volume 425 (2022)

Metou, B. M.: Le contrôle international des dérogations aux droits de l'homme, 9-294.

Silva Romero, E.: Legal Fictions in the Language of International Arbitration, 295-423.

(ISBN 978-90-04-51770-7)

Tome/Volume 426 (2022)

Kuijper, P. J.: Delegation and International Organizations, 9-240.

McCaffrey, S. C.: The Evolution of the Law of International Watercourses, 241-384.

(ISBN 978-90-04-51771-4)

Tome/Volume 427 (2022)

Kaufmann-Kohler, G.: Indépendance et impartialité du juge et de l'arbitre dans le règlement des différends entre investisseurs et Etats (leçon inaugurale), 9-50.

Boyle, A.: International Lawmaking in an Environmental Context, 51-108.

Weller, M.-P.: La méthode tripartite du droit international privé : désignation, reconnaissance, considération, 109-210.

Mourre, A.: La légitimité de l'arbitrage, 211-288.

(ISBN 978-90-04-52770-6)

Tome/Volume 428 (2023)

Laghmani, S.: Islam et droit international, 9-128.

Oyarzábal, M. J. A.: The Influence of Public International Law upon Private International Law in History and Theory and in the Formation and Application of the Law, 129-525.

(ISBN 978-90-04-54440-6)

Tome/Volume 429 (2023)

Moreno Rodríguez, J. A.: Private (And Public) International Law In Investment Arbitration, 9-702.

(ISBN 978-90-04-54462-8)

Tome/Volume 430 (2023)

Casella, P. B.: Droit international, histoire et culture, 9-610.

(ISBN 978-90-04-54463-5)

Tome/Volume 431 (2023)

Yeo, T. M.: Common Law, Equity and Statute. The Effect of Juridical Sources on Choice-of-Law Methodology, 9-88.

Frigessi Di Rattalma, M.: New Trends in Private International Law of Insurance Contracts, 89-200.

Roosevelt III, K.: The Third Restatement of Conflict of Laws, 201-284.

Sands, P.: Colonialism: A Short History of International Law in Five Acts, 285-410.

(ISBN 978-90-04-54464-2)

Tome/Volume 432 (2023)

Ruiz Fabri, H.: La justice procédurale en droit international, 9-44.

Shaw, M.: A House of Many Rooms: The Rise, Fall and Rise Again of Territorial Sovereignty?, 45-78.

Kovács, P.: L'individu et sa position devant la Cour pénale internationale, 79-421.

(ISBN 978-90-04-54465-9)

Tome/Volume 433 (2023)

Eyffinger, A.: The Hague Academy at 100: Its Rationale, Role and Record, 9-97.

Thorn, K.: The Protection of Small and Medium-Sized Enterprises in Private International Law, 99-205.

Moollan, S.: Parallel Proceedings in International Arbitration. Theoretical Analysis and the Search for Practical Solutions, 207-303.

(ISBN 978-90-04-54469-7)

Tome/Volume 434 (2023)

Stephan, Paul B.: Applying Municipal Law in International Disputes, 9-214

Casado Raigón, R.: La contribution des juridictions internationales au développement du droit de la mer, 215-511.

(ISBN 978-90-04-69182-7)

Tome/Volume 435 (2023)

Salam, N. : Rethinking the United Nations : 75 and Beyond, 9-32.
Hascher, D. : Le rôle du droit international dans le contrôle des sentences arbitrales, 33-72.
Blokker, N. : Legal Facets of the Practice of International Organizations, 73-324.

(ISBN 978-90-04-69432-3)

Tome/Volume 436 (2024)

Corten, O.: Le champ juridique interntational, Cours général de droit international, 9-389.

(ISBN 978-90-04-69912-0)

Tome/Volume 437 (2024)

Lim, Chin Leng: The Aims and Methods of Postcolonial International Law, 9-193.
Tanzi, Attila M.: The Principle *Jura Novit Curia* in International Judicial and Arbitral Proceedings, A Window on International Adjudication, 195-382.

(ISBN 978-90-04-69913-7)

Tome/Volume 438 (2024)

Lehmann, M.: Crypto-économie et droit international, 9-384.

(ISBN 978-90-04-70670-5)

Tome/Volume 439 (2024)

Hey, E.: Making Sense of Soft Law, 9-114.
Galindo, G. R. B.: The Inviolabilities of the Diplomatic Mission, 115-288.
Gomez-Robledo, J. M.: Le droit international du désarmement: entre idéalisme et réalisme, 289-3974.

(ISBN 978-90-04-70671-2)

Tome/Volume 440 (2024)

Sicilianos, L.-A.: La dimension humaine du droit international, Cours général de droit international public, 9-768.

(ISBN 978-90-04-72244-6)

Tome/Volume 441 (2024)

Stanivuković, M.: Property Rights of Individuals after Changes of Territorial Sovereignty, 9-351.
Reyes, A.: The Use of Domestic Law to regulate the Conduct of Individuals, Corporations and Governments Extraterritorially, 353-495.

(ISBN 978-90-04-72245-3)

Tome/Volume 442 (2024)

Kamto, M.: Le droit international et la décolonisation inachevée, 9-78.
Reinisch, A.: The Settlement of Disputes Involving International Organizations, 79-342.

(ISBN 978-90-04-72246-0)

Tome/Volume 443 (2024)

D'Avout, L.: La cohérence mondiale du droit. Cours général de droit international privé, 9-724.

(ISBN 978-90-04-72247-7)

Tome/Volume 444 (2025)

Tigroudja H.: Conflits armés et droit international des droits de l'homme, 9-304.

Österdahl, I.: The Regulation of the Internet, 305-496.

(ISBN 978-90-04-73473-9)

Tome/Volume 445 (2025)

Rodríguez Benot, A.: Le régime économique des couples en droit international privé, 9-288.

Martinez-Fraga, P. J.: Settlement and Risk Assessment in International Commercial Arbitration, 289-616.

(ISBN 978-90-04-74172-0)

Tome/Volume 446 (2025)

McLachlan, C.: On the Interface Between Public and Private International Law, General Course on International Law, 9-304.

Dickinson, A.: Natural Justice in Recognition and Enforcement of Foreign Judgments, 305-546.

(ISBN 978-90-04-74173-7)

Tome/Volume 447 (2025)

Klabbers, J.: Disagreement Reduced to Writing: Rethinking the Law of Treaties, 9-186.

Hobe, S.: Perspectives for Space Law in the Twenty-First Century, 187-352.

(ISBN 978-90-04-74174-4)

Tome/Volume 448 (2025)

Kamto, M.: Droit international et polycentrisme normatif, la règle internationale dans tous ses états. Cours général de droit international, 9-557.

(ISBN 978-90-04-74874-3)

Tome/Volume 449 (2025)

Esplugues, C.: New Dimensions in the Application of Foreign Law by Courts (and Arbitrators) and Non-Judicial Authorities, 9-426.

(ISBN 978-90-04-74875-0)

Tome/Volume 450 (2025)

Couvreur, Ph.: Le Statut de la Cour internationale de Justice: bilan et perspectives, 9-447.

(ISBN 978-90-04-74876-7)

Tome/Volume 451 (2025)

Garcimartin, F.: Responses to a Legally Fragmented World: A Private Law Perspective, General Course of Private International Law, 9-328.

Reichler, P.: Practicing before the International Court of Justice: What I Learned since the *Nicaragua* Case, Inaugural Lecture, 329-348.

(ISBN 978-90-04-74877-4)

Tome/Volume 452 (2026)

Benedettelli, M. V.: Power(s) in International Arbitration, Balancing Party Autonomy and State Sovereignty Through Arbitral Authority, 9-389.

(ISBN 978-90-04-76343-2)

Tome/Volume 453 (2026)

Chimni, B. S.: International Law and Global Justice: The Imperative of Climate Justice, 9-72.

Pinto, M.: Le droit international au temps de la mondialisation. Contextes, réseaux, pratiques. Cours général de droit international, 73-434.

(ISBN 978-90-04-76446-0)

Tome/Volume 454 (2026)

Racine, J.-B.: Arbitrage et droits humains, 9-605.

(ISBN 978-90-04-76965-6)

Printed in July 2026
by Brill,
(Netherlands)

Setting: R. Mirland,
59870 Warlaing (France)

www.ingramcontent.com/pod-product-compliance
Lightning Source LLC
Chambersburg PA
CBHW071442230926
51846CB00001B/309